Penguin Books

The Seventies

Christopher Booker, aged 42, has written as journalist, essayist and author on politics, the arts, psychology and a wide range of subjects. He was the first editor of *Private Eye* (1961–3), and in 1969 published *The Neophiliacs*, a history of the Fifties and Sixties. Throughout the Seventies he wrote and campaigned widely on all aspects of urban development. He published *Goodbye London* in 1973 (with Candida Lycett Green), and in 1974 won an award as 'Campaigning Journalist of the Year' for his work with Bennie Gray for the *Sunday Times* and the *Observer*. More recently he was the author of a widely acclaimed BBC-TV documentary *City of Towers* (February 1979) on modern architecture and the destruction of Britain's cities. He is at present working on a major book on 'the Jungian psychology of stories' and 'the basic plots of literature'. He lives in Somerset.

D1340287

Christopher Booker

THE SEVENTIES

Portrait of a Decade

Penguin Books

Penguin Books Ltd, Harmondsworth, Middlesex, England
Penguin Books, 625 Madison Avenue, New York 10022, U.S.A.
Penguin Books Australia Ltd, Ringwood, Victoria, Australia
Penguin Books Canada Ltd,
2801 John Street, Markham, Ontario, Canada L3R 1B4
Penguin Books (N.Z.) Ltd,
182–190 Wairau Road, Auckland 10, New Zealand

First published by Allen Lane 1980
Published in Penguin Books 1980

Copyright © Christopher Booker, 1980
All rights reserved

Made and printed in Great Britain
by Richard Clay (The Chaucer Press) Ltd,
Bungay, Suffolk
Set in Intertype Lectura

For Christine

Contents

Part Four Culture Heroes – Nostalgia and Self-deception

Part Five Cultural Collapse

As long as one is within a certain phenomenology one is not astonished, and nobody wonders what it is all about. Such philosophical doubt only comes to the man who is outside the game.

(C. G. Jung, 'Psychology and National Problems', *Collected Works*, Vol. XVIII, p. 509)

Author's Preface

What is the true nature of the times we are living in?

Ten years ago I wrote a book called *The Neophiliacs*, a detailed, analytical account of the astonishing changes which had come over Britain in the Fifties and Sixties. This is a very different kind of book about a very different decade. It does not set out to give a detailed history of the Seventies. Anyone looking for such an overall picture would instantly notice a great many glaring omissions.

What I *have* tried to do, through a linked series of essays and profiles (many of which have already appeared elsewhere), is to penetrate rather more deeply to what the Seventies were about; to pick out the underlying themes which shaped our thoughts and our lives in those years, and to show how an understanding of the Seventies in this historical context may help us to see where we are going next.

The book begins with a specially written section, entitled 'The Death of Progress', which attempts to give a brief overall framework to the decade, and to show why I think that, far from being just the rather depressing, drifting interlude they often seemed at the time, the Seventies were in their own way 'the most important decade of the twentieth century'.

I then go on to draw some 'Global Perspectives', on some of the major issues which have affected mankind. This is followed by a section on Britain in the Seventies, 'The

Politics of a Sad Little Island'. The fourth section, 'Culture Heroes — Nostalgia and Self-deception', looks at a number of significant figures — Kenneth Clark, David Frost, Tom Wolfe, Arthur Koestler, Germaine Greer — whose writings or careers in the Seventies seem to me to have shed particular light on the changing mood of the times.

The fifth section, 'Cultural Collapse', looks in a less personal way at some broader aspects of what was undoubtedly one of the most revealing characteristics of the decade — the collapse of cultural self-confidence, the strange exhaustion of the Modern Movement in architecture and the arts, the general flight into nostalgia and love of the past, the great 'natural craze'. This leads into a section on 'Re-appraisals', touching on some of the ways in which I believe the Seventies marked the beginning of one of the most profound shifts in psychological, intellectual and spiritual perspective to have taken place in Western civilization for several hundred years. I conclude with a brief epilogue which, in an oblique way, may I hope be taken as a summing up of what the whole book has been about.

Acknowledgements

A substantial part of this book is made up from essays which I wrote during the Seventies for a variety of newspapers and magazines — notably the *Daily Telegraph*, to which I have contributed a monthly 'Saturday Column' since 1973, and the *Spectator*, for which I have written regularly since 1976, during the welcome revival in its fortunes under the editorship of Alexander Chancellor. I am most grateful both to him and to Bill Deedes, Editor of the *Telegraph*, for permission to reprint so much that originally appeared in their pages.

I am also indebted to Donald Trelford, Editor of the *Observer*, both for permission to adapt the profile of David Frost which he originally published in 1977, and for serializing the opening chapters of this book at the turn of the decade; to Mel Lasky, Editor of *Encounter*, for permission to reprint the essay on Tom Wolfe; and to Kate Wharton, late Editor of *The Architect*, who originally commissioned the article 'The Brave New World of Leisure'.

More specific and personal thanks are due to all those who helped me in various ways to make the book possible: to Malcolm Muggeridge (father of all 'decadologists'), Arianna Stassinopoulos and Simon Jenkins, who all in different ways suggested I should write it; to Philippa Harrison, of Allen Lane/Penguin, who gave the idea such a warm welcome; to Brigid Hardman-Mountford, Loraine Philip and Serena Booker, who helped to assemble the contents; to Michael Dover, Tim Binding and Annie Lee of Penguin Books, who assisted so efficiently in its editing and production; and to my agent, Felicity Bryan.

Finally, my very particular thanks to Bennie Gray, for kindness and friendship throughout the decade, for helping to sharpen up so many ideas in conversation and for being London's most generous landlord; and to Shirley, Cassian, Lucan, Rosie and Sebastian for providing such happy diversion while the book was being written.

Hampstead Hill Gardens, October 1979

Part One

The Death of Progress

1

A Most Important Decade

If it were not for our quasi-religious modern obsession with anniversaries, centenaries, decades and other arbitrary spans of time, it might at first sight seem a crazy proposition to essay an account of the Nineteen Seventies.

Of all the decades of the twentieth century, it would be hard to pick out one with a less distinctive, recognizable character.

We have no hesitation, for instance, in summoning up a mental image of the Twenties – the Charleston, the wail of saxophones, Model T Fords, flappers in waistless dresses, silent films and Charlie Chaplin's 'little man', the Wall Street boom.

Similarly, the Thirties, the Forties, the Fifties, all carry with them their own, clearly-defined package of associations, while the decade immediately preceding the Seventies, the 'Swinging Sixties', instantly evokes perhaps the clearest set of images of all – Beatlemania and mini-skirts, Carnaby Street and 'Swinging London', Harold Wilson's 'dynamic new Britain', the assassination of President Kennedy, the horrors of Vietnam, LSD, 'flower power' and the rest.

But what in years to come will evoke the sober, gloomy Seventies – which in so many ways seemed like little more than just a prolonged anti-climax to the manic excitements of the Sixties? What was the Seventies sound, the Seventies look? What was the Seventies 'image'?

Of course memorable things happened. We shall remember the Seventies as the years of Watergate, and the first resignation in history of an American President. We shall remember the ending of the Vietnam War, the final, tragic ignominy of America's catastrophic bid to keep South-East Asia from falling under Communist domination, the horrors of Cambodia and the mass-evictions of the 'boat people'. We shall remember the onset of the worst and most intractable economic recession since the war, the first serious signs of the great gathering world energy crisis. We shall remember the toppling of the Shah and the rise of the Ayatollah Khomeini, the end of Franco's Spain and Salazar's Portugal, the countless wars, coups, rebellions, hi-jackings, acts of terrorism and other lesser disorders which daily filled the headlines from almost every corner of the globe. Here at home in Britain, we shall remember the end of the Wilson—Heath era in our politics, the steady rumble of trade union power continually threatening chaos in almost every area of national life, above all perhaps a decade of unending hard slog through the quicksands of inflation.

But altogether, if this constitutes an image, it is a pretty blurred, depressing one. The Seventies were scarcely a decade to cheer about, to quicken the pulse, to remember with excitement — hardly a time which in years to come is likely to inspire us with an overpowering sense of nostalgia. Indeed this in itself is scarcely surprising, since such an enormous amount of our cultural energy in the Seventies seemed devoted — on our television and cinema screens, in the booming antique shops and salesrooms, in the unprecedented fervour with which we sought to preserve and do up old buildings — to dwelling on the charms of almost every time except our own.

Against the steady background drizzle of grim global warnings from Solzhenitsyn, from the ecological 'doomwatchers' and other pessimists about the future of mankind, we may in short remember the Seventies primarily as a kind of long, rather dispiriting interlude: a time when, in politics, in the arts or in almost any other field one considers, the prevailing mood was one of a somewhat weary, increasingly conservative, increasingly apprehensive disenchantment.

Yet it is my firm belief – one which underlies almost every essay in this book – that the Seventies were in fact the most important decade of the twentieth century. Something has been beginning to happen to us all in the past ten years – even if most people are as yet only dimly aware of it – which marks out this decade as one of the most profound historical significance, not just in the context of the twentieth century, but over a perspective stretching back many hundreds of years. And the key to understanding just what it is that has been happening to us lies in appreciating the peculiar nature and depth of that disillusionment we have been heading into through the Seventies.

The truth is that, in the past ten years, the old sources of optimism which have sustained the human race throughout the twentieth century (and which began to emerge a very long time before that) have begun to collapse on an unprecedented scale. Men have, individually, been questioning the belief in human progress for generations. But in our own time, as never before, we have actually begun to see the first real death throes of that belief – that underlying conviction that, whatever disasters and mistakes marked the way, the human race, through its own efforts, was climbing out of the darkness and ignorance of the past into some unimaginable future of light, knowledge and material abundance. However dimly, we have in the past few years not only come to see that the future may not be all that light, may indeed hold out to us the greatest range of catastrophes the world has ever known; we have also just begun to see that possibly, in our dizzying, upward flight, we have lost something of inestimable importance to us, that thing whose image at least we seek in our desperate desire to re-create the simplicities of the past, to preserve threatened species, to contemplate the unconscious beauties and harmonies of nature, to visit the last, vanishing 'un-spoiled' human settlements and wildernesses of the earth. At the eleventh hour and fifty-ninth minute perhaps, we are willy-nilly being pushed and pulled into the most dramatic and fundamental change of perspective on where we have come from and who we are that the human race has ever experienced. Over the next twenty years, I suspect, that change of perspective will become one of the most obvious and crucial factors in all our lives. And as its importance becomes more and more evident, we shall look back on the late Sixties and Seventies as the time when, although only a few people may initially have been aware of it, the whole of this fundamental shift in the way we look on ourselves and the nature of our civilization really began.

Two unfailing barometers of cultural optimism in our century have been the height of buildings and the height of girls' hem-lines. In times of high excitement, like the Twenties and the Sixties, when people looked forward to the future with hope, the skyscrapers and the skirts went up. At times when men became fearful of the future, or began to look back nostalgically to the past, as in the early Thirties, the late Forties and the Seventies, they stopped building towers and the skirts came down again. Never, however, did skirts rise so high, nor was there such a universal frenzy for building tower blocks as in the Sixties: and never, in either case, was the reaction so complete as it has been in the Seventies.

Perhaps the most obvious and immediate way to get the Seventies into perspective is to see the extent to which they were a kind of prolonged 'morning after' to the euphoria and excesses of the Sixties. So many of the events and moods which marked out the Seventies were simply a winding-down or reaction to trends which had been set in motion by the Sixties that it is really difficult to draw a firm dividing line between one decade and the other.

In my earlier book *The Neophiliacs*, sub-titled 'A Study of the Revolution in English Life in the Fifties and Sixties', I depicted the shape of post-war history as having been not unlike that of a gigantic wave. It was a wave which began to gather in the mid-Fifties, as the world finally began to emerge from the shadows cast by the Second World War — a wave of expectation, of nervous excitement, born of the growing sense that somehow Britain, the West and mankind were moving forward into a new era, of a kind never known before.

This sense of anticipation was above all generated in the mid-Fifties by the dawning realization that, thanks to the miraculous advances of technology, an entirely new kind of material prosperity was coming into being. Hundreds of millions of people, for the first time in their lives, were able to own cars, buy fridges and washing machines, shop at the new supermarkets for detergents and frozen foods. Television passed into the centre of our homes and our lives. There was suddenly much more money around than would have seemed imaginable to any previous generation, and every year that passed seemed to bring yet more technical marvels, more change — transistor radios, jet airliners, computers, motorways, new kinds of architecture in steel, concrete and glass.

At the same time, in large part generated by this sense that we had all climbed onto an escalator moving ever more rapidly up into the future, sweeping away so many of the traditional landmarks and patterns of life, a new spirit emerged in Western society – a spirit of revolt against the 'restrictive' conventions of the past, and in favour of some new 'liberated' vision of the future. Nowhere did this show more obviously than in the remarkable new importance which in the late Fifties came to be attached to youth – manifesting itself in the emergence of a whole new, rebellious 'youth culture', in Teddy Boys and the rock 'n'roll craze which swept the West in 1956–8, and Britain's 'Angry Young' playwrights and novelists who shot to prominence at the same time.

On a wider stage, across the world, this anticipation of a new age of liberation, and the sweeping away of old restrictive structures, gave rise to that mass of nationalist movements which, in Africa, Asia and the Caribbean, began to work as never before for emancipation from the centuries-old domination of European imperialism. In America, in the mid-Fifties, the same mood gave rise to the Civil Rights movement. Yet despite this world-wide stirring of a new radicalism, in favour of the young, the blacks, the colonially oppressed, and any group which could see itself as an underdog, there still seemed little doubt at the end of the Fifties that the future of mankind lay with the way of life of that country which stood unequalled in material abundance, in military and technological power, in self-confidence of all kinds – America. It was America which was pioneering the road towards a materialist Utopia that the rest of the world – including the countries under Communism – might eventually hope to follow.

In the Sixties, the tidal wave of change and euphoria rolled ever higher. If there was one man above all who seemed to embody the radical youthful idealism and energy which was to carry mankind into a new age of boundless prosperity and peace, it was that inexpressibly glamorous figure who, in November 1960, was elected the youngest-ever President of the United States, John F. Kennedy. In Britain, as the Conservative Macmillan government collapsed in a turmoil of TV satire, security and sex scandals, and general irreverent rage at a tired old 'upper-class Establishment', Harold Wilson's promise of a 'classless, dynamic New Britain', forged out of 'the white heat of technology', seemed to offer our own prospect of a bright 'New Frontier' future.

On all sides, standards, sensibilities — even the landscape — seemed to be changing faster than at any time in history. The cities of the world in the Sixties, from London to Liverpool, from Melbourne to Moscow, from Paris to Peking, were going through the most dramatic transformation they had ever known, as the bulldozers moved in, as the tower blocks and new housing estates rose in their tens of thousands, and the 'Brave New World' visions of the Modern Movement-inspired planners and architects finally came into their own. In the heyday of Beatlemania, the Rolling Stones and all that was implied by 'Swinging London', the heroes and values of the new 'youth culture' came to exercise glamorous sway over half the globe. Before the triumphant onward march of 'permissiveness', age-old conventions of dress, language and behaviour seemed to be dissolving like snow, as the Western world plunged ever more obsessively after a vision of complete sexual freedom — while, in books and magazines, on the cinema screen and the stage, the image of sex (and of sexual perversity) emerged into the open as never before.

The Sixties were certainly a time when it was still possible for most people to look forward in hope to an as yet unrealized future. But as that frenetic decade wore on, it became increasingly apparent that not all was well with the dream. After the world-wide shock of President Kennedy's assassination in 1963, America in particular seemed to be floundering deeper and deeper into trouble. Year by year, as civil rights aspirations turned into the horrific series of race riots, as the growing shadow of the 'escalating' war in Vietnam lengthened across the world, the dream became more of a nightmare. President Nixon's election in 1968 represented at least in part a desperate yearning by 'the silent majority' for a return to quieter, more peaceful, more orderly times – and when America finally managed to land two men on the moon in the summer of 1969, this astonishing technological triumph was already not without undertones of deepest irony, as the world viewed the impotence of American technological power elsewhere.

In Britain, the bright hopes held out by Harold Wilson's promises of 'dynamism' had swiftly faded, as it became clear that Britain's long industrial and economic decline was not to be halted by mere bureaucratic tinkerings – nor by a Prime Minister who, more than any of his predecessors, seemed to be acting out a mere fantasy-version of his role, concerned primarily with the kind of image he would create in the receding-mirror world of the media.

As the 'youth culture' ran through an ever more bizarre series of permutations – Flower Power and hippiedom, LSD and hard drugs, the wave of student protest and pseudo-Marxism of 1968 – it increasingly lost its glamour, and became shadowed by violence (e.g. the Manson murders) and by the strains which led to the arrests, suicides or simply the fading away of many of its leading figures.

In the Third World, the dreams of the 'liberation' which would follow independence increasingly gave way to disillusionment, as one newly-independent state after another fell foul of military coups and tyrants, civil war, or just the intractable problems of poverty and even mass-starvation which the coming of independence alone had failed to solve.

Above all in the West in the late Sixties there were abundant signs of a new countervailing spirit to that great tidal wave which had swept up mankind since the Fifties in its onward rush. There were the first signs of a conservative reaction, of a growing weariness with the relentless battering of change. Around 1967, we suddenly began to hear a new set of words – 'conservation', 'the environment', 'pollution', 'ecology' – expressing a growing sense of horror at what our wonderful, runaway technology was doing to our cities, to our countryside and rivers and seas, to other species, to the whole balance of nature on the planet. Somehow, the feeling ran, things seemed to have got out of hand. The paradise we had all been moving towards so rapidly in the late Fifties and early Sixties seemed to be proving curiously elusive. And so, on a deep note of questioning, did the Sixties come to an end.

It has been a fairly general rule in this century that each decade in turn has turned out very differently from what was generally predicted at its outset. At the end of the Forties the outlook for mankind was taken to be very gloomy indeed. Ten years later, at the end of the Fifties, *The Economist* caught the almost universal mood of optimism when it declared, 'at the gates of the new decade, the main peril, blinding our eyes to what we could achieve, seems almost to be smugness'.

At the beginning of the Seventies, few people could imagine that the new decade would be all that different from the Sixties. *Time* magazine, for instance, predicted that young people would continue to rebel, that Women's Lib would get more strident, that 'gays', old age pensioners and other groups would climb on the protest bandwagon, that stage nudity would get more daring, that the Western world would continue to enjoy an economic boom, that technology would continue to produce new triumphs – in other words, that the mixture would be much as before, only more so.

Indeed, for the first year or two of the Seventies, this was pretty well how things turned out – even though the difficulties of sustaining the onward rush became more and more apparent.

The world economy did continue to boom, partly as a result of the way America was choosing to finance her war in South-East Asia. Increasingly desperate about her impotence in Vietnam, the United States made a last attempt to bludgeon her way to victory, as in 1970 President Nixon ordered the invasion of Cambodia, and stepped up still further the blasting of those unhappy lands with high-explosive, napalm, chemical defoliants and every kind of sophisticated technological horror. At the same time, as if foreshadowing her eventual weakening of will, America pursued *détente* with the rest of the Communist world more fervently than at any time since the Second World War, leading to the SALT disarmament talks, Helsinki, the Nixon–Brezhnev summit and, most surprising of all, Nixon's visit to Mao's China in 1972.

In Britain likewise in the early Seventies, the new Conservative government under Edward Heath (elected in 1970), far from reflecting that desire for quieter, more conservative times which had already begun to show in English life, made a last effort to bludgeon Britain into a bigger, brighter, more 'efficient' future, by a series of grandiose bureaucratic and technological gestures only too typical of the wishful thinking of the Sixties. For a time the economy boomed in all sorts of rather sick and unreal ways. The property boom unleashed on Britain's cities the greatest concentra-

tion of redevelopment they had ever known. Inflation rose
alarmingly. The trade unions, already at odds with the
Heath government over its maladroit Industrial Relations
Act, became more and more aggressive.

The world in general, as an explosion in commodity
prices pushed up inflation across the globe, was passing
into a strangely jumpy state. And so, in 1973, began that
period of general disorder which, in many ways, we can look
back on as having been a kind of grand climacteric to the
whole of the vision of a new age opened up twenty years
before, and the attempt to achieve which had already, since
the mid-Sixties, begun to produce such signs of strain.

The most obvious place where the climacteric showed
was, of course, America. As Dr Kissinger prepared at the
beginning of 1973 for the United States' final, ignominious
scuttle from Vietnam, the country was suddenly plunged
into the shadow of that miasma known generically as
'Watergate', which in just over eighteen months was to
lead to the resignations of Vice-President Agnew and of
President Nixon himself.

Just as significant, however, were the consequences of
the Yom Kippur war between Israel and her Arab neighbours, which broke out in October 1973. It was almost
eerie how the ripples from that event were to spread out
across the rest of the Seventies. The immediate reason for
the Arab world's quadrupling of oil prices over the succeeding twelve months was simply to show disapproval for the
West's support of Israel. But at the same time, it seemed
like the most dramatic example yet of the non-industralized
world's growing desire to protest at the reckless exploitation by only a fraction of mankind of the earth's finite and
rapidly diminishing natural resources. Indeed it was the
first really serious, practical symptom of that approaching
crisis for mankind of which the 'environmentalists' had

been warning for six or seven years. And the most immediate and obvious consequence was that the world's economy was plunged into its deepest recession since 1945.

As on all sides we began to hear talk of 'zero-growth' and 'diminishing expectations', country after country took drastic steps to contain the new threat to their economies. Almost the only exception was Britain which, thanks to peculiar political circumstances, was over the next eighteen months to drift into an unreal little climacteric of her own.

Initially, in his typically rather wooden way, Prime Minister Edward Heath attempted to follow other countries in taking steps to meet the crisis. But as his government's authority dissolved in the early months of 1974, amid industrial chaos, power cuts, food shortages and the 'Three Day Week', events could scarcely have conspired more effectively to complete the work of financial chaos which the Heath government had already begun.

For eighteen months, Harold Wilson's new Labour government in effect gave way to the unions in everything they asked for. Wage demands and government spending went through the roof – as did inflation, public borrowing and the huge balance of payments deficit that were their inevitable price. By the summer of 1975, with an inflation rate of 27 per cent, higher than any other country in the industrialized world, Britain stood on the edge of what eventually even Mr Wilson himself, though lost to the last in his own imperturbably self-regarding fantasy world, warned could become 'a catastrophe of unimaginable proportions'. The unions, led by the man now widely described as 'the second most powerful figure in the country', Jack Jones, at last agreed to moderate their wage demands. But it was not until after a further autumn of crisis in 1976, when the IMF stepped in and some attempt was made to cut government spending, that the threat of the 'unimaginable catastrophe' finally, for the time being, receded.

The rest of the world, during these watershed years of the mid-Seventies, had not been without rather more serious troubles of its own. While America, the leading champion of capitalist democracy, had been introspectively locked in the gloomy toils of Watergate, the other great ideology holding sway over mankind, Communism, had enjoyed its greatest series of advances since the late Forties. Most spectacular, of course, was the collapse into Communist hands in just a few weeks of the spring of 1975 of the whole of Indo-China. Over countries which for years had been bathed in the glare of the world's publicity, there suddenly fell a black wall of censorship – through which percolated rumours, from Cambodia in particular, of the most frightful aftermath to the Communist victory, with perhaps anything up to *two or three million* of Cambodia's population of seven million being effectually put to death in 1975–6.

Two countries which for forty years had embodied for the world the other extreme of the ideological spectrum, Spain and Portugal, briefly seemed likely so to over-react to the end of their right-wing dictatorships that they too might teeter over into Communism, although both eventually pulled back. But certainly Portugal's two largest and richest African colonies, Angola and Mozambique, both fell quickly after independence under semi-Marxist, totalitarian regimes, as did other parts of Africa, including Ethiopia and Somalia. It was perhaps hardly surprising that, emboldened by their burgeoning military and political strength, while America flagged, the leaders of the Soviet Union should finally in 1974 have begun to seize the nettle of that internal dissent which had grown up since the early Sixties by expelling the most powerful of all Russian dissidents, Alexander Solzhenitsyn, who came to the West as a prophet of terrible doom.

Certainly as the world emerged from those turmoils of the mid-Seventies, and as America emerged from the long dark night of Watergate, electing as President the almost unknown Georgian evangelist Jimmy Carter in token of the general desire for a 'fresh start', the global landscape began to seem very different from the way it had looked only a few, brief years before. Gone were the expectations that mankind was heading up into an ever more glorious, prosperous future, on an ever-rising curve of production and consumption. Gone was the old unchallenged standing and pre-eminence of America, whose self-confidence indeed was to diminish even further as the somewhat ghostly, milk-and-water nature of the Carter presidency emerged.

Almost without it being noticed, a tremendous change had come over the world's mood. Already so many of the more garish and strident phenomena which had marked out the Sixties and the early Seventies seemed to have faded away so far that they belonged almost to another era. The great heyday of youthful protest was now so much a historical memory that occasional nostalgic television programmes would appear, showing how the 'hippies' and 'flower children' and 'Marxists' of the late Sixties had become transmogrified into short-haired computer programmers or prosperous antique dealers or even, as in the cases of the 'Black Power' leader Eldridge Clever, singer Bob Dylan and others, committed Christians. If 'Gay Lib' continued to flourish, as *Time* had predicted in 1970, certainly Women's Lib had lost much of its initial dark energy, and the great wave of 'protest' and demands for 'rights' which had once seemed likely to engulf the whole of Western society had markedly lost momentum.

Of all the cultural symptoms of the late Seventies, few were more revealing than the spectacular collapse of that ideology which, for twenty years, had sought to bulldoze our cities into a 'Brave New World'. Certainly the economic recession following the 1973 oil crisis had played its part in bringing re-building to a sudden standstill. In Britain, for instance, the years 1974–6 had seen a wave of bankruptcies of unprecedented size, affecting a whole series of major property companies, 'fringe banks' and other institutions which had gambled recklessly on the 'property bubble' of the early Seventies. But running much deeper than these mere financial factors, the same years had seen a quite astonishing reaction to the 'Modern Movement dream', that vast areas of the older parts of the world's cities should be swept away, to be replaced by mighty towers, concrete housing estates, motorways, multi-storey car parks and all the other outward expressions of the age of Technology Triumphant. Although the ideas derived from the Modern Movement might still be a long time in dying among the architects and planners primarily responsible, the reaction to the more inhuman excesses and horrors of the years of the great 'concrete explosion' was an almost world-wide phenomenon.* The desire to preserve old build-

---

* When Britain's Environment Secretary Peter Shore formally proclaimed to the 1976 Habitat Conference in Vancouver that 'Britain has pensioned off the bulldozer' he was applauded by delegates from many countries. In France an edict in 1977 prohibited future building above seven storeys, except in special circumstances. In America the disillusionment with the Modern Movement expressed itself in such books as *Form Follows Fiasco* by Peter Blake, once one of its most fervent champions. Even in East Germany the only form of social criticism occasionally permitted on television was that relating to the difficulties of living in tower blocks and the social problems caused by vast new housing estates (cf. 'A Tale of Three Cities', BBC-TV documentary, 1978).

ings, or at least only to build in future on a smaller, more
'human' scale, had suddenly become one of the great driving forces of the age. And nowhere did this loss of confidence in the Modern Movement go further than in the
country which, in some ways, had embraced its ideas for
comprehensive redevelopment more wholeheartedly than
any, Britain.

In all sorts of ways, in fact, Britain reflected the new
mood of the late Seventies more obviously than many
countries. This was not least made apparent in the fact
that, within little over a year in 1975–6, both Britain's
major political parties had chosen new leaders. Those two
typical 'fantasy-figures' of the Sixties, Heath and Wilson,
had departed (as at much the same time, though for rather
different reasons, had the leader of Britain's third largest
party, Jeremy Thorpe). And in many ways, the two figures
who succeeded Wilson and Heath could not have provided
a greater contrast.

However much his detractors claimed that the 'bluff,
avuncular style' of Jim Callaghan, who succeeded Harold
Wilson as Prime Minister in April 1976, was just a façade,
in reality hiding a weak man, prone to panic, the fact remains that the atmosphere of British political life did change
markedly after Wilson's departure. Seeing himself initially
as 'Moses', come down from the mountain top to utter
stern truths to his people, Callaghan did run a tighter, more
orthodox monetary policy,* and unlike his predecessor

---

* One of the 'success stories' of the Seventies was the influence of
the monetary theories of Milton Friedman, which by 1977 were even
carrying weight with the British Labour government. In the inflation
of the early Seventies, almost every country in the Western world
had seen an unprecedented expansion of its 'money supply'. The later
success of 'Friedman-ism' could be seen as a reaction to that, and as
one of the many symptoms of the end of the 'Keynesian era' whose

was not afraid on occasion to spell out to the unions the economic facts of life. Inflation did come down a long way from its traumatic peak in 1975 (in fact to 9 per cent by 1979) and, assisted by that greatest unlooked-for bonanza of the Seventies, North Sea oil, which only four years after it began to flow in 1974 was already meeting four-fifths of Britain's needs, the country's financial picture by the late Seventies looked, at least outwardly, rather more rosy.

Even more interesting, in terms of the changing mood of the times, was the emergence of Mrs Margaret Thatcher, symbolizing a very different kind of conservatism from that which Mr Heath had stood for. By the late Seventies, indeed, it was widely accepted that the revival of conservative attitudes which had begun to show as early as ten years before had at last reached the point where it was the most powerful, even intellectually vigorous force in English life. Certainly it seemed a long way from the days of that triumphant onward march of 'permissive' morality, 'progressive' attitudes in education, and general neophilia which in the Sixties had dominated English life in all directions.* Similarly there was a widespread and deep-seated reaction to those heady days of the Wilson government in the mid-Seventies, when it had seemed that the trade unions and an ever-expanding bureaucracy were carrying all before them. Various former left-wing writers, such as Paul John-

---

orthodoxy had been that governments could and should 'spend their way out of trouble'.

* Another reflection of Britain's more conservative mood in the late Seventies was the extraordinary nationwide rejoicing which surrounded the Queen's Silver Jubilee in 1977. It is hard to imagine that such an occasion would have been celebrated in quite this way in, say, the mid-Sixties. The mood of nostalgia was quite explicit. The *Times* report of one East End street-party quoted a participant as saying, 'It's like the old days – before the planners came.'

son, and politicians, like the one-time Labour Foreign Secretary Lord George-Brown, were now in the forefront of those warning that the power of the unions and the over-mighty spread of government (which by 1975 had come to represent or control 60 per cent of the entire British economy) might be just the forerunners of Britain's possible eventual collapse into the kind of Marxist, totalitarian state which many of the more extreme members of the Labour Party, such as Mr Anthony Wedgwood Benn (who had changed his name during the Seventies to plain Tony Benn), seemed to see as increasingly desirable.*

By the last two years of the Seventies, the thought that at least one more last-ditch attempt should be made to save Britain from such a fate, by giving a try to Mrs Thatcher's 'new Conservatism', had for many clearly become irresistible. If there were any doubts that she might be pre-empted by the success of Mr Callaghan's 'Moses' act in talking tough to the newly-quiescent unions, they were rudely dispelled in Britain's 'winter of discontent' in 1978–9, when the lower-paid unions in particular plunged the country into the kind of social chaos it had never known before. Amid three months of the worst winter weather of the decade, and a flood of newspaper headlines and television interviews reflecting a mood of surly, inhuman aggression among the strikers and their leaders that was almost entirely unprecedented in English life (e.g. the

---

* One of the more remarkable features of the latter part of the decade was the collapse of Labour's moderate or social democratic wing. As late as 1974, it would have seemed incredible that within five years the parliamentary Labour Party would be without Anthony Crosland and John Mackintosh (dead); Roy Jenkins and David Marquand (retired to well-paid employment in Europe); Brian Walden (retired to well-paid employment in television); Shirley Williams (defeated at the 1979 general election); and Reg Prentice (joined the Conservatives).

ambulance-drivers' spokesman who said, 'If it means lives lost, that is how it must be ... we are fed up of being Cinderellas, this time we are going to the ball'), hospitals were closed, ambulance services withdrawn, water supplies and sewage shut off, even bodies remained unburied; while a combination of strikes by lorry drivers and petrol tanker drivers seemed for a while to threaten that the country's entire economic activity might be brought to a standstill.

In May 1979, Mrs Thatcher's election victory seemed to mark an appropriate break with much of the kind of thinking which had dominated English life for twenty-five years. As for whether it might be a real turning point, or just a short-lived interlude, only the events of a new decade, the Eighties, could tell.

2

The End of the Twentieth-century Dream

The crisis which may develop as early as 1988 will be of such magnitude as to make the current situation appear like a mere passing event of trivial consequence.

(Sheikh Yamani, 19 June 1979)

It is time to look a little more deeply at what had really been happening to Britain, the West and mankind in the Seventies.

As we have seen, the late Fifties and Sixties, with their tidal wave of change and euphoria – the coming of affluence and television, the Kennedy era, the youth and pop 'revolutions', permissiveness in social mores and the arts, the rebuilding of our cities according to the ideology of the Modern Movement – were the last great moment when it was possible for most people in our culture to look forward in hope to an as yet unrealized future. But if we look more closely at the nature of that optimism, that wave of expectation which so markedly died away in the Seventies, we may see that in essence it was rooted in precisely those same sources of hope that have sustained the human race throughout the twentieth century.

The 'Twentieth-century Dream' has had three central, interwoven strands:

1. the belief that, through science and technology, we should be able to unlock all the 'secrets of the universe', we should be able to 'master' nature, and thus create a materi-

ally secure and comfortable life for the majority of mankind;
2. the Utopian belief that, through drastic social and
political re-organization, aided by the greater use of state
planning, we should be able to create an entirely new
kind of just, fair and equal society;
3. the belief that, through the dismantling of all the old
repressive 'taboos' and conventions of the past – whether in
social attitudes or the arts – individuals would be able to
enjoy a much greater degree of freedom and self-realization.

The importance of the Seventies was that, in each of
these great avenues of human exploration, they had marked
a 'moment of truth', a point at which, more obviously and
inescapably than ever before, the dream ran out. As a friend
put it to me recently, 'the Seventies were the time when our
bluff was called' – not least in the extent to which, in being
actually realized, the dream had turned out (like the 'Brave
New World' visions of tower blocks) to produce such a
very different kind of reality to that originally promised.

Let us consider each of these strands in turn.

1. The Technological, Scientific Dream

Some time in the Seventies a profoundly significant moment
was passed in the history of mankind – the moment when
it became apparent that, even on their own terms, science
and technology were no longer necessarily making life
better, easier, more efficient for us all. Of course there
continued to be technological advances – from the avail-
ability of cheap electronic calculators to the world's first
'test tube baby'. But for the first time in centuries, if not
in millennia, it became apparent in the Seventies that the
whole advance of human technology was beginning to
operate on the law of diminishing returns.

On the one hand, there was nothing new which could really startle us any longer. A deeply symbolic moment, casting its shadow over the Seventies, was that which occurred just before the decade began, when men first landed on the Moon. For the first time (as I analyse in a later essay) technology had literally carried men so far outside their frame of reference that they no longer knew how to relate to it. Never again in human experience could there be such a moment. And even on a more mundane level, the Seventies could offer nothing like a continuation of that avalanche of change which had transformed our lives out of recognition in the Fifties and Sixties. We had shot Niagara – it was impossible that our lives could ever be so deeply, radically changed again.

On the other hand, it became evident that, after all the advances of the previous twenty years, our societies were actually, in countless ways, becoming less efficient; we were actually, for all our computers, labour-saving devices and electronic gadgets, beginning in many ways to get less service, less benefit. If you had asked the average Westerner whether, taking all things into account, the quality and ease of life had improved in those ten years, the chances are that for the first time since the Fifties, he might well have replied 'no'. And not the least ingredient in making life seem more difficult, more unreal, more strained, was inflation.

No account of the Seventies would be complete without some attempt to analyse this extraordinary world-wide phenomenon which has come so much to dominate our lives, our news, our politics, our conversation that we are scarcely any longer aware of just how strange it is. Why is it that, just as we appeared to be standing on the edge of the ultimate consumer Utopia, that world of universal abundance dreamed of by mankind for thousands of years,

we should have become bedevilled by this extraordinary joke we have played on ourselves, that has made the quiet enjoyment of our materialist paradise like one of those mirage-oases which constantly recede before the traveller in the desert?

If we look at the history of inflation, one of the most remarkable things is how comparatively stable over long periods in the past the value of money remained. The value of a pound sterling in 1910, for instance was very similar, in terms of what it could buy, to what it had been two and a half centuries before, in 1660. Almost the only times when its value had declined were during wars, when governments inflated the currency by massive borrowing, or printing paper money (a disguised form of credit) – and in fact more people had lived in periods when prices were falling than the reverse. The two world wars of this century pushed up prices considerably, so that by 1956 the 1910 figure of 100 had risen to 301. But from that moment on, as the Western world climbed onto the escalator of the Fifties consumer boom, prices began to shoot up in a way they had never done in peacetime before. By 1970, in Britain, they had reached 500, by the end of the Seventies they had easily topped 1000 – an increase bringing in its wake such a state of social neurosis and instability that it was not unusual to hear sage commentators like Mr Peter Jay warning that inflation had become a threat to our civilization potentially as great as over-population or the H-bomb.

Yet the economists. for all their talk of 'Phillips Curves', 'cost-push' and 'demand-pull', were ultimately quite baffled by this new problem – in a sense not surprisingly. For its real causes ran much deeper in Western civilization than anything which could be explained by mere economics. At root the great inflation was a psychological phenomenon –

an inevitable consequence of that great unleashing of material expectations that had taken place since the Fifties, which had led people more and more to lose touch with the inexorable fact that you cannot spend what you have not got. Not only had the great consumer boom (like the near-tenfold increase in house prices between 1970 and 1979) been fuelled by an unprecedented expansion of credit – the 'fantasy money' that is spent today and earned tomorrow. The trade unions (not to mention almost everyone else) had come to expect more money as a matter of course, regardless of whether the goods or the production were there to justify it. The whole spiral of financial unreality, increasingly separating money from any true criterion of value (a process assisted on its way by the introduction of decimal coinage in 1971) had become self-perpetuating, the symptom of a gigantic act of collective make-believe. Inflation thus became one of the most obvious measures of the way our material expectations had begun to outrun our capacity to justify them.

An even more fundamental danger sign in the Seventies that mankind could no longer hope to look for an unlimited upward spiral of 'economic growth' was the abundant host of 'early warnings' that for the first time in history the earth's supplies of energy and natural resources were coming under severe and genuine strain. One of the most significant statistical landmarks of the Seventies (apart from the fact that the world's population for the first time reached 4,000 million – it had reached 3,000 million only as recently as 1950) was that for the first time since our civilization began to develop its astonishing dependence on oil a mere eighty years ago, the rate at which new oil reserves were being discovered was overtaken by the rate at which we were consuming oil. By the end of the decade that world energy crisis (which at the end of the Sixties had still

seemed little more than an environmentalists' 'scare story') had already begun to become a reality. With that, and sober forecasts of the exhaustion of other resources, such as a number of metals, within thirty, forty or fifty years, it began to become apparent that the whole technological explosion of the twentieth century, far from preparing the way for some Utopian future, might well turn out before long to have been just a very short-lived phase in the story of mankind.

At a deeper level still there was growing evidence in the Seventies of a new kind of questioning and re-appraisal of the whole role played by technology and science in Western culture since the Renaissance. This was not just a matter of the widespread revulsion against the deadening, destructive character of technology itself, its power to inflict untold harm on nature, the increasing noise, ugliness and pollution it had brought into the world. Such feelings were largely neurotic, since there were few signs that those who experienced them were actually prepared to deny themselves the benefits of technology. What was more interesting was the growing recognition by a good many scientists and others (cf. the essay later in this book on Professor Ehrenfeld's *The Arrogance of Humanism*) that the scientific and technological modes of relating man to nature and to the universe *might in themselves have severe and potentially catastrophic limitations*; that the whole tradition of rationality which had dominated Western thought since Descartes, Galileo and Bacon had, even by its own methods, begun to reveal disastrous shortcomings when measured against the boundless and delicate complexities of nature. This was indeed a sign that some absolutely fundamental shift of opinion was taking place, even within the citadels of science itself — and that one of the most substantial underpinnings of twentieth-century thought might be dissolving towards an entirely new way of looking at the world.

2. Political Utopianism

If one Utopian dream, that of the material paradise to be brought about by technology, began to turn as never before into a mirage in the Seventies, another aspect of the twentieth-century dream which took an unprecedented beating was that of the social and political Utopia – that vision of a just, equal and compassionate society associated above all with all the countless variants of Socialism.

Although the late Sixties had seen a last infantile flicker of the tradition of Socialist idealism – in the wave of 'student protest' and pseudo-Marxism that ran round the world in 1968, associated with such idols as Marcuse, Guevara, Trotsky and Ho Chi-Minh – the decade which followed could scarcely have exposed the dark underside of Socialism more starkly. More than ever before in the Seventies was it borne in on us all just how cruelly the Socialist dream could betray the originally proclaimed humanitarian ideals of its leaders and their hundreds of millions of not always willing followers.

Solzhenitsyn's *The Gulag Archipelago*, published between 1974 and 1978, revealed to the world in an entirely new way just how horrific had been the experience of Russia under Socialist totalitarianism – not only at the height of Stalin's purges in the Thirties, but from the earliest days of the Bolshevik Revolution: how the systematic policies of enslavement, extermination and genocide carried out against the peoples of the largest country on earth for fifty years had amounted to the greatest crime in the history of humanity, dwarfing even the more familiar atrocities committed by Hitler.

As if to demonstrate that such savagery was by no means

a matter of history, the aftermath of the Communist take-over in Indo-China in 1975 (cheered on by many young Western sympathizers) led to the almost unbelievable nightmare of Cambodia, where even on Communist figures, over a third of the population were in effect put to death by the new Pol Pot–Ieng Sary regime in just two or three years. By the end of the Seventies, the spectacle of the 'boat people' fleeing in their hundreds of thousands from Vietnam gave the world at least some tiny glimmering of the sufferings inflicted on that country by its new 'Socialist' masters. In Mozambique, Angola, Ethiopia – wherever Marxist regimes had taken over during the Seventies – reports of slave camps and massacres trickled out.

Such distant horrors across the world may have seemed a far cry from the rather cosier politics of our own little island. But even in Britain, one of the most conspicuous developments of the Seventies was the way that Socialism showed a little more of its ugly underside. The trade union movement became more and more of a dark presence in our national life, showing itself more than ever before concerned with little other than money, power and the winning of privilege above the law, capable on occasion of exercising brute force to achieve its ends quite as ruthlessly as the stereotyped capitalist villains of old. Many trade union leaders, such as Jack Jones, Clive Jenkins and Arthur Scargill, now displayed quite open sympathy with the Soviet Union and the Communist world – as when, in 1976, the TUC received a fraternal visit from Shelepin, the head of the KGB. At the end of a decade in which the Labour Party had become increasingly synonymous with trade union power, the dead hand of bureaucracy and Trotskyite infiltration, it was harder than ever to recall how deeply it had once been associated with the humanitarian ideals of liberty and compassion.

In fact one of the most graphic illustrations of the evaporation of that twentieth-century dream of a fairer, juster society, planned to give a better life for all its citizens, lay in the astonishing disillusionment which now surrounded the attempt in the Fifties and Sixties to rebuild our cities. Inspired like Le Corbusier and others in the early decades of the twentieth century by the vision that that we could sweep away the old cities of the past and replace them with an entirely new kind of city, planned down to the last detail to give a better, healthier, fuller life for all its inhabitants, the politicians, architects and planners of Britain had produced little more than a series of bleak, grimly regimented wastelands. Vast areas of cities such as London, Liverpool, Glasgow and Newcastle had been transformed into inhuman moonscapes of tower blocks, set in a sea of dereliction. The millions of (mostly poorer) people who had been herded into the concrete Gulags of the new housing estates were victims of one of the most dramatic of all attempts to realize the twentieth-century dream of Utopia. In the Seventies it became clear how profoundly this version of the dream, like others, had failed.

3. The Dream of 'Individual Self-realization'

Alongside the dream of salvation through technology and of a collective Utopia, the twentieth century has been haunted by a third — although it was closely linked with the others and, like them, its roots in fact went back much further in history than just the twentieth century, at least to the time of the Industrial and French Revolutions at the end of the eighteenth century. This was the dream that if only we could throw off the repressive shackles of convention, and 'bourgeois', socially imposed morality, we should arrive at a wonderful new age of 'liberation', in which human beings would at last be free to 'be themselves'.

In essence this mighty impulse, first appearing in the form of the Romantic Movement, was a revolt against structure, order, discipline – a reaction in the name of 'life' against the dehumanization of an increasingly machine-dominated, money-conscious, bureaucratic civilization. And it showed itself nowhere more than in the arts and in the realm of sexual morality.

In the nineteenth century the Romantic revolt against 'bourgeois respectability' took the form of wave after wave of 'Bohemianism', 'Aestheticism' and the self-conscious pursuit of 'Decadence'. At the beginning of the twentieth century it made a further huge leap forwards, particularly in that *avant-garde* explosion which convulsed the arts, that whole reaction against Victorian academicism which marked the birth of the Modern Movement in music, painting, literature and architecture. Amid the frenzied *avant-garde* 'experiments' and sexual 'liberation' of the Twenties it reached still further heights – but even these were to pale into insignificance when set against what was to follow in the late Fifties and Sixties.

In the 'youth revolution', the 'permissiveness', the general world-wide hysteria of the 'Swinging Sixties', the collective impulse that had begun with the rebellion of the early Romantics reached its peak. In the flashing lights and blaring cacophony of the discotheques, in the four-letter words and displays of nudity, in the drug obsessions, the 'love festivals', the cults, the crazes, the dazzling patterns of Op Art and the infantile playthings of Pop, the children of the Sixties sought to shake, deafen, blind and drug themselves into the 'ultimate experience' on a scale never before seen – until there was almost nowhere further to go. To put it at its simplest, the mini-skirts could go no higher, the pop music could get no louder, even the available permutations on 'sexual normality' must eventually be exhausted. One of the main reasons why the Seventies had such an air of hangover, of aftermath, was that a psychological climax had been passed which could never be worked up to with the same frenzied excitement again, simply because so many of the 'kicks' had come from the very act of 'pushing back frontiers', dismantling 'taboos' and 'flouting conventions' which could never again, in the same way, be re-erected.*

At the same time in the Seventies a strange exhaustion settled over the Modern Movement in all the arts. As I point out in a later essay, it is remarkable how many of the giants of the Modern Movement died in the ten years between 1965 and 1975 – from Le Corbusier to Picasso, from Eliot to Stravinsky – leaving very few major figures left on the world arts scene. The truth was that the Modern Movement had exhausted itself for precisely the same reasons as the other manifestations of our modern neo-Romanticism. For decades it had gone on pushing back frontiers of form, structure and tonality, until there was no structure left to topple. The concert halls were still full, the theatres busy, the queues outside the art galleries longer than ever – not so much in honour of the masterpieces of our own time, as because the appetite for the music, the plays and art works of the past had never been greater. After tens of thousands of years of seemingly endless fertility, the artistic imagination of humanity had at last reached, for the time being at least, a more or less gaping void. It was perhaps the most profound reflection of all of the strange plight of late-twentieth-century man.

---

* One of the more pitiful shadows of all this in the Seventies were the so-called 'Punk Rockers' who, with their safety pins stuck through noses, their circus-clown make-up, their abysmal music, showed how virtually impossible it was any longer to exceed the 'bounds of convention' in order to excite some last vestige of sensation.

3

On Dover Beach

... the world, which seems
To lie before us like a land of dreams,
So various, so beautiful, so new,
Hath really neither joy, nor love, nor light,
Nor certitude, nor peace, nor help for pain;
And we are here as on a darkling plain
Swept with confused alarms of struggle and flight,
Where ignorant armies clash by night.

(Matthew Arnold, 'Dover Beach', 1867)

Just before the Seventies began, one of the more interesting symptoms of that groundswell of reaction which was already beginning to form against the frenzied contemporaneity and rude disorder of the Sixties was the astonishing popularity of Kenneth Clark's *Civilisation*, the most successful series television has ever produced.

A powerful ingredient in the immediate impact of *Civilisation*, particularly in America, was the contrast it struck with the strange times in which it first appeared. There, on television screens which had been purveying nightly images of Vietnam, race riots, protest demonstrations and pop festivals, was this urbane figure, in his beautifully cut suits, taking us back into a different world – a realm of exquisite paintings, tapestries, cathedrals, palaces, the rich, ordered harvest of a thousand years of European culture. Amid the chaotic nightmare of the present, Clark seemed a symbol of all that sense of permanence and stability we thought we had lost, and were beginning again to yearn for.

Indeed as he magisterially surveyed the whole sweep of Western civilization since the Middle Ages, not the least appealing thing for many viewers was the way Clark did not conceal his distaste for the way the story had ended up. Apart from stray asides directed throughout the series at modern architects, playwrights, psychiatrists, 'hellish traffic' and 'all those forces which threaten to impair our humanity – lies, tanks, tear gas, ideologies, opinion polls, mechanization, planners, computers', Clark's fear that we were no longer civilized, his suspicion that we were sinking into a new barbarism, constantly intruded on his survey of the glories of the past like a spectre at the feast. In Chartres Cathedral, he could not help remarking, 'even the tourists have not spoiled its atmosphere, as they have in so many temples of the human spirit'. From the octagon-room at the top of Greenwich Observatory, surrounded by all the noble impedimenta of seventeenth-century science, his gaze strayed out across the trees and the elegant buildings of Wren's Royal Hospital below, to a distant skyline of smoking factories and high-rise flats, 'the squalid disorder of industrial society'.

Why should we have come to such a pass? This might well have been one of the major underlying themes of such a series; indeed, up to a point, Lord Clark seemed to be giving his answer. The trouble with our present civilization, he implied, was that we have lost touch with our spiritual roots, our sense of human scale, our sense of man's proper place in the frame of nature. We have become, in short, materialists on a heroic scale, defying the universe, but at the same time losing that sense of proportion in all things which has been the secret of all those societies along the way which may be held to have been truly civilized.

So where did it all start to go wrong? If we are to see the past thousand years of our civilization as an evolutionary development, and not just as a set of disconnected episodes, there must have been certain points along the way where those disruptive tendencies now bearing such unwelcome fruit began to show themselves. But here Lord Clark showed himself strangely reluctant to accept the full implications of his own evidence.

He began his story with a somewhat melodramatic account of how civilization was brought through the Dark Ages following the fall of Rome, 'by the skin of its teeth'. He made no bones about what constituted this holy relic, being carted about on the extreme Western shores of Europe by a handful of barbarian monks. It certainly had little to do with Christianity, the latest of those 'mystery religions', full of 'meaningless rituals', that had 'destroyed the self-confidence' of the antique world. It was the humanist tradition of Graeco-Roman culture.

Around A.D. 1000 this frail flame was fanned back into life. 'Civilization' was re-born. And the moment Clark chose to illustrate this was particularly significant — the re-emergence in Christian art of a 'recognizably human' figure. From then on, despite his previous lukewarm sympathy for Christianity, the Church passed into favour as the chief pillar of Western civilization, and over the next two episodes, describing the Middle Ages, it could do little wrong. But even here, despite his passing insistence on the 'civilizing' importance of the Christian view that the spiritual world was ultimately more real than the material, it was again revealing what incidents and people Lord Clark chose to illustrate this. He homed in with particular delight, for instance, on the figure of the Abbé Suger of St Denis (whom he compared to 'Van Horne, the builder of the Canadian-Pacific railways'), the man who had consciously revived the Greek belief that men's minds could only come to appreciate the spiritual world through material beauty.

Even the sculptors of Chartres must have drawn their original inspiration from Greek models.

In short, for all his apparent sympathy for the world-view of medieval Christendom, Clark's real admiration for the Middle Ages was centred on the way they marked the beginning of a revival of the humanistic values of the classical world. All of which might lead one to suppose that, as the Middle Ages drew towards their close, and as civilization reached that mighty turning point where men reached out to find still greater significance in the material world (and in themselves) without necessarily retaining the all-embracing framework of religion, Lord Clark would have found himself increasingly at home; indeed that, in the Renaissance, that time when the old Graeco-Roman culture was revived more fervently and consciously than ever before, and when (as he borrowed from Protagoras for the title of one of his programmes) man might again become 'the measure of all things', Clark would find his true centre of gravity.

Yet here was a curious thing. Of the Middle Ages themselves, Clark had spoken with almost unreserved enthusiasm. They had almost everything he regarded as a necessary condition of 'civilization' – 'a sense of permanence', of 'eternity', of man's place in nature and so forth. But in each of the three programmes covering the Renaissance and the Reformation, in which he represented man bursting forth from the constrictions of the medieval frame, he so chose to arrange his evidence that, after an initial wave of optimism, liberation and creativity, they ended in blackest pessimism. From the order and light of Urbino and Alberti's Florence to the romantic, almost nihilistic gloom of Giorgione's *Tempestà*, from the glories of the High Renaissance to Leonardo's world-destroying deluges, from the sun-lit humanism of Erasmus to what Clark rather curiously took to be Shakespeare's conviction that life is ultimately meaningless, each time the great leap forward and upward of these two centuries in which our modern world came to birth was represented as ending in doubt, if not total despair.

Why should Clark have portrayed that very moment which saw the triumphant re-emergence of his own highest values, the leap of the Renaissance into a newly liberated, man-centred world-view, in this way? Was it that he unconsciously sensed this to be the crucial moment of the birth of that restlessness, that refusal to accept the restraints of a universal order, that insatiable curiosity about and desire to 'master' the external, material world, which had finally led to his nightmarish vision of the present?

Certainly in the next episode, on the Counter-Reformation, Clark seemed to take unusual delight in running counter to the modern grain, as he extolled the partial re-establishment of authority and religious certainty in the Tridentine Church. But even here, as he surveyed the attempts of Bernini and Co. to give their spiritual visions material expression, he was driven to end his story unhappily on the dissipation of the ceilings and paintings of the late Baroque into swirling clouds of illusion.

From there on, as the modern world grew closer, Clark found it ever harder to keep a secure foothold. He rejoiced briefly in the re-ordered universe of Newton and Descartes, of Vermeer's prosperous Holland — but even this was an order based ultimately (except for Rembrandt) on the materialism of emergent capitalism and scientific observation, and as he gazed out from Greenwich, he was only too gloomily reminded of what that love of wealth and scientific knowledge was to lead to. He found universal truth in the masters of eighteenth-century music, Bach, Handel, Haydn, Mozart, but saw them leading inexorably to *Don Giovanni*:

'the pursuit of happiness and the pursuit of love, which had once seemed so simple and life-giving, had become complex and destructive, and [Don Giovanni's] refusal to repent, which makes him heroic, belongs to another phase of civilization.'

Loth to plunge on such a perfect cue into the whirlpool of nineteenth-century Romanticism, Clark returned to the 'Age of Reason' – but again the smile of Voltaire faded into the self-destructive make-believe and irrationality of the French Revolution. He tried the revolutionary ideals of brotherhood and liberty themselves, but found them fading faster than ever into the 'Fallacies of Hope' and totalitarian violence.

Increasingly, in his final episodes, Clark was forced to clutch at straws for anything he could really call 'civilization' – Balzac's defiance of 'fashionable opinion' (really? – was that why Balzac so liked living in a large house and being invited to smart dinner parties?), the technological Romanticism of Brunel, the 'heroic materialism' of the Manhattan skyline (as long as you don't look at it too closely), the 'love of nature' which he traced from Rousseau and Wordsworth to the cloud studies of Constable, the gaseous canvases of Turner, and Monet's lily pools, where the figurative image finally and delicately hovers on the edge of complete abstractionism. All this was pretty thin stuff when measured against that confident universality which Clark had found in the past, above all in the Middle Ages; only by shutting the best part of both eyes was it possible to see in those closing episodes anything more than the faintest vestiges of those ideals of 'harmony', 'proportion', 'a sense of permanence' and 'eternity' which in earlier programmes he had claimed were essential to any definition of 'civilization'. And so, with this increasing sense of dissipation, of a reluctance to lift his head, we reached Lord Clark's melan-

choly peroration on the whole series, his quotation from
Yeats:

> Things fall apart; the centre cannot hold;
> Mere anarchy is loosed upon the world,
> The blood-dimmed tide is loosed, and everywhere
> The ceremony of innocence is drowned . . .

As if finally reluctant to end his story on quite so bleak
and despairing a note, he showed some 'idealistic' students
at Essex University (vintage 1968), and then, as he later
put it in his autobiography, 'I walked into my library,
patted a wooden figure by Henry Moore, as if to imply that
there was still hope, and it was all over.'

Perhaps the most apposite comment on this superbly
polished performance, which was greeted in 1969–70 with
near-universal rapture (but noticeably by almost no attempt
to discuss what Clark was actually saying), might have been
some lines from the dialogue of Plato named after that same
Protagoras who had once pronounced that 'man is the
measure of all things':

> 'Do you think it a beautiful and well-written poem?'
> 'Yes, both beautiful and well-written.'
> 'And do you think a poem beautifully written if the poet con-
> tradicts himself?'
> 'No.'
> 'Then look at it more closely.'

Almost everyone at the beginning of the Seventies took
the view that *Civilisation* was a 'beautiful and well-written
poem' – indeed it remained throughout the decade the *beau
idéal* of the 'intellectually prestigious' (and money-spin-
ning) series which all good little TV chiefs were constantly
seeking to repeat. But at the heart of the series was a contradiction so glaring that it might be thought astonishing
it was not picked up more widely at the time. On the one

hand, Lord Clark was arguing that the rise of Western civilization in the Middle Ages had rested on the revival of the humanist ideals of Greece and Rome. On the other, he could not conceal his intuition that somehow the 'drowning of our innocence' may have begun at precisely the moment when those values again became uppermost; when to the heroes of the Renaissance it seemed possible that man and his works, to a degree which not even the ancient world could have imagined, might become truly 'the measure of all things'. Clark hated much of the way the story had ended up. Yet somehow he seemed unable to draw the connection between all these things.

Of course one reason why Lord Clark was not picked up on such a fundamental hiatus in his argument was that his position is one almost universally shared. As they consider the contemporary plight of mankind, it is not uncommon these days for people to opine that the modern world appears to be going to hell in a handcart. They believe that civilization is in decay. Certainly the state of our arts shows that we have culturally lost confidence on a scale which is quite unprecedented (imagine a world in which we were condemned only to listen to the music, look at the pictures and live in the buildings of the last twenty years – a definition of hell?). Yet the last thing which most people are prepared to accept is that possibly such an outcome might have been absolutely inevitable from the whole course Western civilization has taken over the past five hundred years. Of course we revere the past, as an escapist refuge from the spiritual dissonance of the present, as a source of reassuring images to shore us up against our present ruin. We admire Chartres Cathedral more than the New York World Trade Center, Rembrandt more than Mark Rothko, *War and Peace* more than *Last Exit to Brooklyn*. Yet we refuse to put the whole picture together with a proper sense of intellectual consistency, to admit that the ugliness, noise, pollution, triviality, totalitarian horrors and threatened catastrophes of our world may spring just as surely from our view of man and his relations with the universe as did the Gothic cathedrals from the medieval view of those things. And the chief reason why we do this is our last-ditch reluctance to abandon our one-sided belief in the religion of Progress – that belief that somehow our mighty voyage out of the past has only been a journey out of darkness up into light, out of ignorance into knowledge, out of helpless dependence on nature towards some fondly imagined state of omnipotence. We cannot imagine that we may have got it, at least half, very seriously wrong.

It took a very long time for that gigantic shift of psychological perspective that was implicit in the ending of the Middle Ages and the coming of the Renaissance really to work through in our culture. In a sense it did not fully work through until the middle of the nineteenth century, when the religion of human Progress finally emerged in all its self-congratulatory splendour. The triumphant advance of nineteenth-century industrialism, bringing unimaginable material comfort to millions, the Macaulayan 'Whig' view of history, which saw the past as a gradual winning of individual liberty from ancient tyrannies, the Darwinian theory of evolution, which saw the whole history of creation as an impersonal, ineluctable process whereby lower beings evolved into higher (culminating of course in the final glory of mid-nineteenth-century *Homo sapiens* himself), were all the underpinnings of that world-view whereby mankind seemed to be being carried up into an ever more delightful, comfortable, omniscient future.

Yet even at that very moment when the doctrine of Progress was finally burgeoning forth, there were a few who recognized that something very fundamental was going astray, that something very important to humanity was being lost. In 1867, the year Karl Marx published the first volume of *Das Kapital* (which he originally wanted to dedicate to his fellow 'progressive', Darwin), Matthew Arnold wrote 'Dover Beach'. This remarkable poem, as poignant as anything in Victorian literature, was an elegy for the lost certainties of those past ages when men still felt themselves to be a part of nature, and religious faith was an expression of that fact:

> The Sea of Faith
> Was once, too, at the full, and round earth's shore
> Lay like the folds of a bright girdle furl'd.

Now, in the high noon of Victorian industrialism, as the human race was being carried forward by the irresistible advance of new technology, new knowledge, that old simple, largely unconscious faith was, scarcely surprisingly, vanishing like a fast-ebbing tide:

> . . . I only hear
> Its melancholy, long, withdrawing roar,
> Retreating, to the breath
> Of the night-wind, down the vast edges drear
> And naked shingles of the world.

A new faith had arisen, a faith in man himself – the religion shared by Macaulay, Darwin, Marx and almost all the leading prophets of that age. Yet, as Arnold sharp-sightedly perceived, the vision of a future world which that religion held out to its devotees, though it

> . . . seems
> To lie before us like a land of dreams,
> So various, so beautiful, so new,

would ultimately bring to mankind

> . . . neither joy, nor love, nor light,
> Nor certitude, nor peace, nor help for pain.

Exactly a hundred years after Arnold wrote those words, in 1967, Kenneth Clark began writing his *Civilisation* — taking a very much less one-sidedly rosy view of where Progress had led us all to than would have been fashionable in the mid-nineteenth century. Today, a mere thirteen years or so after that, we are in an even better position to appreciate Arnold's scepticism, just as, when we look around our contemporary world (or even just switch on the TV news) we can only too easily recognize what he meant by the poem's closing lines, when he said:

> . . . we are here as on a darkling plain
> Swept with confused alarms of struggle and flight,
> Where ignorant armies clash by night.

Today we are all on Dover Beach, with a vengeance.

Of course we can all see the benefits which Progress has brought us — hot baths, colour television, jet air travel, kidney transplants, frozen food and all the rest — largely those material advances which have cocooned a minority of mankind from the vicissitudes of nature, and made their lives more comfortable, on a scale which even the most fervent of those Victorian preachers of the Progressive religion would have found unimaginable.

On the other hand, we can also see more clearly than ever before just where that short-lived religion has been taking us, how astonishingly limited it was in its view of the totality of human nature. Even if we do not consciously accept these things, we have begun to express our implicit sense of loss in all those countless hankerings which were perhaps the supreme characteristic of the Seventies, hankerings after a lost wholeness, a lost simplicity, a lost innocence — whether they took the form of passions for 'whole-food' or 'nature', for the preservation of old buildings, the following of 'new religions', or just those innumerable television serials set amid the cosy reassurance of past ages, from *Upstairs Downstairs* to dramatizations of Hardy, Dickens and Tolstoy. However superficially, every one of these things was in its own way a symptom of that overwhelming desire to take refuge from the dreadful spiritual oppression and vacuity of the world technology and Progress had led us to. Never before in history had there been an age so distrustful of the present, so fearful of the future, so enamoured of the past. Therein lay the true significance of the Seventies.

But however unconsciously or semi-consciously we betray our feelings, our intuitions about these things, we still have not consciously worked out, any more than Kenneth Clark, just why we should have come to this pass. To do that will require as gigantic and profound a shift in our psychological perspective as that which marked the four centuries after the ending of the Middle Ages and the coming of the Renaissance. It cannot be a shift back to what has gone, it can only be a shift forwards to an entirely new view of human nature. To find that new centre of perspective is the most urgent challenge confronting mankind today. I hope the rest of this view of the Seventies may be seen as making some tiny contribution to that immense task.

Part Two

Global Perspectives

Some time in the mid-Seventies, I recall a year-end television discussion in which various commentators were asked which of the events and personalities of the previous twelve months they thought would still be remembered in a century's time. One of the contributors was Malcolm Muggeridge who, in his customarily sweeping way, said that the only figure of our time who would have the remotest claim on the interest of our descendants was Alexander Solzhenitsyn.

At the time I was rather disposed to write this off as a typical example of Mugg overstatement. Five years later, however, I have entirely come round to his view. Solzhenitsyn *has* towered over the past decade like no one else.

As we have watched the story of mankind unfolding through the Seventies, three great themes have consistently overshadowed almost everything else that has been going on.

The first has been the quite startling decline in the power, world standing and self confidence of America – battered by virtual defeat in South-East Asia, the Watergate scandal, the thin, well-meaning but watery leadership of the Carter presidency – and the corresponding advance of Communist power and influence, in Asia, in Africa and throughout the world, in terms of military and naval might.

The second has been the steadily looming prospect of the

exhaustion of the earth's natural resources, above all oil, from their reckless, seemingly unstoppable exploitation by mankind's runaway technology.

The third has been the increasing shadow cast over the individual human spirit (to an extent which few recognize because most people are themselves so deeply and unconsciously affected) by every conceivable form of collectivism and collective thinking – urging men to take illusory refuge from the complexities and instabilities of contemporary existence by submerging themselves in every kind of 'groupthink', from the trivial values of consumer capitalism to militant trade unionism, from the neurotic clamour for 'rights' to openly violent terrorism.

On all three of these themes, Solzhenitsyn has raised his voice with unrivalled eloquence. There has been no other spokesman for humanity to touch his stature (although the startling election of Karol Woityla as Pope in 1978, bringing the papacy back into the centre of the psychic drama of mankind in a way which seemed inconceivable, promised that another such figure might be in the making).

Not only was Solzhenitsyn, for obvious reasons, in a position to warn of the terrible dangers implicit in the growing weakness of the West and the advancing influence of the totalitarian East. He took a lofty enough perspective to perceive that, at root, the two great ideologies which have come to divide our modern world – the 'Consumer Capitalism' of the West, the 'State Socialism' of the East – are very similar; they are merely superficially different expressions of that humanistic materialism which marks the final phase of mankind's great 'post-Renaissance adventure'. Both are ultimately committed to the same fundamental view of man, and the purpose of his existence on earth; both are equally inimical to the flowering of man in his individual fullness and spiritual maturity; and both are trying to do something which, in terms of human nature and of the earth's resources, cannot be done.

For this reason I have no hesitation in placing at the head of this section two essays analysing Solzhenitsyn's Harvard speech of June 1978 (in fact it was only when these two essays were published in the *Spectator* that the speech came to be properly reported in Britain at all*).

The remaining essays in this section each bear the mark of Solzhenitsyn's pre-occupations. There are two on Western attitudes to totalitarianism in China. The essay on that conspicuously world-wide psycho-political phenomenon of the Seventies, terrorism, is concerned with the West German Baader–Meinhof gang – but the same points could equally have been made about the IRA in Northern Ireland, the Palestinian Liberation Front or any other of those countless symptoms of 'collectivist' thinking at its most brutally anarchic that chequered the history of the decade. There is an essay on the moral collapse at the heart of Nixon's America represented by Watergate, and another on the hideous moral ambivalence of the Vietnam war (written just before the fall of Saigon in 1975, although its conclusions have only been underlined by events in South-East Asia since, including of course the world-wide horror aroused by the escaping 'boat people' in 1979).

'Ex Africa Semper Id' is a survey of Western attitudes to

---

* This was a curious affair, reflecting one of Solzhenitsyn's own points of alarm when he arrived in the West – to discover just how astonishingly sheep-like was the 'free' press of the 'democracies'. The Harvard speech was originally given only a few trivial paragraphs in the British press. With enormous difficulty I managed to secure a copy (from Malcolm Muggeridge). After my articles had appeared I was invited by a number of influential people and newspapers, including the editor of *The Times*, to supply them with cyclostyled copies (almost like a form of *samizdat*). As a result the speech was eventually printed in full in *The Times* and elsewhere.

Africa, where the decade ended in the overthrow of three of
the most horrendous tyrants even that unhappy continent
had thrown up in the years following 'emancipation' from
'imperialist tyranny' — President Amin of Uganda, President
Nguema of Equatorial Africa, and the self-styled Emperor
Bokassa of the Central African Republic; while the same
year, 1979, also of course saw the beginnings of 'black
rule' in Zimbabwe-Rhodesia, a story whose outcome remained as uncertain when the decade ended as the future
of the rest of Southern Africa.

The section ends with an article written in 1979 on that
theme which was likely to dominate the world's politics in
the Eighties even more than it had done in the Seventies, the
gathering global 'energy crisis'.

4

The Warnings of Solzhenitsyn

(15 July 1978)

After soaring into the Western heavens in the late Sixties
and early Seventies like a skyrocket, as the most glamorous
'dissident' of them all, there is no doubt that the trajectory
of Solzhenitsyn's reputation is now on a downward curve.
He is still of course the most famous writer in the world.
But since the zenith between 1970, the year of his Nobel
Prize, and 1974, the year of his expulsion from Russia,
when he was besieged by the engines of Western publicity
as if he were a Jackie Kennedy or a Marilyn Monroe, he has
unmistakably begun a slip back into eclipse. On all sides
there has been a rising chorus of puzzlement and impatience
at some of his more extreme utterances, even of downright
hostility. He is dismissed as a 'mystic', a 'self-righteous
prophet', a 'cold warrior'. People are beginning to say that
he was much over-rated as a novelist, that his books are
turgid and unreadable. Now that he is holed up in Vermont,
behind a security screen, earning all that money, he has lost
both roots and role. We need not be bothered by him much
more.

All this has been beautifully illustrated in the past month
since, on 8 June, Solzhenitsyn gave at Harvard his first
major public speech since his arrival in America three years
ago. There was a time when Solzhenitsyn breaking silence to
give his first considered observations on the Western way of
life would have aroused tremendous interest. In fact, the
speech was given only the scrappiest coverage in this

country (more attention was paid to Mrs Rosalynn Carter's 'reply' to Solzhenitsyn than to his own remarks). And as for America's more general reaction, the comments of Harvey Johnson in the *Washington Post* appear to have been not untypical. He accused Solzhenitsyn of being 'arrogant', 'infuriating', lacking humour. 'His tone is annoying.' 'He lectures us severely and tiresomely.'

What on earth did Solzhenitsyn say to arouse such ire? I believe that his Harvard speech is worth consideration in some detail, because it is a remarkable document. Nothing Solzhenitsyn has said previously has made it so abundantly clear why his message is arousing increasing hostility in the West — nor indeed why, in a sense, it is right that it should do so.

Solzhenitsyn prefaced the first two-thirds of what he had to say by remarking that if he were speaking to an audience in his own country, he would of course be concentrating on the 'calamities' of the Soviet way of life; but since he has now been in enforced residence in the West for four years, it might be of more interest for him to speak about those aspects of Western life which, since he came to live here, have struck him most forcibly. Of these there are essentially five.

The first is what he describes as 'the decline in courage': 'The Western world has lost its civil courage, both as a whole and separately, in each country, each government, each political party . . . political and intellectual bureaucrats show depression, passivity, perplexity in their actions and their statements . . . and even more so in theoretical reflections to show how realistic and reasonable, as well as even intellectually and morally warranted it is, to base state policies on weakness and cowardice.' It would be easy to parody this as merely a plea for such futile displays of power as Suez, Vietnam, or even Heath's confrontation with the miners — but most of us have a suspicion what he means. One of the more eerie things about the past thirty years has been that all-pervasive loss of authority, of the courage of their convictions, by politicians, academics and social leaders of all kinds — and their replacement by a kind of weak geniality, a desire to placate, to say what people want to hear rather than what they ought to hear. It is no accident that the word 'courage' must have been more often used in our society in recent years to describe some highly-paid film-maker extending 'the frontiers of expression' with pornographic films than of any politician, with the possible exception of de Gaulle.

The second thing which startled Solzhenitsyn, coming to the West from the Soviet Union, was to find, in a society which has managed to give its citizens a degree of material comfort which even thirty years ago would have seemed inconceivable, how strained and unhappy so many people look. 'The constant desire to have still more things and a still better life, and the struggle to obtain them, imprints many Western faces with worry and depression, though it is customary to conceal such feelings.'

The third point which struck him about the West is how legalistic our social relations have become. Everyone operates to 'the extreme limit' of the legal framework. 'One almost never sees voluntary self-restraint.' This observation is shrewder than might at first appear. Quite apart from all the public arguments about pay guidelines and the 'protection of employment', it is quite true that what Solzhenitsyn calls 'legalism' has penetrated right down to the smallest details of life: people (as for instance the garage which mends one's car) are no longer motivated by the pleasurable desire to do a job properly (which in the end makes everyone much happier), but only by the sullen-faced desire to do the minimum that is legally necessary – in return, of course, for the maximum reward that can be legally exacted.

Solzhenitsyn's fourth, not unrelated point, is the quite extraordinary degree to which our society has come to place importance on 'rights' rather than 'obligations' (forgetting that one cannot exist without the other). The chief example he gives may seem fairly obvious: 'when a government starts an earnest fight against terrorism, public opinion immediately accuses it of violating the terrorists' 'civil rights.' But again this is something which goes much deeper in our society than just the obvious examples of emphasis on the 'rights' of terrorists or criminals. The speed and regularity with which we are prepared to see any social relationship in terms of the 'rights' of one side rather than the 'obligations' of both is reminiscent of nothing more than a mass of petulant small children.

The last shock Solzhenitsyn had on coming to the West was to look at our newspapers and television. Only someone who has read the Communist press, with its heavy diet of enormously lengthy speeches, no gossip, no crime, and an almost eerie lack of hard facts, can imagine the eagerness with which Solzhenitsyn looked forward to reading for the first time in his life a press that was 'free'. But two things soon depressed him beyond measure. The first was the relentless triviality of so much of even what is still laughably known as the 'serious' press. The second thing that struck him about the Western press, despite the fact that it is 'free', was how astonishingly conformist it is. 'Without any censorship, in the West fashionable trends of thought are carefully separated from those which are not fashionable; nothing is forbidden, but what is not fashionable will hardly ever find its way into periodicals or books or be heard in colleges.'

Now it must be remembered that Solzhenitsyn was merely recording here, in the briefest possible way, some of the main points which had most surprised and shocked him about Western society, as he came upon it directly for the first time in his life. Many people will dismiss his observations as little more than trivial clichés. Others may recognize in this picture of an immature society, full of greedy, self-righteous, squabbling, unhappy children, a reflection of the profound spiritual sickness which they sense has come over Western civilization in recent decades, and which gives the whole flavour of our public and private life a sickly, strained, superficial quality, as if something terrible has happened to us all, without our really daring to admit it.

But Solzhenitsyn then went on to draw a conclusion to the first two-thirds of his speech which really must have endeared him to his American hosts no end. Not only could he no longer recommend Western society, he said, as 'an ideal' for the transformation of Communist society. He would now, as a result of his direct experience of life in the West, have to go much further than that. 'Through intense suffering, our country has now achieved a spiritual development of such intensity that the Western system in its present state of spiritual exhaustion' looks singularly unattractive. 'A fact which cannot be disputed is the weakening of human beings in the West, while in the East they are becoming firmer and stronger.' In the six decades since the Revolution, 'we have been through a spiritual training far in advance of Western experience. Life's complexity and mortal weight have produced stronger, deeper and more interesting characters than those generated by standardized Western well-being.'

It is not difficult to see why the plastic battalions rose up behind Rosalynn Carter when she howled in outrage at this suggestion that, morally and spiritually, Americans might actually score less points than Soviet slaves (she pointed out that last year alone, Americans gave more than $35 billion in 'philanthropic contributions'). But Solzhenitsyn was still not finished in his almost desperate attempt to find some response in that bland complacency: 'There are meaningful warnings which history gives to a threatened or perishing society. Such as, for instance, the decadence of art or lack of great statesmen. There are open and evident warnings too. The centre of your democracy and of your culture is left without electric power for a few hours only, and all of a sudden, crowds of American citizens start looting and creating havoc . . . The fight for our planet, physical and spiritual, a fight of cosmic proportions, is not a vague matter of the future. It has already started. The forces of Evil have begun their decisive offensive, you can feel their pressure, and yet your screens and publications are full of prescribed smiles and raised glasses. What is the joy about?'

Thus saying, he switched for the last third of his speech onto a new, and rather more startling tack. What he had to say here was, I believe, so interesting that I would like to reserve it for separate discussion.

5

Crisis for the West

(22 July 1978)

Up to this point, it is clear that Alexander Solzhenitsyn has laid claim on the attention of mankind primarily as a critic of the Soviet system of government in his own country, and of the various forms of Communism which in the past sixty years have imprisoned a third of the peoples of the earth under a new and unique degree of totalitarianism. Although he has done this by means of innumerable novels, speeches, articles and interviews, no one who has read the now completed *Gulag Archipelago* can doubt that this majestic and sombre book is the crown of his literary work – with its shattering portrait of a whole society transformed into a Kafka nightmare: a world where, in the name of the People, the people have been enslaved; where, in the name of Man, untold millions of men have been cruelly murdered; and where all the highest human values, truth, love, a sense of the fundamental meaning of existence, have been stood on their heads and turned into their grotesque opposites.

But now, during four years of enforced exile, Solzhenitsyn has had an opportunity to take a much more penetrating look at the West. And, as became clear from his widely unreported speech at Harvard, his world-view has consequently completed a most important transmutation. In the first two-thirds of the speech, he set down the chief aspects of contemporary life in the West which had most surprised and shocked him. All this had led him to a sense that the

West is suffering from a profound spiritual sickness much deeper than he had ever guessed from the other side of the great gulf which divides mankind; he had even been forced to recognize that, in certain fundamental respects, the hell of living under sixty years of Socialism had produced in the East a much greater spiritual strength and resilience among ordinary people than is readily evident anywhere in the West (as the bearing of Scharansky and Ginsburg in recent days, he would no doubt suggest, well illustrates).

In the last third of his speech, Solzhenitsyn seeks to inquire how it is that, after centuries of its apparently triumphant march as the spearhead of man's progress, our Western civilization should have been reduced to this appalling state of spiritual debilitation. He sees us as a weak man who wants to cling onto his easy life and to hide from reality, desperately hoping that somehow the status quo will be preserved — as year by year, one 'faraway little nation' after another (Vietnam, Laos, Cambodia, Angola, Mozambique, Ethiopia) continues to slip into the totalitarian darkness, and the shadow of Soviet power lengthens ever longer over the future of mankind. He sees us even pathetically hoping that somehow China, a worse totalitarian power than the Soviet Union, will prove to be an ally in preserving our fragile freedom and our material comforts. Again and again the force of his argument is strikingly reminiscent of those words of Yeats which, with only a shift in tense, could still become the epitaph for our twentieth-century civilization: 'things fell apart, the centre could not hold . . . the best lacked all conviction, while the worst were full of passionate intensity'.

In short, Solzhenitsyn sees approaching for mankind a moment of crisis, a watershed, more important than any since the end of the Middle Ages and the dawn of the

Renaissance. No longer is it just a matter of blithely hoping, as did he and his friends thirty years ago during the darkest night of Stalinism, that somehow the superior moral values of the West would one day prevail, and that the Communist system would become gentler, more liberal and more humane. The day when any of us could indulge in such foolish hopes is long since past. We must now take a much deeper, more honest and more painful look at the whole tendency of the West's development over the past five hundred years. 'The West kept advancing socially in accordance with its proclaimed intentions, with the help of brilliant technological progress. And all of a sudden it found itself in this present state of weakness. This means that the mistake must be at the root, at the very basis of human thinking in the past centuries.'

The point Solzhenitsyn is making here is not a wholly unfamiliar one. He addresses himself to that 'prevailing Western view of the world which was first born during the Renaissance and found its political expression from the period of the Enlightenment [which] became the basis for government and social science, and could be defined as rationalistic humanism, or humanistic autonomy'. He is certainly not saying that the Renaissance was anything other than 'historically inevitable'. In the Middle Ages, man's spiritual nature was exalted above his physical needs; and sooner or later what Heraclitus described as *enantio-dromia*, the tendency of all things in human nature to 'run about' into their opposites, was bound to take place. But Solzhenitsyn then asks us to consider the consequences of that fundamental shift in man's view of himself which took place after the Renaissance, a view which has so come to dominate the thinking of our civilization that most people are scarcely aware that there is any alternative – namely the view of man as a creature whose chief and overriding purpose is to create a materially comfortable life for himself on the largest possible scale.

And here, more forcefully than ever before, Solzhenitsyn expresses a conviction which has clearly been growing in him in recent years – which is that, seen in such a light, the apparently glaring differences between the two ideological poles which now divide the earth shrink into insignificance. Both the Eastern and Western ideologies are fundamentally materialist and humanist in their view of man. For a long time, our Christian heritage, with its 'great reserves of mercy and sacrifice', appeared to give a spiritual underpinning to the whole forward thrust of Western civilization. But increasingly those resources have been exhausted, to the point where we are being forced finally face to face with the fact that the real driving force behind both the Socialism of the East and the 'despiritualized humanism' of the West is nothing more noble than the desire to live as long as possible in the greatest degree of material comfort.

Now, about this process, two very important facts may be observed. The first, Solzhenitsyn argues, is that built into this 'current of materialism', there will always be a fundamental drive to the Left. The 'logic of materialist development' dictates that the Left will always end up being 'stronger, more attractive and victorious, because it is more consistent. Humanism without its Christian heritage cannot resist such competition. We watch this process in the past centuries, and especially in the past decades, as on a world scale the situation has become increasingly dramatic. Liberalism was inevitably displaced by radicalism, radicalism had to surrender to socialism, and socialism could never resist communism.'

Certainly if we survey the political history of this country over the past hundred years, it cannot be denied that the 'leftward drift' has invariably made the running in our own political development – since the heyday of Gladstonian Liberalism, the onward march of state control, bureaucracy, welfarism, social engineering ('egalitarianism') has been pretty well unchecked; and despite occasional illusory flurries of 'reaction', such as the de-nationalization of steel, or Mrs Thatcher's present attempts to provide Conservatism with a 'new philosophy', the underlying process is still continuing at remarkable speed. It now seems quite extraordinary to contemplate that in 1959, less than twenty years ago, influential members of the Labour Party were contemplating the abandonment of nationalization as something 'no longer relevant'. In those days most people in Britain still looked on America as the most likely model for our future social development; whereas, a year or two ago, when I was watching a Robert Kee TV film about life in East Germany, showing a society with full employment, no inflation, no taxes and cheap subsidized housing for all, I could not help reflecting that the picture Kee presented would probably now strike most people in this country as rather enviable.

The same general pattern (again with comparatively trivial exceptions such as Greece after the war, or more recently Chile and Portugal) is observable all over the world. The overriding political tendency of mankind in the twentieth century has been to move to the totalitarian left, with the proportion of the earth's nations living under such regimes rising at an ever increasing speed. The chief odium of our century has been reserved for those governments which, in attempting to stand out against the tide, have seemed to lurch to the opposite extreme of the political spectrum – above all, of course, Hitler's Germany, but also South Africa, the juntas of South America, and America's intervention in Vietnam. Indeed the most dramatic development of all in the past twenty years has been perhaps the extent to which the United States itself, the chief flagship of 'democracy' which twenty years ago seemed to be the undisputed 'super-power' of the world, both in terms of its military might and its material achievements, now seems to have faltered and fallen away to the point where it now seems only to be *primus inter pares* among that small group of Western nations who are all, in different ways and to differing degrees, going through the same prolonged crisis of internal confidence.

Are we then to assume that somehow it is built into the whole underlying tendency of our late, post-Renaissance, materialist civilization that sooner or later the superior confidence and single-mindedness of the totalitarian left will conquer everywhere; that all attempts to stem the tide will look as petulant, absurd and short-lived as America's adventure in Indo-China, or Ian Smith's stand against black nationalism; and that ultimately the whole globe will languish under the same totalitarian night as do Russia, China and some thirty or forty other countries today?

I do not think that Solzhenitsyn himself has really thought through this question in his own mind – any more than he has really faced up to the curious difficulty which the West appears to have in attempting effectively and with conviction to stand up for its own values (he is far too blithe, for instance, in his insistence that America should have taken a much 'tougher' line in Vietnam. What does he really mean – that they should have dropped the H-bomb on Hanoi?). He appears to think that some great final confrontation between the two schizophrenically-split halves of mankind may come about; but again he seems to have convinced himself that such a war need not be nuclear (although he is prepared to consider the possibility that, if the United States were foolish enough to enlist the help of China against the Soviet Union, the Chinese would then turn round with their newly-acquired American weapons and 'America itself would fall prey to a genocide similar to the one perpetrated on Cambodia in our own days').

Where Solzhenitsyn is on much stronger ground, because it is based on his own profound experience and observation, is in emphasizing that ultimately the whole humanist, materialist view of man's existence and purpose on earth simply does not work. It may seem to 'work' politically, in that sixty years later the oldest-established left-wing totalitarian regime in the world is not only still in existence but stronger than ever. But even the Communist world itself is far from being a monolith, and is riven by every kind of nationalistic discord (Russia *v.* China, China *v.* Vietnam, Vietnam *v.* Cambodia) which could sooner or later break out into wars just as terrible and destructive as any between East and West.

Much more important is the fact that the materialist view of man does not work simply because it is based on a total misreading of the fundamental nature of man and his relations with the universe. If the Soviet experiment has demonstrated one thing more clearly than anything else it is that, if you subject men to the very extremes of material and spiritual deprivation, if you force lies into their ears and surround them from birth to death with nothing but the materialist, humanist view of man in its most grandiloquent and exalted form, you will find that in the end many of them discover an entirely new spiritual centre to their existence *within themselves*, because it is imprinted within us to an extent that is beyond the power of any earthly force to eradicate.

Perhaps mankind as a whole will have to endure prolonged and terrible suffering of the kind which so far in our century only the Russian people themselves have had to undergo, in peace and war. One thing that is certain is that our materialist, technologically-based, post-Renaissance civilization can be ultimately seen only as a very short-lived phase in the history of mankind, whether it is destroyed violently and quickly by war, or slowly by the exhaustion of natural resources, or a degree of both. That is why Solzhenitsyn can end his Harvard speech on a note of such unshakeable confidence in saying: 'If the world has not come to its end, it has approached a major turn in history, equal in importance to the turn from the Middle Ages to the Renaissance. It will exact from us a spiritual upsurge, we shall have to rise to a new height of vision, a new level of life where our physical nature will not be cursed as in the Middle Ages, but, even more importantly, our spiritual being will not be trampled on as in the Modern Era. This ascension will be similar to climbing onto the next anthropological stage. No one on earth has any other way left but – upward.'

6

The Destruction of China

(28 July 1978)

> You are all old enough to remember our old towns – towns
> made for people, horses, dogs – and the trams too; towns which
> were humane, friendly, cosy places, where . . . there was a gar-
> den to almost every house and hardly a house more than two
> storeys high.
>
> (Alexander Solzhenitsyn, *Letter to Soviet Leaders*, 1974)

According to the late-lamented Marshall McLuhan, we live
in the age of the 'global village'. It might be more apt to
say that we live in the century of the 'Potemkin village'.
Grigory Potemkin, it will be recalled, was the favourite of
Catherine the Great who, in 1787, when his sovereign was
about to make a tour of the newly annexed Crimea, ar-
ranged for a number of large, prosperous-looking fake villages to be erected along the line of her route, so that
Catherine would believe her new dominions to be much
richer and more populous than they in fact were.

Anything Potemkin could do, his twentieth-century suc-
cesors have done far more effectively and on an infinitely
grander scale. We are all now familiar with the success of
the Soviet propaganda campaign in the 1930s, to convince
gullible Westerners that starving, oppressed Russia was a
land flowing with *crèches*, power stations and happy and
contented citizens; or with the famous occasion in particular when, in 1944, Henry Wallace and Owen Lattimore
were taken round the slave-camps of the Kolyma and Maga-
dan, and shown NKVD office staff dressed up as swineherds

on a model farm, and healthy, smiling 'prisoners' working in a gold mine.

The most eerie thing about the flood of reports which have come out of China in recent years, whether from distinguished Western journalists trotting round with Nixon, Heath or Thatcher, bringing us first-hand reports on the menu at banquets in the Great Hall of the Peoples, or BBC-2 films showing the smiling peasants of the Kwangho commune indulging in 'healthy self-criticism', has been how astonishingly reminiscent they have been of the general image that so many Western visitors gave of Soviet Russia thirty or forty years ago.

I make no apology for returning to the new Penguin *Chinese Shadows* by Simon Leys, because it is a very remarkable and moving book, which deserves the widest possible audience. For the first time we have a portrait of Chinese life today as it actually is (or at least as it was six years ago, when Leys was last there), written by an art historian who is soaked in Chinese culture, is married to a Chinese wife, loves the country 'more than my own' (he is Belgian), and certainly was able to observe what happened to China in the crucial period between 1955 and the end of the Cultural Revolution more intimately than anyone else who has so far been able to give us an account of it.

Not the least telling thing about Leys's book is the way he prefaces it with a delightfully scornful account of just how the 'Potemkin village' trick is worked on Western visitors. The visitor's trail lies along the same tiny handful of well-trodden paths – the same three or four cities, the same half-dozen 'model' communes, hospitals, factories – meeting only specially selected and groomed 'workers' and 'representatives of the people'. He stays in hotels which are completely insulated from the rest of Chinese life. He is taken to the same carefully preserved 'monuments of the past', proudly shown the same archaeological relics dug up during the Cultural Revolution, as evidence of respect for China's artistic heritage. If he is a Roman Catholic, he may even, as proof of the survival of religious freedom, be taken to a celebration of the Tridentine Mass by a Chinese priest, nostalgically surrounded by all the trappings of Catholic ceremonial such as one would scarcely find surviving in the West. And it is all, of course, a carefully staged sequence of charades, a series of 'Potemkin villages', giving absolutely no indication of the terrifying cultural and spiritual desert to which modern China has been reduced.

In fact the real theme of Simon Leys's book is the story of the destruction in less than twenty years of what, even as late as the 1950s, was probably the richest and most deep-rooted popular culture in the world. Consider, for instance, the old Chinese passion for opera which, in city and country, at all levels of society, played a part in everyday life as nowhere else on earth ('no ceremony, no celebration, no solemn or joyful or exceptional circumstance in life was complete without some piece of opera'). By the end of the Cultural Revolution, the whole of that vast repertoire of traditional opera had simply been abolished. By 1972, the only operas being performed in China, endlessly and identically repeated from one end of the country to the other, down to the tiniest production detail, were six 'feeble Punch and Judy shows, whose only "revolutionary" daring is to manoeuvre on stage, to languorous, Khatchaturian-like music, platoons of the Peope's Liberation Army complete with banners and wooden rifles'. If you went to the cinema, apart from the occasional documentary, the only feature films you could see were of those same six 'revolutionary model operas'. If you were unfortunate enough to study Chinese literature at Peking University, the only texts you would have had to study (apart from the works of

Mao) were the 'childish' librettos of those same six 'operas'.

When Mr Heath admired the 'mediocre Rachmaninoff *pastiche*' piano concerto known as 'The Yellow River', he was probably not aware that this (in fact pre-revolutionary) work may well have been the *only* piece of music in the pianist's repertoire. And have you ever wondered at the apparent irony that so destructive an upheaval as the Cultural Revolution should also have allowed people the time off to engage in such a harmless and admirable pursuit as archaeology – to produce all those wonderful old Chinese art objects which are now hawked about the world as publicity for the regime (*pace* the famous 'Jade Princess' exhibition mounted by the *Sunday Times* in 1973)? The explanation of course is simple. 'The Chinese soil is an inexhaustible mine of archaeological treasures, whose sites are very well and precisely known.' When in the late Sixties the vandals set about destroying tens of thousands of temples, looting hundreds of once venerated tombs, it is hardly surprising that the regime was shrewd enough to save a few gems from the sack, to be later used as evidence for the 'vitality' of revolutionary culture.

But the most haunting image of all is Simon Leys's picture of what has happened to the old city of Peking. When he first knew Peking in 1955, it was architecturally one of the most beautiful cities in the world, 'a cultural legacy of all mankind'. Its ancient walls, its great gates, its delicately-roofed *pailous* (or street arches), enclosed vistas and arrangements of temples and palaces were one of the most breathtaking and harmonious examples of Chinese art. The streets themselves were humming with life, 'jugglers, booksellers, storytellers, puppeteers, the thousands of craftsmen, the inns, the little shops, the antique dealers and calligraphy shops', giving 'Peking its lovely, diverse and wonderful face, all that made it into an incredibly civilized city'.

Twenty years later, with a few carefully preserved exceptions (including the Forbidden City itself), it is all gone. *Pailous*, gates, walls have simply disappeared (Leys movingly describes his disbelief when, in 1972, he went to look for the ancient gates, as famous throughout the Chinese world as the Great Wall, and found just the 'obscene stump' of the last of them being demolished). 'Whole blocks were razed to assuage the hunger of socialist town planners for immense avenues, boulevards and squares . . . intended for parades, mass-meetings, pageants and rallies.' Endless acres of empty asphalt lead past serried rows of tatty new concrete slums. The street life has been reduced to glum-looking, identically-garbed grey crowds moving to and from work, like the shuffling toilers in Lang's *Metropolis*.

Now, when I read this description of a city which twenty-three years ago seemed 'full of youth and life', but where everything today seems 'old, run-down and ramshackle', this account of the transformation of the rich, organic past of humanity into a grim, concrete wilderness, dominated by bureaucracy, technology and stupefying boredom, I was reminded of a number of things. I was reminded of a passage in Solzhenitsyn's *Letter to Soviet Leaders* in which he talked about the reconstruction of Moscow in the Fifties and Sixties: 'we have dirtied and defiled the wide Russian spaces, and disfigured the heart of Russia, our beloved Moscow . . . The irreplaceable face of the city and all the ancient city plan have been obliterated, and imitations of the West are being slung up, like the New Arbat; the city has been so squeezed, stretched and pushed upwards that life has become intolerable.' I was reminded of one of the most remarkable images I have ever seen on television, in a recent documentary — mile upon mile of vast grey concrete slabs of new workers' flats in East Berlin, stretching in seemingly endless, inhuman ranks to the horizon. I was also reminded of a good many parts of London, Liverpool, Glasgow, Newcastle, Birmingham and other cities in Britain.

We all these days have a certain image fixed somewhere in our minds of the incredible transformation which has come over the life of mankind in the past thirty years – and of which the fate of so many cities of the world has seemed to be only one of the more dramatic outward reflections. The destruction of Peking and the destruction of Birmingham have only differed in degree. Who, thirty years ago, would have thought it conceivable that the Manchester of *Coronation Street* back-to-backs or even the Glasgow of the old Gorbals slums would one day be looked back on as 'human', 'colourful', 'alive', almost as objects of nostalgia?

Quite regardless of political ideology, or cultural tradition, it seems as though what has happened has been somehow implicit in the very nature of what mankind as a whole has been doing to itself in the late twentieth century. As Solzhenitsyn was recently saying at Harvard, 'the split in the world is less terrible than the similarity of the disease plaguing its main sections'. And the most remarkable thing of all is the extent to which this tremendous cultural catastrophe has almost universally been carried out, I do not say necessarily always with the best intentions, but certainly in the name of 'humanity', and the 'People'. The most eloquently deceptive 'Potemkin village' of them all has proved to be that vision – whether it took the form of a revolutionary manifesto or an architect's drawing for a new block of council flats – which promised in advance a truly 'brave new world', in which human beings could live purer, fuller, richer, happier lives. Just why that vision should so universally have proved such a tragic lie is one of the most profound and important questions we can ask about the time in which we live.

7

Big Brother Hates Everyone

(12 October 1976)

The city's loudspeaker system took up the refrain, 'Down with Chiang Ching, Wang Hung-Wen, Chang Chun-Chiao and Yao Wen-Yuan' – the four chief targets. Fireworks went off as tens of thousands of people raised their voices in a deafening chorus of slogans above the sound of the horns and drums.

> (News report from Peking, 1976)

The horrible thing about the Two Minutes Hate was not that one was obliged to act a part, but on the contrary that it was impossible to avoid joining in. Within thirty seconds any pretence was always unnecessary. A hideous ecstasy of fear and vindictiveness, a desire to kill ... seemed to flow through the whole group ... and yet the rage that one felt was an abstract, undirected emotion which could be switched from one object to another like the flame of a blowlamp.

> (George Orwell, *1984*)

In recent years the image of Chinese life most frequently presented in the West, particularly on television, has been that of a teeming anthill, of 700 million industrious citizens, all toiling happily under the inspiration of Big Brother Mao to build a new nation, after centuries of oppression, division and misery.

Many Westerners, as with Russia in the 1930s, have been disposed to take China at this face valuation, as a society showing an almost miraculous degree of unity and harmony.

There has, however, been one gigantic contradiction in the picture: namely, the enormous part obviously played in everyday Chinese life (which not even the most sycophantic admirers of Mao's China could disguise) by public expressions of aggression and hostility.

Not only have we been aware in the past decade of the remarkable persistence in such a 'happy and harmonious' society of an apparently endless succession of subversives, 'capitalist roaders' and 'Confucian deviationists', from the enemies of the Cultural Revolution, through Liu Shao-chi and Lin Piao, to the presently hated 'Gang of Four', but few things have been so conspicuous in the television films as the degree to which China's social unity seemed to be expressed not in smiling harmony but in expressions of hatred – even on the faces of the little children in the schools, acting out their playlets against American imperialist aggression and 'goulash deviationism'.

Rarely has the world seen a more vivid example of that phenomenon of mass-psychology which, although it was brilliantly portrayed by Orwell in *1984*, has astonishingly never received proper analysis – viz. the absolutely unchanging requirement of Utopian, totalitarian movements for a constant supply of 'enemies', however imaginary, upon whom they can lavish a continual stream of aggression.

Whether we think of Hitler's Germany, Mao's China or Stalin's Russia, we are aware that any such great collective movement requires three things.

The first is a Utopian vision or fantasy of the idealized future (however vaguely drawn) to which the whole forward thrust of the society can be directed – whether it be the perfect Communist state, or the thousand-year Reich.

The second is the semi-deification of the superhuman leaders, or 'dream heroes', who will lead and inspire the struggle – the Fuehrer under the searchlights of Nuremburg, the icons of Lenin, Stalin, Marx or Mao.

The third, to provide psychic personification of something to struggle against, is the constant invocation of 'enemies', both external and internal, whose very existence gives both justification to the battle, and a ready explanation for everything that goes wrong in pursuit of the dream – Jews, capitalist roaders, Wall Street imperialists, or whatever.

But even though all extremist political movements, whether of the Left or the Right, conform to this psychological pattern, we should not of course only be ready to perceive it in its extreme forms.

It is in fact one of the most basic psychic patterns in the political and social life of any society, particularly ones which are threatened by any degree of violent change or disintegration, which inevitably leads to the desire by various groups in that society for simple, instantly compelling and largely fantasy-based 'solutions'.

We see it, for instance, wherever a conflict arises which tempts each side to exaggerate the other into a monstrous caricature. In British politics, we saw a particularly striking example in 1963/4 in the considerable psychic energy which was generated around Harold Wilson's vision of a 'New Britain', which would somehow be dynamic, classless, efficient and forged in 'the white heat of the technological revolution' – as opposed to the bumbling stagnant, 'old-school tie' and 'grouse moor' complacency of 'thirteen years of Tory rule'.

We saw it in the late 1950s and 1960s in the great imaginary struggle of those who wanted to be thought 'young' and 'swinging' and 'with it' (with their 'dream heroes' from the world of pop culture), against the 'squares' and 'blue meanies', later translated only too readily by some into 'Fascists'.

In the end, however, all these expressions of the same

psychic phenomenon are perversions of the same, fundamentally religious archetype. The 'promised land' to which
we aspire (like the 'lost Eden' of the past) are symbols of a
sense of wholeness and unity from which we obscurely
feel that we have been exiled.

To admit that any of those detestable qualities which are
standing between us and the perfect world might actually
lie in ourselves is obviously impossible. It is so much more
comforting to project them on to other people, and other
groups, because it makes our view of the world so much
simpler. All that is wrong is the fault of 'the others' – the
Fascists, the Jews, the 'squares', the 'reds under the bed'.
If only these villains can somehow be got out of the way,
the paradise we deserve will be ours.

The great religions (in their highest expressions) tell us
that these things can only be achieved by each individual,
in his struggle to recognize his own 'darker' side and thus
to work towards a 'whole' view.

But as soon as the battle for salvation becomes collective
rather than individual (whether it takes on religious, political or social expression) then the enemies are always outside us. Thus, in the comfort of knowing that we are the
elect, do we launch on the world persecution, war, collective
hatred and all the other hideous consequences of our own
psychic disintegration.

8

Descent into the Maelstrom

(7 June 1975)

It may seem a far cry from Shakespeare to the great terrorist trial now going on in West Germany. But in recent days my thoughts have been running on these apparently incongruous rails – partly because I have been reading Mel Lasky's fascinating study of the Baader–Meinhof gang in the June issue of *Encounter*, and partly because I have been re-reading what I believe to be the best book about Shakespeare ever written.

The most haunting ingredient in Lasky's article is his account of the 'downward descent' of Ulrike Meinhof, the beautiful, highly intelligent daughter of two art historians, from fervent young Christian pacifist, through increasing radical chic sympathy with the underdog (expressed in a highly-paid magazine column) to infatuation with the terrorism of Andreas Baader. The devoted mother, who once burst into tears when her brother-in-law fired off a pistol in a wood, ends up as a ruthless terrorist herself, flinging around 'Mollies' (Molotov cocktails) with gay abandon, and prepared to commit almost any murder for the sake of her gang.

The book I have been reading about Shakespeare was published in 1959, never sold more than a few thousand copies, is out of print and its author, John Vyvyan, died in February this year almost without remark.

In recent times it has been fashionable to see Shakespeare as a man without a moral point of view, and without any profound convictions. According to the Jan Kott school, he was so convinced of a random, meaningless universe that he was virtually the founder of the Theatre of the Absurd. Even Kenneth Clark in *Civilisation* described Shakespeare as 'the first and maybe the last supremely great poet to have been without a religious belief, even without the humanist's belief in man'.

'Who else,' asks Clark, 'has felt so strongly the absolute meaninglessness of human life?'

But Vyvyan says rubbish to all this. Shakespeare, he claims, had a completely clear and consistent moral view of 'the meaning of human life'. His plays are not just 'magical poetry' and 'excellent theatre' but 'ethical theorems of Euclidean logicality', and in *The Shakespearian Ethic*, Vyvyan demonstrates with unanswerable lucidity just what that moral view was.

Each of the seven plays he analyses in detail — four tragedies and three late comedies — shows the spiritual progress of a hero who is put to the test.

In the tragedies — *Macbeth, Othello, Hamlet, Julius Caesar* — the hero succumbs to the temptation. The play shows a battle taking place in a noble soul. Gradually light fades, hatred replaces love, all moral and spiritual values are inverted, and finally comes a physical death which only underlines a spiritual suicide which has already been committed.

The comedies on the other hand, *Measure for Measure, A Winter's Tale, The Tempest*, show a similar process of testing, through which the hero eventually takes not the downward but the upward path, through love, mercy and self-understanding, towards realization of his 'proper self', that 'own self' to which a man must be true.

I cannot even begin here to summarize the rigorous detail with which Vyvyan traces a parallel nine-stage pattern through both the tragedies and the comedies, or the skill with which he shows, for instance how Desdemona and Ophelia are not just characters but also allegorical figures representing love, so that as both Othello and Hamlet turn on them, rejecting love, we can see a meticulous reflection of their downward spiritual progress.

Vyvyan's explanation of the underlying theme of Hamlet is particularly powerful – that it is the tragedy of a man who succumbs to the temptation of the Ghost, representing the Old Testament morality of an eye for an eye, a death for a death, and losing knowledge of his true self in the process, goes to pieces.

The very next play, *Measure for Measure*, shows us precisely the opposite – the triumph of the New Testament, as the pure moralistic Angelo tries to impose on Vienna the Old Testament 'law that killeth', is exposed as a vicious hypocrite, and is only released at the end by repentance and the 'creative mercy' of the wise old Duke of Vienna.

What has all this to do with Ulrike Meinhof? Simply of course that Shakespeare's 'ethical theorems' are not just the stuff of academic study, but are acted out every day, in ways large and small, all around us. His plays are great art precisely because they are based on a profound perception of those archetypal patterns which govern both art and life – they are psycho-analytical case-studies of the utmost accuracy.

In talking of the downward descent of Ulrike Meinhof, Lasky says that the process whereby she became a terrorist 'defied analysis by police psychologists and political pundits'.

But it would scarcely have puzzled Shakespeare. In the Meinhof story, like that of Charles Manson, or Trotsky, or even for that matter that of the American involvement in Vietnam, we see what happens whenever human beings set off, individually or collectively, in the name of whatever noble-seeming, Brutus-like cause, to turn against love and self-awareness, to project all capacity for evil outwards onto 'the others', and to succumb to the temptation to become harsh and hard.

Gradually, we see light extinguished, fair become foul, and all that spiritual inversion which Shakespeare described so vividly and so often – concluding in the ultimate madness of total consumption by hatred (one of the Baader–Meinhof slogans was '24 hours of HATE each day'). 'Untune that string', drive out love – and the only ending can be death.

Great art is so precisely because it shows us how life actually works – and what makes great criticism is that it tells us so.

9

Nixon and the Darkness of Watergate

(Based on articles originally published in 1973 and 1974)

Looking back over our view of America in the Seventies, we can see how it was overshadowed by one thing above all else – the almost incredible events of those two years, 1973 and 1974, which are summed up by the word 'Watergate'.

More than ever as we look back a few years later can we see how the great black cloud of Watergate seemed to settle over America like a kind of grand judgement, not just on Nixon himself, but on the whole of post-war America. For twenty years after the Second World War, the United States had seemed to tower over the rest of the world like a rock of prosperity, stability, unequalled political and military power. But the hubristic Kennedy years of the early Sixties seemed to lead inexorably to the growing nightmare of Vietnam, racial violence, youthful protest and all those symptoms which, in the late Sixties and early Seventies, betrayed a condition of terrible sickness. In clinical terms, Watergate was the 'crisis' – since when the rest of the world has never been able to look on America in quite the same way again, any more than the Americans have been able to recapture the same confidence in themselves.

It was of course something of an irony that Richard Nixon should have been cast as the ultimate 'tragic scapegoat' for this period in American life – the President whose election in 1968 had itself been widely regarded as symbolizing an end to the corruption and sickness which had crept up on America in the mid-Sixties. Pledged to bring an

honourable end to the war in Vietnam, he had ended up
by extending it even more devastatingly than before, and
then finally scuttling off to leave South-East Asia to precisely that fate the whole war had been fought to avert.
Pledged in the name of his 'silent majority' to restore law
and order, he ended up showing more contempt for legality
than any President before him. Supported in 1972 by the
largest democratic vote in American history, he ended up a
bare twenty months later as the first American President
in history to be forced out of office in disgrace.

Certainly the dark years of Watergate presented the
world with one of the most amazing public dramas of the
Seventies – and 'drama' is the exact word, for one of the
more haunting aspects of the Watergate affair was the way
literary parallels kept on intruding.

On the most superficial level, as the drama began unfolding in the summer of 1973 with the televised Senate Committee hearings under Senator Sam Ervin, was simply the
eerie sense that we were seeing a 'real life replay' of one of
those *Advise and Consent*-type Washington political thril-
lers with which Hollywood had so often entertained us
during the years of America's unquestioned self-confidence
– with Charles Laughton playing the wily old Southern
Senator, and all the other parts – the jowly 'heavies', Haldeman and Ehrlichman, the 'betrayed idealist' John Dean,
the comic relief of the Brooklyn cop Ulascewicz, almost too
neatly cast.

But as the true gravity of what was at stake began to sink
in, with the gradually emerging picture of just how deeply
rotten the state of the whole Nixon adminstration had become, it was clear that Watergate was one of those moments in history when we see how great drama and life
ultimately spring from the same profound mysterious
source.

An obvious parallel was *Hamlet*. Certainly in many ways the picture of life at Nixon's court which emerged during Watergate was remarkably reminiscent of that other more ancient court at Elsinore. One of the most conspicuous features of *Hamlet* is the way everyone is engaged in plotting. The play is full of 'plots' – Polonius commissioning Reynaldo, like some Howard Hunt-type C.I.A. agent, to spy on Laertes in Paris; Polonius twice trying to 'bug' Hamlet's conversation behind the arras; Rosencrantz and Guildenstern, the 'two Germans', being ordered by the king to compile a secret 'psychological profile' of Hamlet. While over the whole play hang the two ultimate plots – that of Claudius to usurp and hold on to supreme political power, and that of Hamlet to avenge his father – which between them lead to the grand tragic nemesis in which they are all brought down.

In fact the point about the intrigues in *Hamlet* (there are nearly a dozen of them in all) is the way every single one of them is shown rebounding on the plotters' heads. This is one of the central themes of the play, which Shakespeare constantly underlines, that of 'purposes mistook fall'n on their inventor's heads', 'the enginer hoist with his own petar', the schemer caught 'like a woodcock' to his own 'springe'.

And this of course was the central theme of the unfolding drama of Watergate, just as it is the essential theme of all classic tragedy – that in life, just as on the stage, purposes mistook *do* fall on their inventors' heads, that *hubris* of any kind *does* lead in the end, by an almost mathematical pattern, to nemesis, just as we saw, by such a pattern, the 'law and order' President being eventually caught up in the toils of his own proudest boast. Never before in history had there been quite such a devastating and public contemporary exposure of the life of a court, reeking with plots, paranoia and intrigue – all rebounding on their perpetrators. And just as *Hamlet* is shot through with famous lines underlining the moral, we even had Senator Ervin on hand in that Senate caucus room to provide appropriate choric comment – 'as a man sows, so shall he reap', 'God is not mocked'. Perhaps the only biblical quotation lacking, at the moment of the revelation that Nixon had been 'bugging' the White House with the very tape recorders that were to provide the evidence for his own downfall, was the observation of the psalmist, 'in the same net which he hid privily is his foot taken'.

But as the mighty drama of Watergate wound remorselessly through 1973 and 1974 to its conclusion, a still deeper parallel to some of the great tragedies of the world began to present itself.

It was the late John Vyvyan, in his excellent little book *The Shakespearian Ethic*, who first pointed out one of the most uncannily perceptive ingredients in some of Shakespeare's plays. The unfolding of tragedy does not always just consist of the hero committing a simple act of *hubris*, followed by nemesis. When the first 'act of darkness' has been committed – as when Macbeth kills Duncan – it may well be followed by a second 'act of darkness' – as when Macbeth kills Banquo – in a desperate bid to shore up his false position. And it may well be this second act – the attempt to 'cover up' – which actually triggers off the coming together of those forces which ultimately bring the hero down, dealing him the final, catastrophic blow.

This is something we have seen so often acted out in real life in our times that we must accept it as a crucial ingredient in those secret patterns which shape the individual and collective behaviour of men. It was not John Profumo's venial and remarkably short-lived affair with Christine Keeler which brought about the greatest political scandal in post-war Britain (even if, at the same time, she was friendly with the Soviet naval *attaché*); it was his attempt to 'cover up' what he had done before the House of Commons. Similarly it was not the pitiful little break-in at the Watergate which brought down President Nixon; it was the attempt to 'cover up' which drew him ever further into that hideous, nightmarish web of self-deception that eventually made his fall inevitable.

There is no question that it is one of the hardest things in the world for any of us to face up to the consequences of our own past acts of moral weakness: to attempt to 'brazen it out' is one of the subtlest and most powerful of all temptations (particularly if one's whole career seems to be at stake – it is so easy to forget the ancient truth that if we set out to deceive others, we end up only by deceiving ourselves).

One of the greatest 'tragedies' in the world is the story of Oedipus, who sets out, promising to leave no stone unturned, to unearth the true cause of the terrible plague that has fallen on his kingdom of Thebes. President Nixon, of course, made precisely the same public boast in 1973 about the Watergate affair – he was prepared to go to any lengths, even, in the immortal words of Jeremy Thorpe, to the point of being prepared to 'lay down his friends for his life', in order to drive away the plague that had fallen on his administration. But of course the psychological greatness of Sophocles' play hangs on the fact that, when Oedipus set out to find the cause of the plague, he really meant it. There was to be no 'cover-up' in Thebes, even though all the evidence Oedipus uncovered increasingly pointed to himself as the chief suspect.

That is why Oedipus is ultimately, in the purest sense, not a tragedy. It does not end in the destruction of the hero, simply because the very reason for his gouging out his eyes is that he has seen the light. Sophocles was himself to underline this point many years later in the sequel, *Oedipus at Colonus*, which showed us a man who, having plumbed the very depths of self-examination and made a full admission of his own guilt, has been thus illumined and made wise, eventually finding reconciliation and wholeness.

In a brilliant essay published some years ago, A. E. Dyson re-interpreted Kafka's *The Trial* not as the surrealistic story of an innocent man who finds himself quite unjustifiably on trial and cannot make sense of what is happening to him – but, in some mysterious way, as that of a man who has found himself in a nightmarish, inexplicable world precisely because the one thing he cannot admit to is his own guilt.

In 1973 and 1974 President Nixon presented such a tortured face to the world for precisely the same reason. Imbued to the end with a fatal sense of his own righteousness, he was Joseph K., not Oedipus. He was simply not prepared to face up to something which had ultimately become inevitable: the conflict between his fondly-imagined *persona* and his dark underside was something he just could not accept; and the main reason why he has remained such a shallow and uninteresting human being ever since (*vide* the pitiful interviews with David Frost) is that, even despite his fall, he appears to have learned nothing, is still at heart totally self-justifying, and still seeking the explanation for all the ills that befell him in the acts and moral weaknesses of others. The unseeing ego has become just a dried-up husk, and its owner nothing more than a lifeless self-parody – for reasons which the great playwrights of the world would scarcely have found difficult to understand.

10

Vietnam – A Black Fairy Tale

(16 April 1975)

Some years ago I recall seeing a film of the Viet Minh pre-
parations for the siege of Dien Bien Phu in 1954. It was an
awe-inspiring sight – the tens of thousands of Vietnamese
peasants toiling through jungles and across mountains, like
an army of ants, carrying shells, parts of enormous guns,
supplies of all kinds.

As I watched, I found myself being more and more reminded of something. This spectacle of tens of thousands of
human beings all working selflessly on one enormous common enterprise was reminiscent of nothing so much as that
extraordinary episode in twelfth-century France when from
every corner of the country tens of thousands of peasants,
monks and aristocrats came together to devote years to the
building of Chartres Cathedral.

Corruptio optimi pessima. In one instance, of course, the
end was to build a great cathedral to the Virgin which seven
centuries later would still remain the most miraculously
beautiful expression of the 'age of Faith'. In the other, it was
to assemble a huge engine of destruction, whose only
memorial was a pile of corpses.

But it was a parallel which has often recurred for me
since – because it was for me a clue as to just why, over the
past thirty years, we have followed the unfolding tragedy of
Vietnam with such a peculiar sense of horror.

It has been because, in a particularly horrible way, Vietnam has been a kind of 'looking-glass war', or rather look-

ing-glass morality play, upsetting all our deepest-rooted moral assumptions and expectations.

The Second World War has sown in all of us the pattern of war as a battle between undisputed good and absolute evil, in which eventually, after all sorts of trials and tribulations, good triumphs.

Similarly, in the fairy tale, which embodies our earliest notions of how the moral structure of the world works, we are accustomed to seeing the hero ultimately triumphing over all his adversaries. 'The good ended happily, the bad unhappily. That is what fiction means.'

But the war in Vietnam has been a kind of perverted fairy tale, in which the 'hero', against terrifying odds, has continued to win through to the point where he now seems in sight of final victory – and yet in which all the moral values have been completely upside down.

All attempts by the 'good' have ended up either in the good losing, or being corrupted, or, as it now seems, both at once – the most horrific example of all, of course, being the utterly impotent intervention of the Americans.

Riding in like Sir Galahad to save the beautiful maiden of South Vietnam from the clutches of the dragon, it is undeniable that the Americans gave to the world one of the most frightening spectacles of the twentieth century. Like the fairy-tale character who gets caught in one of those magic traps, which snare first one limb, and then, with every attempt to get free, each of the rest in turn, the Americans became enmeshed in a mess that was uniquely horrible – above all because it was like an allegory of all that is most destructive in man's attempts to cocoon himself in technological power and insulate himself in jargon.

Has anything in our time, even the concentration camps, been more terrible than the spectacle of fresh-faced young Americans flying off from the 'Coca Cola, Color TV' comfort of their carriers to blast at random a few distant dots – Vietnamese peasants – into eternity? Was anything more chilling than Lieutenant Calley's dismissal of his victims as merely 'oriental human beings'? Was anything more horrible than the debauching of that beautiful country and that ancient, delicate culture with all the detritus of American affluence, the drugs, the defoliation, the bar girls, the black market, the deliberate creation of tens of thousands of refugees as a propaganda weapon?

All this has been truly a paradigm of hell. But does one then turn with relief and gratitude (as one should in the fairy tale) to the gallant spectacle of the Viet Cong fighting heroically for the liberation of their country? Unless one is some dotty student or dim-witted actress, of course not.

For of course the spectacle of that fanatical, ascetic force, seeking remorselessly since 1946 to impose its will on Vietnam, regardless of any moral consideration whatever – spreading tyranny like a cancer, along an unbroken trail of torn-up agreements, massacres and lies – has, in human terms, been just as terrible as anything the Americans have presented, and in the possibility that it may be ultimately successful, much worse.

What is it about Communism which in all its aspects makes it such a uniquely horrible thing? It is precisely its power to turn all normal human values upside down – to corrupt what is best in the human spirit for the worst ends – its capacity with all the force of a perverted evangelical religion to weld men together into an inhuman mass, based always on hatred and enmity, and subordinating every traditional human virtue – truth, loyalty, justice, love, to that end.

The reason why we look on the agony of Vietnam today with such horror – why, quite apart from the sufferings of the refugees and the continuing killing, we look forward to the end of a war, for the first time in our lives without any sense of relief or rejoicing – is because, in a way that is somehow far more shocking than the mere brutal power politics of Hungary in 1956 or Czechoslovakia in 1968, our comfortable fairy-tale world has been turned inside out. We are appalled, not because 'the West' has suffered some 'political defeat', but because the moral foundations of our universe have been disturbed. Not unnaturally, it is hard to take.

11

Ex Africa Semper Id

(11 November 1978)

To anyone who sees the story of modern man as that of a kind of Faustian delving into dark, 'forbidden' realms from whence heaven knows what strange monsters may erupt to engulf him, the story of the relationship between European civilization and the 'dark continent' of Africa may provide an unexpectedly rewarding field of study.

Let us cast our minds back briefly to those crucial decades around the turn of the last century. As we can now see, something very odd was happening to Western man, as he stood on the edge of the fateful twentieth century. On all sides, as men unlocked the secrets of nature as never before, astonishing new inventions were bursting forth – aeroplanes, motor cars, wireless, even the first breakthroughs in nuclear physics which were to lead eventually to the H-Bomb. In music and painting, the European unconscious was incubating that tremendous eruption of disintegrative forces which marked the rise of twentieth-century art. In view of these, and the many other developments then laying the ground for our own explosive century (e.g. the eruption of workers' and womens' movements), it was scarcely inapposite that in the very last year of the old century, Freud should have chosen to preface the first dramatic announcement of his researches into the dark forces of the unconscious, *The Interpretation of Dreams*, with a quotation from Book VII of the *Aeneid*: '*Flectere si nequeo superos, Acheronta movebo*' ('If I cannot bend the gods above to my will, I will stir up the waters of Hell').

It was equally apposite that the same years should have seen the powers of Europe taking part in that other conspicuous act of intrusion into an age-old 'heart of darkness' known as 'the scramble for Africa'. For more than two thousand years, the mysterious 'dark continent' had for European civilization been a gigantic, timeless metaphor for a dark, unconscious realm. It was out of this strange, unknown place that for the Greeks (and Pliny) one could 'always expect something new'. Despite da Gama's circumnavigation, Africa's shadowy interior had still, for post-Renaissance Europe, been the place where lived 'the Anthropophagi and men whose heads do grow beneath their shoulders', not to mention those more tangible freakish creatures – giraffes, elephants, hippopotami – who in the eighteenth and nineteenth centuries were the wonder of Europe's fashionable new zoological gardens. Right up to the second half of the Victorian era, the great African explorations, the wars of conquest (e.g. the Zulu and Ashanti campaigns) and a spate of such popular fiction as *King Solomon's Mines* had continued to delight a seemingly increasingly safe and cosy European civilization with tales of heroism in the face of dark, mysterious forces.

In the very act of exploring and 'opening up' the 'interior', however, Livingstone, Speke and Co. had finally prepared the way for the opening up of that quite different relationship with Africa which has characterized the past eighty years. As never before, the once dark continent has been brought into our conscious awareness. And it is an unvarying rule of human psychology that whenever some important, previously buried or unconscious element is brought partially into the light, the process is likely to bring about a potentially catastrophic split between the new, 'one-sided' state of consciousness thereby achieved, and those elements which remain, now inevitably repressed and distorted, back in the unconscious. For those to whom this sounds the merest psycho-babble, may I hastily proceed to illustrate something of what I mean. Doing so, I hope, may shed a little illumination on just why, in the twentieth century, Europe's relationship with Africa has proved, through two quite distinct phases, to be so fraught with psychic confusion and 'one-sidedness' (and thus, as their inevitable political corollaries, by the kind of hypocrisy, self-deception and double-think of which both Dr Owen and Ian Smith are in their opposing ways, such conspicuous practitioners).

The first phase, from the 1870s to the 1950s, saw Europe in the 'age of imperialism' conquering, dividing up and imposing its rule over almost the entire continent. From the 'light' or conscious point of view, we were bringing the inestimable blessings of civilization and Christianity to a lot of ignorant, barbarous savages, developing rich natural resources which only Western technology could exploit, and generally dragging a 'backward' continent into the mainstream of human progress. In reality, the unconscious or dark side of what we were doing was utterly different. When we arrived, to complete and immeasurably extend the process begun by the earlier Portuguese and Boer settlers, here was an 'unspoiled' continent, full of thousands of tribes, living under age-old, organic social systems, infinitely more at one with themselves and with nature than European man had been for centuries. Into this rich, unconsciously-integrated *matrix* had intruded the greedy, psychically-disintegrated, *ego*-driven white men, with their guns and their Mosaic-Evangelical version of Christianity, ruthlessly destroying the tribal infrastructure, imposing their alien culture and institutions, and in general smashing up beyond recall a harmony between man and nature, in order to expoit the earth of Africa for its metals, precious stones and other 'products' to gratify the ego-drives of a civilization now more than ever emerging in its true colours as the ultimate cuckoo in the nest of creation.

So much for the fundamental hypocrisy of phase one. But then, in the Fifties, came phase two, when with a combination of forced, foot-dragging reluctance and smug self-congratulation the Western nations began to 'liberate' the new 'nations' which they had artificially imposed on the old 'map of Africa'. In terms of the great political cycle described by Plato in Book VIII of *The Republic* – Monarchy, Oligarchy, Democracy, Tyranny – the Western nations had now firmly reached the stage of 'Democracy', where freedom was the highest value. Their imperial conquests in Africa, however, had got stuck at the stage of 'Oligarchy', where a tiny minority of white outsiders (the 'Oligarchs') enjoyed a handsome standard of living by virtue of having neatly divided society into themselves, on top, and below them, as a helot class, the blacks – now largely alienated from the sense of significance once given them by their old tribal structures, their relationship with the soil and their ancestral gods.

On the conscious surface, what was intended to happen was that these Africans would now be liberated to enjoy all the blessings of that phase of social organization which at the time seemed most admirable to the peoples of the West. Ballot boxes would be imported, franchise lists drawn up, and the once benighted continent would be filled with agreeable little replicas of the home-grown European democracies, in full working order. Oh blessed self-deception! Once again, beneath the surface, the reality was quite different. For, as the independence movement gathered way, the African peoples had already, to a greater or lesser extent, been turned by the process of alienation not into a heterogeneous collection of autonomous little potential democrats, but into a mass, defined simply by their external characteristic of being black as opposed to white. Their old tribal loyalties had largely ceased to be something life-giving, providing meaning to their lives, but had turned into something potentially destructive, a mere external badge of division. They had in short begun to develop (despite the many striking and admirable individuals thrown up in all parts of Africa) the collective characteristics of a rootless proletariat, with new loyalties centred on the independence movement or 'Party'. Psychologically, the moment of winning independence thus became very similar to that moment of 'revolution' in the Platonic cycle, the moment when 'Democracy' gives way to 'Tyranny', when, in the name of the 'People', the 'Party' finally overthrows the old order and takes control – no longer a heterogeneous, organic people, so much as a mass following that supreme expression of the collectivized or group *ego*, a charismatic leader.

The first well-known example of this phenomenon was Kwame Nkrumah of the old Gold Coast. Full of revolutionary rhetoric and talk of 'the People', he swiftly took the new state of Ghana along that only too familiar road to 'Tyranny'. The whole point about the 'Tyrant' (as opposed to the old 'Monarch', or his more shadowy later manifestations as 'Constitutional Monarch', or 'Democratic President') is that he is no longer subject to a belief that he is the symbolic cornerstone of an infinitely subtle framework, relating his society to the patterns of nature and ancestral wisdom. He is simply (like Stalin or Mussolini) a great bull-frog, puffed up by the collectivized *ego* of his people, inflated by the conviction that this glorious new society is all a function of his own will (as Nkrumah put it 'I am the Redeemer'). And of course all over Africa we have seen the same process repeated countless times since, from Equatorial Guinea to the Empire of Bokassa I, from Mobutu's Congo to Amin's Uganda.

Despite all the lessons of the past twenty years, we still see Dr Owen cavorting about under the impression that 'one man, one vote' means something other than just the fact that, sooner or later, there will only be one man left in the country whose vote carries any weight — the tyrant. When Dr Owen uses that phrase 'majority rule', meaning a 'black majority', he is still of course thinking of 'majority' as it is defined in the liberal-democratic phase of the Platonic cycle — a preponderance of free, autonomous citizens. In practice, however, in Africa just as in many other parts of the world, it all too often comes to mean simply that tyranny of the 'People', the *demos*, over the mass of actual people — a deadly abstraction which may be used to cloak and to sanctify every kind of atrocity and 'civil wrong' practised by a part against the whole (and in many parts of Africa this has been given a new twist, as the members of one tribe have, in the name of the 'whole', been able to tyrannize over the rest, through their control of the party or state apparatus).

The most interesting thing of all is that, because of the stage of political development the world in general has today reached, it has now become virtually impossible to defend the 'oligarchic order' of the old white-settler domination — any more than it would have been possible to freeze Britain's development at its stage of aristocratic, landowner domination, against the rising tide of parliamentary reform, universal suffrage and welfare egalitarianism. That is why Ian Smith is on the way out, and why the white South Africans (amid a bloodbath which could equal that of the 1917 Bolshevik Revolution and its aftermath) are eventually likely to follow.

We need no longer be under any illusion as to where this tide leads. It has nothing to do with 'democracy'. Nor does it ultimately have anything to do with allowing 'the blacks to run their own show' — except in the sense that the 1917 Revolution allowed the Russian peasants and workers to run *their* own show. It is no accident that the one white race apparently able to operate most freely in large parts of Africa are the Russians, because having been through the full cycle themselves, they are entirely at home, if not with Africans, at least with the 'tyrant state'. They therefore have no difficulty in deploying the hypocritical terminology of that final phase of Europe's relationship with Africa, which allows the setting up of a new kind of imperialism in the name of 'anti-imperialism', just as it permits the imposition of new, much worse forms of oppression in the name of 'popular liberation'. When we see, staring-eyed on our tele-vision screens, the faces of men like Nkomo, Kaunda or Amin, we may wonder at these new freaks and monsters who have emerged from the 'dark continent' — much as our eighteenth-century ancestors marvelled at those camelo-pards and river-horses of old. But let us not forget who, all unconsciously, summoned these new monsters into being. Poor us. Even more, poor Africa.

12

When the Machine Stops

(19 May 1979)

Last year it was the *Amoco Cadiz*, the *Eleni V*, the *Cristos Bitos*, and an unprecedented series of pollution disasters round our shores. This year, it has been the turmoil in Iran, petrol up to £1 a gallon and chaotic scenes around the gas stations of California.

Slowly, almost imperceptibly over the past few years – certainly since the Yom Kippur war of 1973 – the signs have been gathering of some great impending crisis over the quite astonishing degree to which our civilization has become dependent on oil.

What is this extraordinary stuff, laid down by the decaying remains of billions of little creatures in the swamps and seas of 250 million years ago, on which the whole edifice of our twentieth-century existence has come to rest? Eighty years ago, we scarcely needed it at all.

Yet today, if it were all suddenly to vanish overnight, the whole, vast, complex structure of civilization across large parts of the globe – the end product of 10,000 years of human evolution – would simply collapse.

In just a few decades we have constructed in effect a gigantic, world-wide machine, on which more than half the earth's population now depends for life itself – for food, for clothing, for shelter, for the whole apparatus of working and staying alive – and the hidden lifeblood of that machine is oil.

Yet the more one contemplates this machine, for our dependence on which we have traded in a great part of that old, direct inter-relationship with nature which sustained human life through countless millennia, the more one is forced to ask – what has it actually given us?

When I was recently reading of the panic and desperation of tens of thousands of Californians as they faced even a temporary cutting off of their supplies, I could not help thinking of a series of calculations which cast a somewhat chilling light on the absurdity to which oil-dependence may reduce us all.

The average American, the calculation runs, drives 7,500 miles in a year. Yet the same man spends over four hours a day, either driving his car, or earning the means whereby to pay for it – a total of some 1,600 hours in a year.

In other words, for each of those hours he drives only 4·7 miles – which works out at little more than the speed of the average walker.

Of course giving up his car and taking to his feet instead would seem no more thinkable for such a man than it would for most of us – for our whole pattern of life (e.g. taking it for granted that we can live twenty miles from our place of work) has been entirely reshaped and distorted by our wonderful ease of travel.

We could no more do without our motor cars and long-distance lorries and airliners than we could do without fertilizers for our farms, central heating and lighting for our houses, plastics for our clothes, or any of the million and one other by-products of our wonderful new Universal Provider.

Yet the more one looks at the dark underside of this great explosion of energy which has surged through our civilization in the past eighty years, the more dubious a blessing does the dark, viscous muck appear to have been.

A few years ago I spent some time reading about the

history of the oil industry, and I could not help being struck by the extraordinarily unhappy lives which seem to have been led by so many of those individuals most directly involved in it. Time after time, from humble Texan farmers who discovered a gusher in their backyard and ended up committing suicide, to the fabulous John D. Rockefeller himself, spending his last years in a state of miserable, frozen paranoia, the story of oil is that its discovery has fallen on its beneficiaries like some fairy-tale curse.

Do we really think that life in Iran has been immeasurably improved by the great upheaval brought to that country in the past thirty years by its vast reserves of oil? Do the Shetlanders view with unmitigated delight the polluting river of oil and oil-money oozing from Sullum Voe to affect every part of their ancient island culture?

Do we see in the Arabs who flock in such numbers through the streets of London these days, a people who on the whole look contented, at one with themselves and the world? On the contrary, a more rootless, unhappy, bewildered-looking lot of visitors can never have come to these shores.

And if this is true of the more obvious, direct beneficiaries of the great twentieth-century oil bonanza, how much is it also true of the rest of us? The flow of oil may have permitted us to cocoon ourselves from nature in an unprecedented degree of material comfort, but it has also brought to our lives a restlessness and rootlessness the full psychic effect of which we can scarcely begin to be aware of.

The most haunting parable I ever heard about oil came from a friend of mine who, some months ago, paid a privileged visit to Williamsburg in Virginia, the 'living museum' of eighteenth-century life which is financed by Rockefeller money.

Near the town itself is a series of great underground

store-rooms, into which from the salerooms of the world pours a constant stream of furniture, paintings, harpsichords – every conceivable kind of art object which might have been found in Williamsburg in 1776.

The collection is already so great that not more than a fraction of it will probably ever be put on public show – but under the terms of the Rockefeller trust, the flood of treasures must continue to pour in, because it is virtually unstoppable.

In other words, by what horrendous irony, the Rockefeller millions have come full circle. Begun a century ago, when a young man first began to dig dirty black stuff out of a hole in the ground in Pennsylvania, today those millions are simply being stuffed back into the ground – in the shape of a not inconsiderable chunk of the artistic heritage of mankind.

And yet even more ironically, with the oil age still only a few decades old, we are already today having to contemplate the astonishing prospect that the supply of lifeblood for this Greater Mother we have created, the World Machine, may be beginning to dry up. We face the prospect that, in only a few more decades, we may once again have to learn to stand on our own feet, relate again more directly with nature, stay rooted to the soil instead of dashing about willy-nilly in all directions, forgetting who we are.

Of course we find the prospect unthinkable. We would much rather keep our heads buried in the sand, imagining that 'more oil will soon be found', or that we shall soon discover perfectly adequate 'alternative energy sources'.

But at least, amid such wishful thinking, let us begin to think more deeply about what our grotesque, and historically very short-lived dependence has done to us all. Far from this being the century when 'mankind has come of age', it has in a profound sense reduced us more than ever before to the status of rebellious, greedy, not very happy children.

That 'energy' we talk of so glibly, that 'lifeblood', is only a dead outward projection of the real energy and lifeblood that once, to a far greater degree, used to pulse through ourselves. And as it begins to drain away outwardly, over the coming years, it is only in ourselves that we shall be able to recover it again – or our hopes of survival are nil. We may today be just at the beginning, in fact, of one of the most important and truly life-giving lessons the human race has ever had to learn.

Part Three

The Politics of a Sad Little Island

It would be a mistake to suggest that life in Britain in the Seventies was all gloom and despondency. Despite the ceaseless, demoralizing pressures of inflation, the rampant waves of 'collectivism' that swept people up into such phenomena of the age as football hooliganism or some of the more disruptive forms of trade union activity, the passing of the frenzies of the Sixties made the later years of the Seventies in many ways a less strained, neurotic time to live in. It would be impossible, for instance, to measure the relief which followed from the quiescence of the great development mania which in the Sixties and early Seventies had roared through our towns and cities like a hurricane. The slowing of the pace of change manifested itself in countless ways. Even the departure of Edward Heath and Harold Wilson as national leaders brought a relief of its own, and there were many signs of the re-emergence of a quieter, more traditional approach to life, from the longer skirts in women's dress to the pervasive mood of nostalgia which hung over the theatre, the cinema and television.

Nevertheless there was one all-important respect in which, despite the discovery of North Sea oil, the Seventies could hardly be said to have been a time when things improved for Britain.

Over the past twenty-five years or so — since that short-lived, illusionary 'New Elizabethan era' of the early Fifties, when Britain was still able to see herself as one of the international 'Big Three', still ruled 'an empire on which the sun never set', was still (after America and Russia) the third richest and most technologically advanced nation — British political life has been dominated by one thing above all: our painful, often blindly reluctant, but always eventually enforced adjustment to our continual economic and political decline.

In the 1970s, one part of that process — the dismantling of the British Empire — was, with the exception of the 'problem' of Rhodesia, virtually complete. Indeed there were those who saw the most intractable crisis which continued to confront the United Kingdom through the Seventies, that in Northern Ireland, as a last ghostly epilogue to the whole Imperial story, appropriately centred on the unhappy island where Britain's 'overseas expansion' had first begun eight hundred years before.

But another aspect of Britain's reluctance to accept her declining status in the world came so much to a head in the Seventies that it became the dominant factor in our national life: our inability to accept that we were no longer a 'rich' nation, certainly in terms of the prosperity enjoyed by North America and by our European neighbours.

In the Fifties and Sixties, like them, we had been through a tremendous 'revolution of rising expectations'. We had accustomed ourselves to thinking that we 'deserved' the same standard of living as, say, France or Denmark. Yet for all sorts of reasons (some going back a century or more) we were no longer keeping up with those nations in the degree to which our industrial output justified those expectations (by the mid-Seventies our 'gross national product' per head had fallen to twentieth in the 'world-league', behind such countries as Austria, Iceland and Finland). The consequences of this gap between our assumption of what we deserved (both in terms of private and public spending) and what we were actually capable of producing was to colour everyday existence in the Seventies with a sense of strain and instability such as the British had never experienced.

The most obvious symptom of this gap, of course, was the inflation which even officially trebled prices during the decade – though the price of many things, such as houses, went up much further than that, accounting for the curious fact that although on paper we were all more or less supposed to be 'keeping pace' with inflation, many people actually felt by the end of the decade that it was becoming harder to make ends meet.

Just as debilitating as the more obvious strains caused by inflation, however, were those subtler social and psychological stresses it brought in its wake – envy, the constant awareness of how much 'other people were making', the sense of unreality as money literally lost its meaning. As the noughts multiplied in the headlines, and words like 'billion' became commonplace, this applied as much to the spending of public money as of private. It was perhaps a tiny measure of how far this process had gone during the Seventies that the most celebrated 'public spending cut' of the decade was Mrs Thatcher's decision in 1971, when Secretary of State for Education, to economize on school milk – saving the nation an annual total of £7 million. By the end of the decade one local authority, Southwark, could quite cheerfully contemplate spending ten times that sum, £70,000,000, on just one new council building – while the amount of money the government borrowed annually to finance its deficit rose in just five years from nothing in 1970 to some £10,000,000,000 at the height of Harold Wilson's mid-Seventies spending spree (representing a tenth of the entire gross national product).

The most obvious disruptions of all to national life, as the meaning of money evaporated in this way, were those which resulted from the particular inability of the unions to accept that our expectations had outrun our will to justify them. This had already in the late Sixties begun to create in the unions a new mood of aggression and 'bloody-mindedness', a blind 'protectionism', a desire to preserve the status quo in everything except ever fatter wage packets, which in the Seventies, as both inflation and unemployment rose to levels unprecedented since the war, became even more marked.

What it all came down to was a quite straightforward matter of mass-psychology. What was happening was that the British people (and the unions *par excellence*) were collectively slipping into a state of infantilism, where they expected the 'Great Mother' (the State, the 'system', the 'World Machine') to gratify their desire for a continual supply of material good things, as of right, in precisely the way that a small child makes demands on its mother. As with all adult people who are reduced to this condition (e.g. the unruly students of the late Sixties), the result is a state of rebellious dependency, where on the one hand it is expected that 'someone else' shall provide all that is demanded, but on the other there is a continual mood of dissatisfaction, aggression, petulance, born of a fundamental diminution in self-respect, the unconscious knowledge that one is no longer behaving maturely as an autonomous human being. The symptoms of this familiar psychological condition could scarcely have been more obvious in Britain in the Seventies.

I have deliberately placed at the head of this section an essay written on the resignation of Harold Wilson as Prime Minister in April 1976, because Wilson was in so many ways the apt presiding genius over Britain's slide into this condition. His two periods in office as premier conveniently defined that era between 1964 and 1976 which, as

I argue in the essay 'The Age of Mother', can be seen as a kind of self-contained 'phase' in English life, marked out by all sorts of rather morbid psychological symptoms which were in no way diminished by the interlude of Conservative government under Edward Heath in the early Seventies.

In fact, as we saw in Chapter 1, the Seventies really unfolded through three distinct stages. The first, marked by Heath's coming to power in June 1970, was more like a continuation of the Sixties by other means than anything new. Like the Wilson Government of 1964–70, the Heath administration took refuge in typically Sixties 'fantasy solutions', a whole range of elaborate bureaucratic and technological gestures which had little to do with Britain's real problems. The introduction of decimal coinage in 1971, like the great 'metrication programme', was a direct legacy of the Wilson years, as in their own way were the reorganization of local government in 1972, abolishing a number of ancient counties, and the reform of the Health Service (in each case the essence of the 'reform' was the creation of huge new amorphous 'units', leading to the proliferation of bureaucracy, reckless extravagance and a marked decline in efficiency). Equally characteristic of these years were the '£1,000 million projects' – Concorde, the Channel Tunnel, the new 'city' of Milton Keynes, the Maplin scheme (which was far more ambitious than almost anyone realized at the time, involving as it did not just the building of a new, third London Airport on the Essex marshes, but the biggest land-reclamation scheme the world had ever seen, the building of a new city for 250,000 people, a new port equal in size to Rotterdam, the largest in Europe, not to mention the two vast swathes of destruction that would have been involved in driving special new motorway and rail links into the heart of London, across some of the most densely populated country in Britain).

All this seemed perfectly expressive of the rather limited, wilful personality of Edward Heath, seeking refuge from his own lack of ability to make real human contact in grandiose visions of 'bureaucratic reform' and huge, cloudy technological dreams that conveyed the impersonal, pseudo-masculine image of 'efficiency'. It was this same drive which made him such an appropriate candidate in 1972 and 1973 to drag Britain into the great bureaucratic and technological 'dream' of Europe.

But perhaps the most unreal of all Heath's gestures, with his Chancellor Anthony Barber, was a last desperate effort in 1971 to get Britain's industrial production going by relaxing credit (in other words, by releasing a flood of 'fantasy money' into the economy) as never before. Only a tiny proportion of this non-existent 'new money' went into industrial investment. A much greater amount poured into property, of all kinds, with the entirely predictable result (since twice as much money was now chasing virtually the same quantity of assets) that property values soared. House prices doubled in eighteen months, the boom in commercial property was so great that it became a 'bubble', into which the pension funds, banks, 'fringe' banks and insurance companies poured cash with a recklessness never seen in Britain before. It was a very sick period indeed in English life, throwing up all those morbid symptoms which always attend a 'get-rich-quick' psychic epidemic (cf. the article on Jim Slater), and of course the spectacle of all this money pouring into the hands of speculators, not to mention the great redevelopment mania reaching its height in Britain's cities, did little to encourage a sense of financial realism among trade unions.

The unions were already increasingly restive under the Industrial Relations Act of 1971, Heath's forlorn bid to curb their growing unruliness (which ironically went little

further than Harold Wilson's own abortive gesture in the
same direction in 1969). From the time of the 'first' miners'
strike in the early months of 1972, the sense of strain in
English political life became more and more acute – culminating in the turmoil which followed the Yom Kippur War
in October 1973 and the quadrupling of world oil prices.
Amid the greatest collapse in share prices and property
values since 1929, the 'second' miners' strike, the 'Three
Day Week' and all the rest, the Heath government in March
1974 finally fell (Heath himself being simply not psychologically equipped, with his wooden, unvisionary stubborn-
ness, to do anything other than make the situation worse).

Then began the most unreal phase of all, that eighteen-
month period between March 1974 and the summer of
1975 when the Wilson government simply let rip. For a
start, the vacuum of leadership created by Wilson's virtual
abdication after his election defeat in 1970 had helped to
give the Labour Party a decisive push to the left: it was
committed to the most extreme ragbag of left-wing measures, from the nationalization of the shipbuilding and air-
craft industries to the abortive Community Land Act, that
the country had seen since just after the war. Despite the
Labour Party receiving in the October election of 1974 its
lowest share of the popular vote since the 1920s, the
government gave way to the unions on everything – from
wages, which by June 1975 were rising at 25 per cent, to
their demands for unprecedented privileges. The Trade
Union and Labour Relations Act, master-minded by Michael
Foot, granted the unions a degree of legal privilege no body
had enjoyed in Britain since the mediaeval Church.* As

---

* For instance, the passing of TULRA meant that unions were no
longer to be liable for damage inflicted as the result of an industrial
'dispute', even where the victim had nothing to do with the dispute.
This was later to have some sinister consequences, such as the un-

another cabinet minister, Anthony Wedgwood Benn, talked headily of a 'fundamental and irreversible shift of power' having taken place at the heart of our society, and as the unions could be seen virtually dictating a wide range of government policies, this was the time when Jack Jones, head of the largest union, the Transport and General Workers, was widely described as 'the second most powerful man in the country'. Compared with the impotence of Harold Wilson, indeed, it was hard to see that he had a superior.

But in the summer of 1975, under the threat of an appalling financial crisis, there were at least the beginnings of an 'explosion into reality' from this state of fantasy. Within nine months, in April 1976, Wilson himself had resigned (some say pushed by his senior colleagues). Over the next two years, as the Conservatives under Mrs Thatcher (who had succeeded Heath in February 1975) won a long series of by-election victories, toppling huge Labour majorities in seats like Ashfield and Walsall North with ease, there were signs of a gradual subsidence, a steady swing back to the right. By 1978 the Labour government seemed concerned with little more than implementing the policies dictated by the International Monetary Fund, and with the prolonged farce of the great 'Devolution Debate', a last echo of those grandiose bureaucratic gestures of earlier

---

scrupulous 'recruiting campaign' waged by a small print union, SLADE, among London advertising agencies in 1975. A number of firms were in effect forced to submit to SLADE's demands for '100 per cent union membership' under threat of being made bankrupt, and it was only when the members of one large advertising agency, Collett Dickinson Pearce, displayed considerable courage in standing up to these unpleasant threats that SLADE finally began to moderate its tactics. A more widely-publicized effect of the Act's immunity was the national row over 'secondary picketing' during the 'winter of discontent' in 1978–9.

years. Indeed the Callaghan style of leadership was so different from that practised for thirteen years by his predecessor that, by the spring of 1979 (and in the wake of the 'winter of discontent' that marked the final collapse of the Labour government's 1975–9 wages policy), it was perhaps hardly surprising it should seem to many that conservative policies might as well be carried out not by Labour but by the Conservatives themselves.

The series of essays I have chosen to reflect different aspects of Britain in the Seventies all fall within this general framework. The articles on Jim Slater, Milton Keynes and 'The Brave New World of Leisure' look back to some of the follies of those heady high-spending days of the Heath–Wilson era in the earlier part of the decade. The article on VAT ('A Wonderful New Tax'), introduced to coincide with Britain's entry into Europe in January 1973, may be taken as a representative, miniature reflection of that terrifying infatuation with meaningless bureaucracy which characterized the Seventies – although I might just as easily have included articles on metrication, local government reform, waste in public spending or any one of a dozen other symptoms. There are four articles on different aspects of the extraordinary role played in British life by the unions – like giants in the old fairy tales, musclebound, always negative, always causing trouble, grim Holdfasts resisting change.* The first of these, on Jack Jones, was

---

* Two tiny examples from the end of the decade may indicate what an extraordinary state of unreality the unions had got into. In December 1978, the unions at the Ford Motor Company negotiated an 'attendance allowance' as a device for increasing a pay award – in other words, workers should receive a payment simply for turning up at the factory. Having won this concession, however, the unions then became enraged at the suggestion that some workers might be penalized for not turning up to work and thus *not* being considered

written when he was at the height of his power – by the end of the Seventies, of course, he was virtually forgotten (like all union leaders once they have left office and been separated from their 'block vote' – such rarely possess any very great innate stature). The remaining three articles date from the 'winter of discontent' in 1978–9, the beginning of which was symbolized by the closedown in November 1978 of *The Times,* off the streets for the first time in nearly 200 years. Just how this blind Frankenstein's monster would behave in the future was obviously one of the most crucial questions overhanging Britain as we entered the Eighties.

No account of the British political scene in the Seventies would be complete without some mention of the most start-ling political scandal to erupt during the decade – the arrest and trial of Jeremy Thorpe for conspiracy to murder – which ended of course in the summer of 1979 in his unani-mous acquittal by an Old Bailey jury. The essay 'The Two

---

eligible for the 'attendance allowance'. They therefore continued their damaging strike until the management conceded that workers would receive the 'attendance allowance' whether they turned up or not.

In August 1979, faced with catastrophic losses in the nationalized shipbuilding industry, the new Conservative government agreed that a number of shipyards, some without any orders at all, should close. The unions' reaction was to place a ban on overtime, in a deliberate bid to threaten a £100 million order to build ships for the Polish government, which would only pay up if the orders were completed on time. In fact this order had only been negotiated (at enormous cost to the British taxpayer) to placate the unions in the first place.

Contrary to general opinion, however, such attitudes were not only to be found in Britain. The same blind belief that the 'Universal Pro-vider' should go on supplying jobs and sustenance, regardless of economic reality, was beginning to appear all over the industrialized world, indicating that the psychological consequences of the great twentieth-century 'technological revolution' (in reducing men to a state of infantile rebellious dependency) might run much deeper than just the particular form of the disease which affected Britain.

Faces of Jeremy Thorpe' was written in the wake of his arrest in August 1978.

The most startling political innovation of the decade was the arrival in May 1979 of the country's first woman Prime Minister (bringing with her that whole new package of attitudes summed up as 'Thatcherism'). This is discussed in the essay 'The Iron Lady'.

Finally, perhaps the greatest public shock of the Seventies came with the murders on the same day of August 1979 of Earl Mountbatten (with several members of his family) in County Sligo, and of eighteen British soldiers in the worst terrorist outrage of the Northern Irish troubles at Warrenpoint in County Down — and reflections on these events (written the following day) form the final essay in the section 'Mountbatten: The Man and His Murderers'.

13

Farewell to Wilson

(Written in the week of the 'Resignation Honours List' in June 1976, following Wilson's retirement as Prime Minister two months earlier)

The peculiar quality of surrealistic banality surrounding Sir Harold Wilson's valediction – the absurd honours list, followed by howls of 'lies' and 'orchestrated vendetta', at the slightest hint of criticism, the contract with 'Lord Frost' for what the head of Yorkshire TV claims will be 'a television landmark as important and fascinating as Lord Clark's *Civilisation*', the frenzied dinner-party speculation that Lady Forkbender is about to marry Lord Weidenfeld – all this has been so entirely typical of the stamp Wilson has imposed on English public life since the early Sixties that it can only, once again, prompt reflection on the sheer enigma of this extraordinary figure.

Throughout his reign, as Professor Trevor-Roper pointed out in the *Spectator* last week, Wilson has been nothing if not consistent. In the week of Hugh Gaitskell's death in January 1963, I recall writing a *Private Eye* strip-cartoon about 'Harold Willsoon, a very clever little politician. The reason why he is called Willsoon is that whenever anyone has said "Oh, not even Harold would do a thing like that", you can be absolutely certain that he will soon.' And ever since, his most obvious single trait has been the way in which he has invariably managed to strain our collective credulity by always doing that one more unbelievable thing

– like turning Marcia Williams into Lady Forkbender only weeks after the 'land reclamation' affair: with the added refinement, of course, that no sooner have people reacted with entirely predictable astonishment, than they are blamed for being part of a plot got up by the Tory Media.

Yet the most incredible thing has been the way in which, for all his follies and absurdities, for all the appalling collapse in British self-esteem over which he has presided, Wilson has always managed to trot quietly on, pipe in mouth, unchallengeably the dominant figure of English public life. Right to the end, against all the evidence, he has still managed to preserve a kind of grudging respect from the most unlikely people – 'well, you've got to hand it to him, he is the most brilliant political operator' – almost as if it would simply be more than we could bear to admit the full extent of the disaster he has been.

The thirteen years during which Wilson occupied the centre of the British stage can, I believe, be divided into five distinct phases – each casting its own illumination on the nature of the Wilson riddle.

Firstly there were his original triumphant eighteen months of opposition in 1963–4. He had come to power in the Labour Party with little more than a reputation for ruthless deviousness, at a time when, after the somewhat worthy milksop flavour of the Gaitskell years, those qualities seemed desirable rather than the reverse. Through the summer of Profumo, he stood back from the crumbling ruins of the Macmillan government, carefully cultivating an image of disdainful responsibility. And then, with two masterstrokes, he established the effortless dominance that was to carry him to power a year later.

The first was, with little more than a dazzling lick of paint, to erase all the divisions and squabbles which had racked the Labour Party for years past: without so much as a mention of 'Clause Four' or 'the Bomb', he simply lifted the eyes of the Party to the quite meaningless new dawn of 'the white heat of the technological revolution'. The second was to harness all that profound yearning in the closing days of Macmillan's 'stagnant', Edwardian, grouse-moor Britain for a new age of 'classless', 'Kennedy-style' 'dynamism'. Without any meaningful commitment whatever, in the early months of 1964, he created precisely the right kind of vague, exciting, dynamic image for which so many hungered. In his own revealing words at the time, 'the Labour Party is like a vehicle. If you drive at great speed, all the people in it are so exhilarated or so sick that you have no problems.' In 1964, Wilson drove his vehicle so fast that exhilarated intellectuals and journalists crowded onto it without even pausing to glance at the destination-board – and on 15 October, his love-affair with the news media at its height, Wilson's first brilliant stage was consummated.

Stage two was the realities of office. There later grew up a legend among his disillusioned supporters that, in his first two years, Wilson did live up to that promise of 'dynamism', and was only corrupted by the exigencies of power. But the remarkable thing, looking back to that era, is how totally and instantly he established all the broad outlines of the style which was to mark his successive premierships over the next twelve years: the fundamental lack of any broad strategy or solid achievement; the paranoid reflex whereby anything that went wrong had instantly to be blamed on 'the Tory press' or 'the speculators' or the 'moaning minnies' of the 'cocktail circuit'; above all, his obsession with the media and his own image.

Almost immediately, in *Mrs Wilson's Diary*, Richard Ingrams and John Wells brilliantly captured the extraordinary Walter Mitty-like flavour of the Wilson court: the entourage of seedy and mediocre aides and hangers-on;

Wilson's own constant seeing of himself in 'image' terms ('I'm not a Kennedy, I'm a Johnson – I fly by the seat of my pants', or the famous occasion later when Wilson somewhat unguardedly observed to Ingrams himself, looking round the crowd of assorted pop singers and footballers at a Downing Street party, 'Jack Kennedy's soirées at the White House had nothing on this'). His arrival at Number 10, in short, was reminiscent of nothing so much as one of those little men who blow their savings on hiring a famous orchestra, so that they can play great conductor for a night. And as Britain stumbled through the first year of Wilson rule, through a welter of half-baked measures, U-turns and headline-seeking gimmickry (the Harold Davies 'peace mission' to Vietnam, the Beatles' MBEs), it should have become cruelly apparent just how empty all that talk of '100 days of dynamic action' had been.

Nevertheless, somehow the 'Wilson myth' remained intact. During the autumn of 1965, in fact, as he entered into 'eyeball to eyeball' confrontation with Ian Smith over Rhodesia ('my Cuba', as he excitedly told one reporter), he seemed even in some eyes to grow in stature. Flying up to Balmoral to consult with the Queen, or gravely informing the nation on one of his many TV appearances that he had the previous evening 'talked on the phone to nineteen Commonwealth Prime Ministers', he seemed to be quite consciously slipping out of the gritty, dynamic, man-of-the-people role of a year before into a new silvery-haired, 'statesman-like' pose (indeed he confirmed this a few months later when he advised the Irish Prime Minister that 'a political leader should try to look, particularly on television, like a family doctor – the kind of man who inspires trust by his appearance, as well as by his soothing words').

The election landslide of March 1966, and the opinion polls which two months later showed him the most popular

Prime Minister since records were kept, were the high-water mark. And then, all of a sudden, through the seamen's strike — engineered by that famous 'tightly-knit group of politically motivated men' — and the great economic crisis of July 1966, the whole edifice collapsed. The *Observer* mourned 'The Lost Leader' whose 'reputation as a political magician' had vanished overnight. The Walter Mitty Superman was no more. And we were into the third phase of Wilson's reign, the four long grinding years of the late Sixties when, as the government stumbled through an almost unbroken series of by-election defeats, from one silly mini-crisis to another ('D Notices', 'In Place of Strife'), the Prime Minister very noticeably withdrew himself from view.

Perhaps the most extraordinary feature of these years was the almost total lack of achievement of the 1966–70 Labour government (apart from the invasion of Anguilla, the dive-bombing of the Torrey Canyon, the starving of Biafra and the quite unnecessary pulling down of hundreds of thousands of sound houses to make way for tower blocks). In his almost endearingly Mitty-like memoirs, for instance, Wilson at one point proudly lists the great reforming measures which were announced in the Queen's Speech of 1968. The chief items were: legislation to convert the Post Office from a department of state into a public corporation, and to transfer London Transport to the GLC; an Act to set up the new computerized vehicle licensing centre in the 'Welsh Development Area'; the Decimal Coinage Act; legislation on 'the composition and power of the House of Lords'; a Bill to lower the voting age to eighteen; and a Bill to 'encourage tourism'.

It would be hard to conceive a more bankrupt list of mere administrative tinkerings — the only concrete results of which were to accelerate inflation by decimalization, and to subsidize the property developers into filling London with a mass of hideous and largely unnecessary new tourist hotels.

Indeed by 1970 Wilson was at a pretty low ebb. After years of talk about his 'credibility gap', he was probably more widely despised than at any time before or since. He had achieved virtually nothing (except Chancellor Jenkins's rather laborious effort, at the expense of any economic growth, to bring the balance of payments and the budget into surplus). Even so, he was obviously shattered by his defeat at the June election. For months he looked tired and ill, there were rumours of his resignation. He virtually retired from public life to compile those memoirs, Nixon-like in their relentless self-justification. And over the next three years, he seemed to have lost almost all zest for his one-time favourite role as scourge of the Tories (presumably, like all self-fantasizing 'climbers', having once achieved power himself, he no longer saw Heath, as he had once seen Macmillan, as a giant to be toppled, commanding all his adrenalin). By far the most significant development of this fourth phase of his reign was the way his semi-abdication was used by the Labour left as an opportunity virtually to dictate the Party's new manifesto.

The final phase began in March 1974. No one seemed more visibly surprised and bucked up by his sudden return to Number 10 than Wilson himself. Within weeks he was almost back into the swing of his old familiar style. To the seedy and dubious 'land deals' saga, his typical reaction was to envision 'cohorts' of Tory journalists combing the country to dig up any untruth which would embarrass him, swiftly followed by the most ludicrous example of his abuse of the honours system since the ennoblement of Lord Brayley.*

---

* This was of course a reference to the award of a life peerage in June 1974 to his secretary Mrs Marcia Williams, now Lady Falkender.

Much more seriously, however, and worse than any of the faults of the first two Wilson governments, the years of his last two in 1974–6 will almost certainly be looked back on as the time when, thanks almost entirely to Wilson's most characteristic weakness, his invariable wish to avoid immediate trouble at the cost of storing up much worse for the future, Britain was allowed virtually to dig its own economic grave. With the country already reeling from the effects of the 'Barber bubble', rocketing commodity prices and the four-fold rise in the price of oil, 1974–6 will be remembered as the years when, under the appallingly cynical and typically Wilsonian 'Social Contract', wages and government spending were allowed to go through the roof. As other countries took desperate measures to cut back and fight off the crippling effects of the international inflation, Britain alone did nothing. Perhaps the supreme memorial of the whole Wilson style of government was the way in which, in those years, almost any ludicrous pay claim, almost any pressure for new public spending was given way to without a murmur – until finally in the spring of 1975, as the differential between Britain's rate of inflation and others at last yawned into an unbridgeable gulf, the pound began to collapse. Again, Wilson's response was utterly characteristic. On 23 May 1975 he was telling Robin Day that 'to ask for a package that would counter inflation is like a child going round asking Mummy to do something to stop it raining'. Five weeks later, as he ate strawberries and cream at an agricultural show in Warwickshire, he was saying, 'We reject panic solutions.' The following day the pound collapsed to its lowest point ever, and a panic-stricken Mr Healey was announcing his 'package to counter inflation'.

It is hardly surprising that many people interpreted Wilson's sudden decision to resign, after all his Mitty-ish talk about wanting to be the longest-serving Prime Minister since Gladstone, in the most cynical light – as simply a recognition that the game was up. Having enjoyed the indulgence of allowing inflation to let rip, and the public sector borrowing requirement to rise to £10,000 million, Mr Wilson was getting out before the catastrophe.

Such an interpretation, I suggest, does too much credit to his vastly overrated powers of political calculation. The real explanation, I believe, was simply that, deep down, Harold Wilson was bored. After all, in all his thirteen years, he has never given an indication that his ultimate political motivation was anything more than an intense and rather naïve kind of egotism. It has long since been obviously pointless to consider his conduct in the familiar terms of honesty, or vision, or executive ability, or a genuine desire to improve the condition of the country, that one might have applied to previous Prime Ministers. He simply wanted to be Prime Minister, in the way that David Frost (a not dissimilar character) wanted to have a chat show on American television, or a poor man might want a Rolls Royce – and just as that man, having won his toy, eventually finds that it is no more than a car, so Wilson, after two years of his second term in office, simply decided he had had enough.

As for Wilson's chief legacy, it is clearly that he trivialized and debased the currency of English political life – from his abuse of the honours list to his abuse of meaningful language – in a way that has been true of no other Prime Minister in history. Kierkegaard once made a profound observation to the effect that revolutions fall into two categories: there is the really passionate kind of revolution, which tears everything down in a welter of blood and destruction; and there is the other bloodless, passionless kind which leaves everything standing, but 'cunningly empties it of its significance'.

When we think of the almost unbelievable changes

Britain has been through since the Second World War, it is really quite extraordinary how little the outward forms of English life have changed. The Monarchy still rules. The Guard is still changed. The Mace still rests in the Mother of Parliaments. The Lord Mayor still has his Show. The Bank of England still presides over the Pound Sterling. We still have an Archbishop of Canterbury, a Royal Navy, a Foreign Office in its Renaissance palazzo. And yet in a million ways, large and small, the whole show has been 'cunningly emptied of its significance'. The Pound Sterling has become a laughing stock.* The Church of England dwindles, amid meaningless liturgies and 'gay priests'. The Royal Navy, once used to quelling upstart little nations by sending off the odd gunboat, is now cut to ribbons by the gunboats of one of the smallest nations in the world, in the squalid and unworthy dispute known appropriately as the 'Cod War'.

For the British, it has been a depressing time to live through – and over the latter stages of this steady declension of English life into a kind of seedy, Peter Simple dreamworld, the most appropriate presiding figure was Harold Wilson. It would of course be absurd to lay at Wilson's door the responsibility for all that has happened to Britain in the past fifteen years. Partly it has been something inherent in the decline of any world power to comparatively insignificant status (if a very fat man suddenly loses ten stone and continues to wear the same clothes, he is bound to look ridiculous). Partly we are speaking of something which has happened all over the world, connected I suspect with the omnipresence of the television camera,

* Written in 1976, the year when the pound briefly dropped to its all-time low of $1·54. Three years later, of course, thanks to such factors as North Sea oil and the weakness of the US economy, it had risen back to the seemingly incredible level of $2·30.

which has played such a subtle part in diminishing, trivial-
izing and making everything seem less 'real'. Partly it has
been to do with the pace of technological and social change
which has obviously driven everyone slightly dotty (you
can only have a feeling of real social significance in a
stable society).

For all this, perhaps the kindest thing that can be said
about Harold Wilson is a remark Chesterton made of Lord
Northcliffe in 1922: 'it was the fault of his age, rather than
himself, that he lived among shadows, fighting in a shadow
pantomime'. But Chesterton went on to say that 'publicity
consists not of things, but of their vast shadows thrown
upon a wall. To make them so vast, the light must be held
very low down.' And in the case of Harold Wilson, there
was never a moment's doubt as to who it was that was holding the light so low down.

14

Sir Walter Mitty: A Footnote

(26 November 1977)

After ploughing through Andy Roth's somewhat laborious new demi-biography, I fear we all have to face up to the undeniable fact that Harold Wilson, Knight of the Garter, Conqueror of Anguilla and chief architect of that second Battle of the Atlantic, the sinking of the *Torrey Canyon*, has simply become a crashing bore. The real reason for this is plain. It is no accident that not even the industrious Roth himself has had the energy to carry the Wilson story beyond 1964 (with the exception of a preliminary chapter or two on the seedy revelations of the past year and the Honours List). Because after 1964 there really is no story. The fact is that, in terms of any real or lasting significance, Wilson's eight years in office were almost totally nugatory. Apart from certain Home Office legislation (e.g. the 1967 Criminal Justice Act) can anyone name a single positive achievement of those years? Just as it is appropriate that the sole legacy of the great Liberal Revival was David Steel's Abortion Act, so it is appropriate that the chief legacies of the Wilson years were the 70 m.p.h. speed limit, probably more often broken than any Act on the statute book, and Wilson's pet project of 1963–4, the 'University of the Air'. For three terms Wilson presided over a 'Government of the Air', and now that the 'baseless fabric' and 'insubstantial pageant' have faded, they have left 'not a rack behind'.

Nothing, that is, except for what might be called the 'situation comedy' aspects of Wilson's time in office, which continue through the Crossman Diaries *et al.* to provide the nation with a fast-dwindling supply of gaiety (they were always more funnily and accurately scripted at the time by *Mrs Wilson's Diary*). Certainly the Wilson era comes to look more and more like a transfer of *I Love Lucy* to Number Ten, starring Walter Mitty and Marcia Falkender — although the age-old plot of the weak, henpecked husband led astray by a raging virago was the other day inspiring Richard Ingrams, who had just seen *Macbeth*, to draw a rather darker dramatic parallel.

In the end, in fact, the Wilson story was too lacking in substance to provide either real comedy or real tragedy. The only questions which remain, I suppose, are how did this absurd Dickensian caricature (a cross between Gradgrind and Micawber) come to be in Number Ten in the first place; and how far, now that his reputation is crumbling, will it finally collapse (i.e. will further revelations actually lead to disgrace, or will he be just quietly forgotten as a rather embarrassing hiatus?). As Andy Roth assiduously shows, Wilson always was a pretty grey and inhuman figure: the Oxford swot; the eager beaver statistician at the Ministry of Mines during the war; sucking up to Attlee; boasting about his gritty negotiations over the price of animal feed with Mikoyan; the untrustworthy Bevanite rebel of the early Fifties. But this is all familiar stuff. There is no real theme or new insight to the book (no real attempt, for instance, to explain how Wilson came to enjoy his great hour of glory in 1963–4 as the self-appointed 'dynamic' champion of the 'New Britain'). And the only trace of humanity in the story is the forlorn figure of Mary, with her dreams of Rupert of the Rhine, Charles II and Byron, landed by a chance meeting at a tennis club with this strange little womble (who combined all the vanity of her heroes with none of their glamour) and having to stick it out for forty years.

15

Does Europe Exist?

(Written in the week of the first elections to the European Parliament in June 1979)

Quiz question: what world-shaking event was celebrated in January 1973 with the aid of a concert given in York Minster by the Great Universal Stores Footwear Band; an evening of nameless Irish wails 'performed on the bodhran bones, tin whistles and villean pipes' in the dignified setting of Lincoln's Inn; the display by the V and A of a pair of Bronze Age wind instruments dug up from a Danish bog; 'demonstrations of Continental cookery in gas and electricity showrooms' all over Britain; and an exhibition of sweet-wrappers at the Whitechapel Gallery? The answer of course – it could be nothing else – is that all these events were part of the so-called 'Fanfare for Europe', the now totally forgotten jamboree staged by Lord Goodman to add an unconvincing air of national jollity to the great moment of Britain's incorporation into the European customs union.

In fact it was only last Monday morning as I gazed in wonder at those extraordinary election results – the 'Marquess of Douro' takes 'Surrey' with 113,786 votes, 'Sir Frederick Warner' wins 'Somerset' with 120,057, 'Lord Bethell' triumphs in somewhere called 'North West London' with a mere 87,596 – that I at last perceived the true nature of Europe's importance to Britain over the past twenty-five years. Of course – this whole idea of 'Europe' has never been anything other than a gigantic act of make-believe, a harmless fantasy of butter mountains and wine lakes, created to provide our politicians with temporary relief from the boredom and neurasthenic distress of their empty lives.

Consider the three main phases through which our political fascination with 'Europe' has run. First, in the late Forties and Fifties, was what might be called the 'Eccentric Idealistic' phase, almost entirely confined to Winston Churchill and members of the Liberal Party. Indeed that time is most vividly recalled for me by the memory of a Liberal meeting at the Gloucester by-election in 1957. The high spot of the evening was an hour-long, deeply emotional and moving speech on Europe by Mr Clement Davies, which might have been delivered in some Montgomeryshire chapel. To Davies 'Europe' was like a distant vision of Beulah, some celestial vista of eternal peace and brotherhood which had miraculously emerged after centuries of bloodshed. He recalled how, in 1950, when the Schumann plan had first been mooted, he had gone to the Prime Minister and implored him, almost with tears in his eyes – ' "Go in Clem," I told him, "we must go in" ' – like a man exhorting his brother to take the chance of stepping up into heaven.

Stage two – what might be called the 'Cold Bath Pseudo-Realism' phase – came in 1960, when the Macmillan government began looking round for some dramatic new means whereby to prop up Britain's flagging economy and political prestige. The 'economic miracle' of the Market had now caught the imagination of the world, and the growing supposition was that if only we could get into this magical club, the 'icy blasts' and 'harsh winds' of 'ruthless competition' would somehow sweep away all inefficiency in British industry, and that we too should have a booming dynamic economy, like those of West Germany and Italy.

It was only then, as the newspapers dutifully began to fill with enormous 'Common Market Supplements' and Mr Heath began regularly to appear on television droning on about his tremendous negotiating triumphs over sugar and kangaroo meat (thus earning the sobriquet 'Grocer'), that we began to see that other, even more fantastical side to the Common Market — that it was in fact the most wonderful, absurd parody of meaningless bureaucratic activity ever devised. Macmillan's bid to get us in came and went, as did Wilson's in 1967 ('The Great Debate Begins' as the *Private Eye* cover had it, showing a group of old-age pensioners fast asleep in deckchairs).

There was only one man whom history, personality and everything else had cast as the true hero, utterly appropriate to get us into this remote fantasy realm, this enchanted castle piled high with VAT forms, and surrounded by wine lakes. When Edward Heath finally carried the beautiful Princess Britannia yawning and snoring down the Avenue de la Joyeuse Entrée and into the clutches of the monster, we saw the beginning of the third phase when, instead of being looked on as in the Sixties as a day-dream *solution* to all our problems, Europe modulated into being the *excuse* for them. This was the phase of 'Bureaucratic Confrontationism' when it began to become clear that the sole purpose of the Market was to ensnare the stolid British people in a ludicrous web of VAT regulations, put up the price of their food, fill their roads with vast juggernauts labelled 'Antwerpen,' levy astronomically unreal sums from them for something which nobody understands called the 'Common Market Budget', and finally, to add injury to insult, filch all their fish from the North Sea (and probably, eventually, their oil as well).

But the suspicion cannot help intruding that most of these typical late-twentieth-century evils might well have been inflicted on us anyway, Europe or no Europe. Food prices would have gone up. Fish stocks would have run short. Any government capable of re-organizing local government the way Mr Heath did would have been perfectly capable of introducing the absurdities of VAT just for the hell of it. And at this point one cannot help wondering whether belonging to 'Europe' has actually touched the *reality* of our everyday lives at all. Is it even possible that 'Europe' actually *doesn't* exist, that it really is an enchanted Sleeping Beauty-style castle full of superannuated politicians and bureaucrats who have long since fallen asleep on their fairy-tale salaries and fairy-tale expense accounts? Does one not have the feeling that in a very real sense Roy Jenkins has actually ceased to exist since he disappeared off to Brussels? Did Mr Christopher Tugendhat ever exist at all? If it is true that *The Times* still exists on some other plane, then it was appropriate that the rumour should have got about that it was being published in 'Europe' (though no one ever saw a copy). My conviction that Europe is nothing more than a place of fiction was confirmed on Monday morning when I read the result of the Euro-election in 'West Yorkshire':

B. H. Seal (Labour) 76,552
Lord St Oswald (Conservative) 73,555
T. M. S. Cherry (Liberal) 15,460

Obviously none of these characters was real at all. The winner must have been Evelyn Waugh's Basil Seal, 'Lord St Oswald' was presumably taken from P. G. Wodehouse, and didn't young Cherry feature in those school stories Orwell was so keen on? 'Europe' is clearly something devised purely for our entertainment, a pleasing phantasmagoria, and we should be grateful in these dark times that anyone should take the trouble.

16

Jim Slater: The Paper Tiger

(15 October 1977)

Twice in the past fifteen years, London has been over-shadowed by rather nasty outbreaks of collective fantasy. The first was the period between the Profumo affair of 1963 and the end of 'Swinging London' in 1966–7. The second was in the early Seventies, the time of the 'Barber bubble' and the great property boom, when the City and the media appeared to be hypnotized by the belief that money could be conjured out of nothing, and all sorts of rather curious operators, running companies with names like Cannon Street Investments, Vavasseur Securities and Cedar Holdings, briefly enjoyed a strange, unpleasant glamour. The undoubted dream hero of this second period was the boyish financier Jim Slater, who had built up his empire since 1964 with astonishing speed, and was idolized by City and media alike (Patrick Hutber called him in 1972 'cleverer with money than anyone else in the world').

In two books just published, Slater's own self-justification *Return To Go*, and *Slater Walker: an Investigation of a Financial Phenomenon* by Charles Raw, an enormously diligent journalist who has spent three years piecing to-gether the whole sorry jigsaw, we can see why the name Slater Walker has now passed into history alongside that of John Law of the South Sea Bubble and countless others, as a symbol of those euphoric spasms which from time to time seize the financial community, persuading even hard-headed men of business that the laws of nature have been suspended and that the riddle of how to make money out of nothing has somehow miraculously been solved.

Undoubtedly what will come as the greatest surprise to many people in Raw's rather laborious book (although it should not really be a surprise) is his demonstration that the mighty Slater empire was based on nothing more than a confidence trick (in the quite literal sense of those words) all along. Right from the start, Slater's one trump card, apart from a few happy intuitions and many long hours studying other people's balance sheets, was his reputation as a financial wizard, which gave other people the confidence to support his hunches with their money.

Raw in effect takes up the Slater story in 1961–2 when, as deputy sales director of Leyland Motors in his early thirties, Slater begins in a modest way to play the market. As we learn from his own book, he was a fairly likeable but limited young accountant from a modest suburban home, who from his earliest years had always enjoyed a 'deal' (such as swapping birds' eggs for a microscope). Now he has suddenly found his kingdom. He specializes in small companies, with a narrow share market (whose shares are thus sensitive to quite modest interventions). He passes on his tips to richer business associates, like Lord Brabazon of Tara. And often, as they move in, pushing the share price up, he moves out, taking his profit. In 1963, he is able to play this game on a wider scale when he persuades the *Sunday Telegraph* to allow him to contribute a monthly anonymous share-tipping column; again he buys ahead of his recommendation, and takes his profit when his readers move in the following week. Finally, in 1964, with a young ambitious Tory MP Peter Walker (who thereafter plays only a small part in the story) he buys a small public company, changes its name to Slater, Walker, and repeats his familiar strategy, although he is now able to influence the market even more directly by means of the quite large funds that are put at his disposal by clients who use Slater Walker as an investment service.

By 1966, the first phase is over. Many of the clients are not too happy about the Slater Walker service (both the Leyland and Standard/Triumph pension funds, for instance, withdraw their custom). But the company is now prosperous enough to embark on phase two – the 'dream stage' of the fantasy between 1966 and 1969 when, as 'merger-mania' swept through industry and the City (under the benign guidance of Technology Minister Anthony Wedgwood Benn), Slater Walker took over some thirty companies to become the City's leading 'conglomerate'. Profits rose from £370,000 to over £10 million, Slater Walker's market valuation from £4 million to £135 million; and the secret of this phase rested again entirely on confidence.

Slater Walker almost invariably made its purchases by means of its own shares, which of course were hurtling upwards in value almost perpendicularly, as public excitement grew. It was one of those self-generating spirals endlessly familiar from the history of financial speculation: the higher Slater Walker's shares went, the easier it was to use them to buy other companies, and the more companies that were taken over, the higher rose the shares. Every kind of accountancy device was used to show Slater Walker's record in the best possible light (even a deal which lost £600,000 was shown in the balance sheet as a surplus, by writing down the purchase price shares at their nominal rather than market value). And Raw effectively demonstrates that Slater Walker's much vaunted record of improving the efficiency of companies taken over (by selling off surplus assets, and thus showing a greater percentage return on the capital base remaining) was in many cases illusory.

Stage three (the 'frustration stage') came with the decline

of the stock market in 1969–70, when Slater Walker began to run into trouble (it is of course always easier to win a bubble reputation for financial wizardry when the market is rising). The new device to preserve the 'go go' image was the creation of satellite companies, like Ralli International. The paper value of businesses could thus, in Raw's words, 'be blown up by shuffling them from one company to another in the Slater orbit'. One of the beneficiaries from such juggling in this period was Edward Heath, whose anonymous purchases of shares in a Slater satellite company Tokengate, Raw shows, made profits in 1970 of just over £20,000.

At this point, Slater himself sold a great many of his shares in Slater Walker. His intuition was still good; and in 1972, when, after the 'Barber boom' of 1971–2, the market started to slide again, he managed to unload no less than 40 per cent of all Slater Walker's industrial equities, on the grounds that cash was now 'the best investment'. But at the same time, he was still advertising for the public to invest in his proliferating mass of investment trusts, insurance companies and unit trusts (as Graham Serjeant of the *Sunday Times* called it, 'a seething pyramid of escalating paper'). And even though, among other journalists and the City at large, Slater's reputation had never been higher, the fundamental contradictions of trying to keep ahead of the game on a falling stock market were becoming more and more of a nightmare. Slater became fooled by his own propaganda into buying back a lot of the Slater Walker shares he had sold. He plunged heavily into property (I recall writing an article with Bennie Gray in the *Sunday Times* in January 1973, predicting the collapse of the property bubble, at just the time when Slater was wading in).

And then, at the end of 1973, came the greatest collapse in share and property values since 1929. Slater had a temporary success with his investments in gold which, at the Slater Walker Annual General Meeting in 1974, seemed proof of his continuing wizardry at a time when the press and shareholders were desperately searching for reassurance from any quarter. But in fact, as Raw shows, the only thing which had kept Slater Walker afloat at all was the success of its speculations in the Far Eastern stock exchange boom of 1972–3 – and finally, in 1975, the pretence could be maintained no longer. The 'nightmare stage' of the fantasy culminated in the most spectacular financial crash of modern times.

Charles Raw has painstakingly demonstrated that there was not a single moment in its history when Slater Walker, by traditional criteria, could have been accurately described as a 'sound' financial institution. As for Slater himself, the most revealing thing about his ingenuous book is its title, *Return To Go*, which shows that he still thinks the whole adventure has been nothing more than a game of Monopoly (at which in a much-publicized tournament in 1972, incidentally, he lost to Sir Jack Cohen, even though the supermarket king had only learned the game the night before from his chauffeur). Despite Slater's claim that he has gained 'inner strength' from his ordeals (he spares only what appears to be rather perfunctory sympathy for Dick Tarling, his close associate, who may yet be extradited to face charges in Singapore), he appears to have learned almost nothing as to why it was eventually inevitable that the whole paper-fantasy would come crashing down in ruins. The only question which remains is, not why did so many other people get fooled for so long, but why will such a chapter of human folly inevitably one day be repeated, just as such episodes have occurred so often before in history?

But here we move into the province, not of the financial historian, but of the psychologist.

17

The Age of Mother

(22 October 1977)

Reading the plethora of comment on the two books chron-
icling the rise and fall of Jim Slater, I was struck by the
implicit assumption in so many of the reviews that the years
of Slater's success, between 1964 and 1975, constituted a
kind of self-contained 'era' in English life which has now receded into the past. Increasingly, those years, the Wilson–
Heath–Wilson era, do seem to have had all sorts of qualities
which mark them out as a distinct historical, political and
social 'sub-period' – just as the years between 1956
(*Look Back in Anger* and Suez) and 1963 (the fall of Macmillan) formed such a previous distinct entity. Undoubtedly
the prevailing climate of that strange and rather unpleasant
time has now passed away; its heroes, such as Wilson,
Heath, David Frost, the Beatles, Jim Slater, have lost their
glamour and faded, if not into obscurity, at least into
eclipse. And we can perhaps begin to see the distinctive
quality of English life in those years in a new light.

I believe that an important clue to the nature of that
period was contained in a fascinating recent article in the
Spectator by Leo Abse – which suggested that a great
many of the more puzzling phenomena of politics could be
explained, or at least illuminated, by recognizing the
enormous unconscious influence of the psychology of
'Father' and 'Mother' on political attitudes. Right-wing
politics, Mr Abse suggested, with their emphasis on discipline, tradition, individualism and leadership, are 'father-

oriented'. Left-wing attitudes, with their emphasis on permissiveness, welfare and corporatism, are 'mother-oriented'. One can see the truth of such an observation all over the political history of our times. One of the supreme examples of a society dominated by the attitudes of the 'Terrible Father', for instance, has been Afrikaner South Africa – brutally 'masculine' in its orientation, drawing its strength from a sense of historically-ordained hierarchy which must be maintained at all costs against a hostile, namby-pamby, decadent, 'effeminate' outside world. Whereas the attitudes which spring from domination by the 'Terrible Mother' can be seen at their most extreme in the politics of protest – the attitude of children who cannot grow up, who expect society to protect and shelter them indefinitely, while at the same time shrilly rebelling against anyone or anything which can be represented as the brutal tyranny of 'Father'.

Certainly an awareness of the unconscious influence of these two great 'opposites', these two irrational poles, can help to illuminate a great deal more than just politics; for instance, the world of finance and the City. Normally those serried ranks of soberly-suited men who inhabit the banks, stock exchanges and finance houses of the world are heavily under the influence of 'Father'. 'Masculine' qualities such as prudence, firmness and conservatism rule. But from time to time, even such citadels of patriarchy are swept by irrational eruptions of more 'feminine' qualities. Prudence and conservatism are swept aside. There is a sudden heady fascination for intuition, dash, youthful glamour. 'Mothers' boys' emerge as heroes of the hour, who seem to have discovered the secret of conjuring money out of nothing, with none of the stuffy, prudish restraints which normally govern the world of the bank manager. And as the long history of financial scandals shows, from Wall Street in the Twenties to the crash of the Cornfield and Slater empires in recent years, such heady intuitive spasms invariably end in disaster, with the re-emergence of the grey virtues of 'Father'.

Reading Jim Slater's autobiography, one is left in no doubt that he was psychologically a classic candidate for the role of hero in such an hour. He obviously has a very strong relationship with his mother (that vital ingredient in creating the irresistible self-confidence of so many would-be 'world conquering' heroes, from Napoleon to David Frost). Her presence is rarely far away throughout Slater's account of his life, from the early index entry 'encourages Slater to work hard' to the moment of the final crash in 1975, when he writes, 'my mother also gave me tremendous moral support'. For such a man no disaster can ever seem so final as to become real. And anyone who might still be wondering why the proposed merger in 1973 between Hill Samuel and Slater Walker to make 'the largest merchant bank in the world' did not come off, need only look at the picture showing Sir Kenneth Keith, the absolute embodiment of the heavy physical presence of 'Father' (a slightly less grim version of Dr Hans Martin Schleyer*), and Jim, the smiling 'mother's boy', to see why in psychological terms alone the merger was bound to be a non-starter.

But of course it was not just in the City that English life between 1964 and 1975 was so clearly dominated by heroes and qualities with a very pronounced 'feminine' aspect (I hasten to add here that I am not talking about homosexual tendencies, but something quite different, and rather more subtle). It was a period which began with the transmutation of Harold Macmillan from the 'Supermac' of 1959 into the absolute stereotype of a bumbling, unimaginative, tradition-bound 'Father' who had to be pushed out of the way in 1961–3. And for the next eleven years English life was ruled

* The West German industrialist who had been recently kidnapped by a terrorist group, and was later found murdered.

in countless ways by the very worst qualities associated with an 'age of Mother' – narcissism, self-love, weakness, irrationality and permissiveness in all its aspects, from morals to money. Think of the celebrities of that era – Harold Wilson, the Beatles, Frost, George Best, Slater, Heath. Despite Mr Heath's petulant parodies of masculinity in his 'Selsdon phase', and again in the disastrous winter of 1973–4, it was a time when real firmness, rationality, authority and other 'male' qualities were at a very low ebb in English life. Under the supreme guiding star of Harold Wilson, the attributes at a premium were all those of the man with a very strong 'feminine' side – the pursuit of the outward appearance, guile, winning ways, intuition, concili- ation and outward show, punctuated by outbursts of petu- lance, were the very essence of 'the age of consensus', when no one should take too firm a stand or display too rigorous a set of moral priciples on anything. It was altogether an age when 'personality' took precedence over 'character'. And the only really conspicuous flag-bearer for a kind of irrational extreme 'masculinity' of his own in English life during those years was Enoch Powell (with his attendant chorus of racist dockers and 'Father-dominated' Tory ladies).

The symptoms of the collapse of the 'masculine' during this period could be seen in almost every walk of national life – from the reign of a kind of effeminate, unstructured permissiveness in morals, education and the arts (not for nothing was this the heyday of 'Pseud's Corner'), to the craze which swept politics and industry for every kind of 'corporatism', for building up ever larger, more amorphous groups into which everyone could huddle for protection. The search for 'pseudo-Mothers' in these years took every kind of form, from Wedgwood Benn's setting up of British Ley- land to Edward Heath's craving for Britain to become incorporated into the large, sheltering bulk of the European Community, from the 'corporatization' of local government to the bureaucratization of the Health Service, and the desire to close down as many small, local, independent hospitals as possible, in order to merge them into huge 'maternal' entities. Now of course we can look back from the vantage-point of the more sober late Seventies to see how absurd and irrational all this pursuit of bigness for its own sake was. The prevailing climate has changed here as dramatically as it has towards the tower block in architecture or the vast permissive comprehensive school in education, but the damage of the 'age of the Terrible Mother' is done.

One of the most conspicuous symptoms of this weak, self-destructive age was the almost complete collapse of 'fatherly' financial prudence. The belief that money was to be had for nothing infected every kind of group in society, from the City hypnotized by Slater-ism to the town halls on their spending spree, from the get-rich-quick property developers of the 'Barber bubble' to the unions in the age of Jack Jones and Mick McGahey. Obviously the bubble of collective financial fantasy which was so sharply and disastrously deflated in the great crisis of 1974–6 originated in some ways in the early days of affluence in the mid-Fifties, and had just gone on growing ever since – but it undoubtedly reached its height in the years between Barber's 'easy money' policy of 1971 and the wages spree of 1975, the time when the collapse of 'masculine common sense' in money matters finally became so widespread and so complete that even Roy Jenkins could in retrospect seem to have played the role of a thoroughly conservative 'Iron Chancellor' in the late 1960s.

Today there are certainly plenty of signs of what the Jungians might call a change in 'the prevailing archetype' in English life. The 'age of Mother' is discernibly in retreat on all fronts, and, whether 'Moses' Callaghan fits his own bill or not, the virtues of masculine rationality and firmness are more in evidence than they were. But perhaps a last epitaph on the period 1964–75 should be left to Antonio Gramsci, in the comment from his *Prison Notebooks* which is quoted by John Fowles at the opening of his new novel *Daniel Martin*: 'The old is dying and the new cannot be born; in this interregnum a great variety of morbid symptoms appears.'

18

A Wonderful New Tax

(12 March 1973)

Whenever, as happens about twice a week, something happens which leads one to suppose that our civilization has gone clean off its rocker, it is usually a healthy corrective to consult the experiences of L. Gulliver in Laputa. However mad any feature of the modern world may seem, the activities of the Grand Academy in Lagado can invariably be relied on to have included some similar project (such as that for extracting the sun's rays from cucumbers) and it is always reassuring to be reminded that there is nothing new under the sun.

Such a matter has arisen now – as we might all have been given warning by the extraordinary behaviour some months ago of Mr John Bratby, the artist. Something had happened, it appeared, so serious that Mr Bratby had driven his expensive new car into a tree through worrying about it – something so strange and terrible that, had Rembrandt and Van Gogh been exposed to it, we should never have had the fruits of their genius, because they would probably have driven their equivalents of cars into trees and killed themselves.

What Mr Bratby was so upset about was VAT. I know it is too late to do anything about it, and that acres of newsprint are currently being taken up with explaining to us how it all works, and that it is all part of making Britain more efficient and bringing us into line with the Continental way of life. But it is surely not too late simply to stand and marvel at how this extraordinary tax came to be – which, for human ingenuity, must rank with the Gothic cathedrals and the law of relativity and the utterances of Mr Wedgwood Benn as one of the great achievements of the European mind.

For the moment I am not concerned with the nicer metaphysics of whether twelve-year-olds' strapless sandals should or should not be 'zero-rated'; nor even with the problems of the taxi driver who in law might have to issue a separate invoice to his passengers every time he takes a fare. In the past few months my desk has been deluged with pamphlets from agents, publishers and accountants, explaining how VAT affects the self-employed writer.

The general principles of VAT will I am sure by now have been grasped by every school child in the country. For the writer, it simply means that every time he sells something he must make an invoice for an extra 10 per cent on his fee. Every time he pays for something, whether a telephone call or a piece of carbon paper, he must keep a record of how much VAT he has paid. Then, every three months, he has to rummage through hundreds of bits of paper, subtract the total of the latter from the former and submit the difference to his local Customs and Excise office, on pain of a fine of up to £1,000, or two years' imprisonment, or both.

Nothing could be simpler (apart from the complication that his agent then has to charge him 10 per cent on her 10 per cent, and so on presumably ad infinitum). But the real beauty of the VAT system comes in the acres of small print as to what is 'exempt', 'zero-rated' and 'chargeable'. It is not for nothing that one explanatory pamphlet opens: 'The meaning of words in this context are not always as generally understood.'

If, for instance, an author writes a play for the BBC (which is 'zero-rated'), he must make an invoice for 10 per cent of his fee, collect the money from the BBC and

send it to the Customs, who then send it back to the BBC
(because they are zero-rated). If the same play is rejected
by the BBC and sold to a commercial company (who are
Mammon and therefore fully-rated), the same procedure
is gone through, except that Sir Lew Grade does not get his
money back.

I cannot bore you with pages more examples of such delightful philosophical conundra — suffice it to say that Mr
Bratby's point is taken. There was a time a few years ago
when the unhappy writer was tempted to emigrate to Ireland, where in a desperate bid to revive the Celtic Twilight, creative artists were exempted from income tax (the
only contributors to the Celtic Twilight they managed to attract were Len Deighton and Wolf Mankowitz, but that is
another story). I now see, however, that the Irish have
brought in VAT, not even at 10 per cent but at a choice
between 5·26, 16·37 and 30·2 per cent.

It must be confessed that it is a singularly impressive
achievement to have passed into law a tax of such astonishing ingenuity and utter pointlessness, which will put up the
cost of living by several points, and all apparently without having had to put forward a single convincing popular
argument as to why it is a good thing.

But at least we can take comfort from the fact that they
knew all about such things in Laputa, where it was proposed 'to tax those qualities of mind and body for which
men chiefly value themselves, the rate to be more or less
. . . the decision whereof should be left entirely to their own
breast.' 'The highest tax', it was suggested, should be 'upon men who are the greatest favourite of the opposite sex'.
'Wit, valour and politeness were likewise proposed to be
largely taxed.' While 'honour, justice, wisdom and learning'
were for some reason 'not to be taxed at all'. Or, as we
would put it now, 'zero-rated'.

19

The Brave New World of Milton Keynes

(6 July 1974)

These are bleak days for the monster £1,000 million 'prestige projects' which were such a disastrous legacy of the overblown fantasies of the Sixties. The dinosaurs of Concorde, Maplin and the Channel Tunnel seem on the edge of extinction. But there is one project – more expensive, more grandiose and potentially more disastrous than any of them – which, away from the headlines, is still quietly taking shape. Last Sunday I went to look at it.

An hour out of London up the M1, across 40 square miles of countryside, amid the trees, farms and old villages of north Buckinghamshire, it is now becoming for the first time possible to discern the outlines of the 'city of the future', Milton Keynes. To drive through this vast area today is an eerie experience. The first indications are in the sad little town of Bletchley – a tatty tower block, new industrial estates, a forlorn new futuristic 'leisure complex', with its 'freeform leisure pool'.

Beyond, the rolling farmland is criss-crossed with mile upon mile of half-finished roads, labelled V8 or H7. Huge signs indicate 'Milton Keynes Central', and a newly-built road leads to an abrupt halt at a pile of earth in the middle of a wheatfield.

The car stops. Yellowhammers and larks sing. All is still remote rural peace, on the site of what in three years' time is destined to be 'the largest City Centre complex in Europe', a mile long and half-a-mile wide.

On nearby hilltops stand the first housing estates of the new city. Not the sprawling, leafy, affluent suburbia of a Los Angeles, but hundreds of grim little misshapen boxes, in brick or corrugated metal, turned out by machine. It is hard to conceive that one is standing at the middle of what, in fifteen years' time, is to be one of the major cities of Britain, housing a quarter of a million human beings.

Even harder is it to conceive, however, when one turns to the vision of 'MK' conjured up in the mass glossy leaflets and promotional material available from the headquarters of this whole fantasy operation, aptly named Wavendon Tower. The message beamed forth from Wavendon Tower is two-fold. First, that MK is to be a city planned as no city has ever been planned before – right down to the last tree. Second, that it is to be a city dedicated as never before to 'leisure'. 'One of the first European City Centres ever to recognize', proclaims a typical pamphlet, 'that the car is a leisure instrument'.

'The Linear Parks network in Milton Keynes,' runs another, 'is to form a continuous mesh across the city. The basis of this mesh is a movement pattern.'

Clearly one of the problems most worrying the planners is that the wretched citizens will never know where they are. At one point they hope that the 'road network', running 'in vertical and horizontal curves corresponding closely to the land form with a reservation of about 100 metres' will be 'clearly the identity-giving factor at City scale'.

At another, 'to aid navigation, complete areas of the development will have cladding colours in either red, yellow or blue'.

At a third, 'an advanced tree-planting programme is proposed to emphasize the movement pattern of the square so that when the houses are built the green infrastructure of the grid square will have matured sufficiently to form a recognizable overall pattern by which the inhabitants can locate themselves.'

Admittedly, any difficulty the inhabitants have in locating themselves may be hardly surprising when it is borne in mind that 'a system of street furniture which embraces all equipment (from lighting to . . . bus shelters) are [*sic*] proposed with a family solution of structures throughout the city'.

And, as if this is not enough for the home of the Open University, 'at the apartment block it is the focus of the cube in its green square which is the architectural composition. This was Le Corbusier's point.'

While for those office workers who want the opportunity to be 'part of the glitter and the action' at the city centre, 'office buildings are likely to be low-rise and of the Buro-landschaft or open plan type, although there will be some "shiny towers" at locations associated with transport nodes.'

Finally, in this amazing catalogue of 'Linear Parks', and 'scarce resources centres' and 'activity centres' ('where the man can talk about the problems with his car') and a stadium and ten golf courses and sixty-three tennis courts and countless 'leisure complexes', and, of course, buildings just to live in, built of 'white Forticrete block' on 'power floated ground slabs', comes the incredible statement: 'Milton Keynes is derived from the needs and aspirations of its inhabitants, rather than from an intellectual pre-conception of life.'

Here, in short, is the ultimate monument to that schizoid science-fiction dream which has haunted the imagination of twentieth-century man – the 'city in the park', the anthill of shining towers and mass-leisure and humming new modes of transport, the utterly depersonalized nightmare which haunted Aldous Huxley in *Brave New World* just forty short years ago.

Of course there are already signs that this custom-built city for the Deltas and Beta Minuses of tomorrow's Britain is far from living up to its planners' dream. In fact, in the present economic climate, with its gigantic call on public and private resources, the chances must be high that over the next decade Milton Keynes will simply become a pathetic national joke, falling ever further behind its ambitious schedule, and finally grinding to a stop in a sea of mud and rusting contractors' equipment, unsold houses and half-finished factories.

But, in the name of the poor people who will actually have to live there, such a horrible mistake must never be made again.[*]

[*] Six years later, by the end of the decade, these gloomy forecasts were already some way to being realized. It had become apparent that the whole of the basic assumption on which 'the need for Milton Keynes' had been posited – i.e. that the population of South-East England was rapidly rising, and that there would be two million more people by 1991 – was a typical example of the folly of extrapolating from statistics. In fact the 1971 census had already shown that the population of South-East England was static, and later figures showed that by the end of the decade it was in fact falling. In 1976 the government accordingly called a halt to its 'New Towns policy', and the target figure for the population of Milton Keynes was lowered from 250,000 to 200,000. But already the whole city had been carefully planned *only* to work properly if it was fully developed to the original target figure (and so long as fuel prices made public and private transport cheap and viable). Instead of building outwards from existing centres of population, such as Bletchley, the planners had deliberately placed the 'largest city centre in Europe' (opened August 1979) right in the middle of the 'city', surrounded by vast tracts of open countryside. Instead of using the whole site of the city to the full, the planners had placed the greater part of the housing in cramped little estates, miles from anywhere, and the continuing, lavish publicity campaign to persuade people to live there seemed increasingly like a cruel hoax (particularly on those unfortunate council tenants from London who, having relinquished their old tenancies, now found it impossible to move back).

20

The Brave New World of 'Leisure'

(August 1973)

Lenina looked down through the window in the floor between her feet. They were flying over the six kilometre zone of parkland that separated Central London from its first ring of satellite suburbs ... Forests of Centrifugal Bumble-puppy towers gleamed between the trees. Near Shepherd's Bush two thousand Beta-Minus mixed doubles were playing Riemann-surface tennis. A double row of Escalator-Fives Courts lined the main road from Notting Hill to Willesden. In the Ealing stadium a Delta gymnastic display and community sing was in progress ... Ten minutes later they were at Stoke Poges and had started their first round of Obstacle Golf.

When Aldous Huxley conjured up his horrendous vision of the Brave New World, he thought that his nightmare Utopia of genetic engineering, free love and a constant supply of 'happiness' drugs was still 600 years away. Fourteen years later, when he came to write a new introduction to the novel in 1946, he had brought down the timescale of his predictions to a century or so. Today, we recognize, we are in many respects already living in the Brave New World he describes – and in perhaps no respect was his intuition more accurate than in his perception of the central place that would be accorded by the inhabitants of his Brave New World to the mindless pursuit of organized, mass-produced 'leisure'.

Let us, like Lenina Crowne in the passage from *Brave New World* which I quoted at the beginning of this article, take a helicopter ride across contemporary London. There are the gleaming towers, rising through the trees. There are the satellite suburbs, spreading as far as the eye can see. And there, just below us, is the delightful district now known by the Brave New World name of Havering.

What is this that is about to arise in the centre of the charming old world town of Romford? It is a '£3·5 million new arts and recreation complex'. 'The architects and leisure specialists Gillinson Barnett and Partners', according to a handout lovingly prepared by the town's public relations officer, 'are suggesting the creation of ... a 30,000 sq. ft. civic arts centre with flexible purpose hall ... scores of recreational outlets in a new sports hall ... and a leisure swimming pool that would be the first in Southern England'.

'The facilities,' he continues, 'in low blocks with interesting pedestrian flows, will blend in with existing surroundings.' Just what an 'interesting pedestrian flow' might be, I leave to your imagination – but more interesting is the way in which these 'facilities' will 'blend in with existing surroundings'. It appears that the 'first leisure swimming pool in Southern England' will be situated just next to the New Market Place, with a wall of glass in between so that shoppers and swimmers will be able to goggle at each other as they go about respective pleasures.

This is not the only treat promised to the lucky swimmers of Havering. The leisure pool will have 'a transparent roof, shallow beach areas, an irregular shape, a sunbathing solarium, a wave machine, waterfall and play chute'. It will also apparently be stuffed with exotic poolside plants – 'with selected planting inside', say the leisure specialists, 'the leisure atmosphere should be unique'.

The citizens of Kirby, Lancs., are made of altogether sterner stuff. Not for them any such sybaritic comforts as a 'leisure pool'. For them, amid the glories of their Urban District Council's proposed new £350,000 sports complex, it is proposed that there shall be 'an assimilated rock wall in Quettabond, which is achieved by anchoring protruding concrete overhangs to the reinforced brickwork, and includes recesses to resemble niches and chimneys, the whole planned to allow would-be rock climbers to practise in their own neighbourhood'.

The enlightened Borough Council of the Rhondda Valley has lashed out even more extravagantly. In April this year, Major Clifford Jones, 'well known for his great contribution to the international rugby scene', mounted a traxcavator to 'cut the first sod' of a £750,000 new leisure complex to include not just 'a sports hall and lesser halls' but also what are described as 'projectile halls', apparently so that the local miners can indulge in such pastimes as 'archery, badminton or yoga'. The design for this pleasure dome has been decreed by a firm known as Module 2 Ltd, which lives in Piccadilly, London W 1.

At Holmes Pierrepoint in Nottinghamshire, the press was invited in May this year to inspect the £1·5 million 'multi-purpose sports centre', jointly owned by the Sports Council and Nottinghamshire County Council. This 'new national water sports centre', which was to be opened by the Prime Minister on 27 July, offers some of the finest rowing, canoeing, power boating and water ski-ing facilities in the world', linked with a '330-acre country park area which can accomodate up to 50,000 spectators in picnic-style comfort'.

All over Britain, in short, the 'leisure complexes' are sprouting like mushrooms. A 'floodlit £20,000 dri-ski run' for a New Town here; a '10-acre inflatable multi-purpose sportsdrome' for a West Country town there. Even the inhabitants of our prisons cannot escape the flood — for the denizens of Wormwood Scrubs may now take their leisure in two 'glass reinforced polyester, folded plate structures' which are planned on 'a 4 ft. modular grid, each module made of four separate mouldings of GRP jointed at the ridge and hips and erected as three pin portal arches' — not to forget the 'Hume Atkins special Gymnasium fluorescent strip lighting mounted at hip level', and of course the 'two to six air changes an hour' clearly laid down by the Home Office's specification.

Just what the burglars, murderers and assorted rapists of Wormwood Scrubs are expected to get up to in their 'modular structures', I am not quite sure — but one thing quite certain is that the leisure craze is the 'innest' thing of the Seventies after inflation and playing the environment game.

It was no coincidence that this year's first international UNESCO architectural prize (launched as you will recall during the XIth Congress of the Union Internationale des Architectes held last year in Varna, Bulgaria, and won by Russian student V. Kirpichev) was based on the theme of 'Space for Collective Recreational Activities'. Or that the RIBA should have held a special two-day conference in May this year to discuss the whole 'leisure problem', under the heading 'Building for Recreation'.

Among the subjects discussed at the conference were 'the Leisure Revolution'; 'Recreation in Cheshire'; 'Planning Dual Use Facilities in the Urban Environment'; and 'Sporting and Recreational Facilities in the Private and Commercial Sector'. It must have been difficult at times to recall that what was being discussed had any connection with simple fun and games.

The questions posed by the speakers ranged from R. Pickering's challenging 'In the planning of recreational facilities are there anomalies which exist between the provision of facilities for the uncommitted at grass roots level and the needs of sport's elite?' to the dire warning in Norman Collins's 'If the local authorities ignore the serious shortage of leisure facilities and fail to give priority to provide the required facilities, what will be the consequences?' What indeed? Might we have seen steelworkers rioting in the Rhondda, for lack of a place to practice their yoga and badminton? Would the citizens of Romford rush into the streets crying for the administrators of Havering to be hung from lamp-posts, all for the lack of a mere 'leisure pool' (complete with play chute and exotic plants)?

Nevertheless, the conference's winning entry was undoubtedly the thoughtful paper contributed by Colin Bonsey on the theme of 'picnic areas'. Mr Bonsey addressed himself particularly to the problem that 'people like to picnic as near to their car as they can'. Obviously 'to allow cars to drive about indiscriminately' on a designated picnic area can 'wear out the grass and turn the area into a mud patch'. This naturally 'calls for some stage management' by the expert picnic area designer. 'The typical picnic area,' Mr Bonsey concludes, 'should preferably be a collection of small grassed areas or 'nesting sites' sheltered by informal groups of trees and bushes.' These 'individual picnic spots or "nesting sites"' should be connected by a 'simple gravelled circuit track winding round the area'. No detail is spared: 'the layout of the road is important as it should meander from feature to feature, and never be straight'. 'Popular picnic areas might include a lavatory, a drinking water fountain, a limited number of picnic tables ... a barbecue fireplace ... and somewhere for the children to play.'

Even the uniform of the ideal 'picnic area warden' does not escape Mr Bonsey's remorseless gaze. 'Obviously we should avoid the park-keeper style with peaked cap, and I would settle for a workmanlike rig, perhaps battledress with shoulder flashes in the winter, and shirt-sleeve order with shoulder flashes in the summer.' Nor should we expect our warden to be 'a born naturalist or scholar, because if he is he may tend to fight shy of some of the more menial parts of his task, such as picking up litter'.

What on earth is happening to our civilization? The most horrific programme shown on television so far this year was nothing to do with the impending 'eco-doom', nor the 'energy crisis', nor even Watergate. It was the film of a whole city in the Arizona desert, entirely devoted to the playing of golf, morning, noon and night. Here the senior citizens come to live out their last days, living in luxurious bungalows built in a series of huge concentric rings – each ring an emerald-green, well-watered, eighteen-hole golf course. Here each morning every single citizen issues forth in his electric caddy car, to spend every waking moment on the greens – and there was not one who did not hope to die there, too, preferably of a heart attack while still 3 up at the thirteenth.

We should not be surprised soon if we read a little item in the press announcing that Hammersmith Council is to spend £750,000 on building a Riemann-surface tennis court complex for Beta-Minuses at Shepherd's Bush. Or that the mammoth new leisure complex designed by Colonel Seifert for Stoke Poges is to include the latest electronic equipment for playing Obstacle Golf ('you can play any of the Great Courses of the World – just set the indicator, press the button and a film of St Andrews or Sacramento will unfold before you as you play').

The point about Brave New Worlds is that they do not just spring up overnight, or people might see them for what they are. They develop slowly, in such a way that all seems quite natural. A 'leisure pool' here, a press-handout announcing that the Duke of Edinburgh is to open a new '350-acre picnic complex' there. And before we know where we are, we are taking the whole thing for granted, scrambling happily up our Quettabond replicas of the North face of the Eiger, driving into our allotted place in the Snowdonia 'leisure park', dry-ski running down the slopes of the St Paul's 'fun area'. As with Huxley's Brave New World, all passion, all adventure, all truth and tragedy and profundity will have gone out of the world. We shall be nothing more than a lot of beautifully fit, tanned and healthy vegetables, pursuing the sacred cause of 'leisure' all our lives long. And we won't even know what we're missing. Or will we?

21

The Emperor Jones

(8 May 1976)

In the week when, after 750 years, the House of Commons finally acknowledged its surrender to another estate of the realm of the power to determine the level of taxes, it was a shrewd stroke by *Panorama* to profile the union leader described as 'the second most powerful man in Britain'.

The picture of Mr Jack Jones that emerged from Michael Charlton's skilful assemblage was a kind of updated version of Peter Sellers's immortal Kite in *I'm All Right Jack* such as even Peter Simple woud scarcely have dared to envisage a few years ago.

We discovered the great man unveiling a piece of sculpture, a statue of an idealized worker of the type which may be found outside the party headquarters of any large East European town.

'The whole tone of this piece of very fine art,' declared Mr Jones, 'is to demonstrate the strength and in a sense the forward-looking character of our trade union movement, because this man is looking out. He is raising his eyes to the stars. That's what we have to do in our movement – something just far and beyond wages and working conditions, although they are very important. We have to understand that we are working towards a better world.'

We were then shown a kaleidoscope of important landmarks in the great man's life. There was the back-to-back house where he was born ('still without a bathroom'), which has presumably only survived Liverpool's vast slum clearance schemes in order to be preserved as 'The Birthplace'.

There was the ramshackle construction of rusting iron on the Liverpool waterfront, looking remarkably like Vladimir Tatlin's Monument to the Third International, which turned out to be a 'speaker's platform' unveiled two years ago by Mr Jones in commemoration of the First-Ever International Strike against Multi-National Capitalism.

There was the formidable Mrs Jones, sitting Krupskaya-like in their South London flat, telling us that 'Socialism is Jack's religion' and how stupid it was in the Thirties that people did not have enough coal to put on their fires when Britain was an island of coal.

And of course there was the emotional high-spot, the reminiscences of Mr Jones's heroic struggle against Fascism in Spain, as part of the International Brigade.

'You were wounded, weren't you?' asked Michael Charlton. 'Yes, I was wounded in Spain,' admitted the erstwhile freedom fighter. 'Whereabouts?' 'In my shoulder.' All this was conducted in such grave and sepulchral tones that one could almost imagine pilgrimages to view the Sacred Blood of Jones forming spontaneously in a Thousand Workers' Cooperatives.

Nevertheless, if one was to express a reservation about Michael Charlton's excellent profile, it would be that – as so often when trade union leaders appear on our screens – so many crucially important questions really remained unanswered.

It was established, for instance, that Mr Jones has very little time for the English parliamentary system. He admitted that he would only be prepared to cooperate with a Conservative government so long as it pursued Socialist policies.

But is Mr Jones a democrat at all, in any meaningful sense of the word? Michael Charlton raised the question, without getting a real answer, although it was clear that the Jones Philosophy of Democracy is certainly not one that would have been recognized by Plato or Jefferson or Mill – involving as it does not so much the democracy of individual citizens, or the rule of Parliament, as simply the domination of large organized groups, and only large organized groups approved by Mr Jones at that.

Indeed this question as to how much we really know and can know about the views of our new rulers in Britain today is one to which I believe we should all give much more attention.

A few weeks ago, another important union leader, Mr Geoffrey Drain, of NALGO, wrote a highly significant letter to *The Times* on what he called 'the poverty trap'. This means that, the higher people's wages rise, the more they have to pay in taxes and the less they receive in welfare benefits – in other words, they are worse off. Mr Drain's thesis was that taxes should be substantially reduced.

I was so struck by this letter that I asked Mr Drain whether I might interview him. I thought that it would be of some public interest to know how, if taxes were reduced, he proposed to raise the money to pay for his members' salaries, a fifth of which are already being paid for out of borrowed money.

Unfortunately Mr Drain replied that he was 'too busy' to answer any such questions, which I naturally thought was rather a pity.

There are so many questions of the same kind these days to which I am sure millions of people would like some answers.

At a time when it seems likely that the National Debt will double in four years, it really would be quite interesting, for instance, to know quite precisely how our union leaders (let alone the government) propose that we should continue borrowing.

Or again, in recent days, the miners of South Wales have come out in favour of £100 basic rates for faceworkers. Who do they think should pay this extra money — the taxpayers, or the consumers of coal and electricity?

Similarly the agricultural workers want their basic rate increased fom £36 to £60 a week. If the agricultural wages bill is to rise by 64 per cent how much can we expect on the price of a loaf of bread or a pound of butter?

I believe that the press and particularly television (because few union leaders can resist invitations to appear on the magic screen) have a vital duty, whenever possible, to insist on much more precise answers to these sorts of questions than we have been used to in the past.

If there is one symptom more revealing than any other of the state of total financial unreality which is overcoming our society it is the way we forget that whenever *anyone* gets a pay rise (without increased productivity) it *always* has to be paid for by someone else — something which the media should get used to reminding us of, simply as a matter of course.

It is not after all a very difficult calculation to work out, for instance, that 20 per cent on the wages of railwaymen will automatically mean an increase of more than 10 per cent in fares for commuters (or higher taxes). Instead of just reporting a new NUR wage claim blandly as if it affected no one else but the railmen themselves, the media should constantly underline this inexorable example of the law of cause-and-effect.

People like Mr Jack Jones, with their dreams of 'a better world', often resent what they describe as the 'unconstructive' reporting of their activities by the press and television (that is to say, any reporting which is not entirely adulatory). They are even on occasion, if their memories go back that far, rather fond of quoting the late Stanley Baldwin's comment on the press lords of the early Thirties, that the media enjoy 'power without responsibility, the prerogative of the harlot througout the ages'.

In fact there are few psychological rules more constant in human nature than that which might be known as 'the Law of Mote and Beam' — which dictates that we always unconsciously invest those opposed to us with precisely our own worst failings.

In our own society today there is no group which enjoys 'power without responsibility' more conspicuously than that represented by Mr Jones. One might add that this has been the prerogative not just of the harlot down the ages, but even more obviously of the bully.

22

Upstairs, Downstairs at The Times

(25 November 1978)

As I watched last week's brilliant, infinitely depressing *Panorama* film on the battles behind the scenes in Gray's Inn Road as the great Times Newspapers dispute worked towards its present climax, I found a particular image coming more and more strongly to mind. It was of that strange, bleak, intangible mood of despair which hangs over H. G. Wells's vision of the England of the distant future in *The Time Machine*, in which society has become irreparably divided between the 'upper-world' of the weak, pleasure-seeking, powerless Eloi, and the grim, resentful tribe of Morlocks, who live underground amid the constant throb of machinery, making regular forays to the surface to wreak futile havoc before retiring once more into their subterranean depths: 'The Upper-world people might once have been the favoured aristocracy, and the Morlocks their mechanical servants, but that had long since passed away. The two species which had resulted from the evolution of man were sliding towards, or had already arrived at, an altogether new relationship.'

In the past decade or so of Britain's decline, the new bitter, disruptive mood of the 'workers' has become the supreme, all-pervading issue of our society, hovering menacingly behind almost everything else – like an ever-present migraine which simply will not go away. On television, few images have become nightly more familiar than those of one group of workers or another, asserting their power and their 'rights'. Like the Hydra-heads of a great subterranean dragon, the faces of men like Joe Gormley, Alan Fisher, Clive Jenkins, Sid Weighell, have become as familiar as any in the land. Scarcely a week goes by without a bread shortage, a crisis in the hospital service, or a plethora of disrupted rail services, as evidence of the monster's ceaseless stirring into angry, or just petulant activity. As for the shadow this mighty, brooding new power casts over the country's future, it has already reduced significant parts of the motor industry, the largest in Britain, to a state of almost catatonic paralysis. Where will it all end?

Part of the importance of the Times Newspapers dispute, after years when the particularly acute version of the national crisis on Fleet Street's own doorstep has been virtually the Great Unmentionable, is that it has brought into clearer focus than ever the sheer intractability of this wasting disease which has Britain so painfully on the rack. Certainly the picture the BBC gave last week of goings-on behind the scenes on almost any recent Saturday night in Gray's Inn Road showed a kingdom utterly divided into two, quite separate worlds – the 'upper world' of smooth-talking, well-dressed, public-school-educated executives like Mr Marmaduke Hussey, apparently talking the language of reason, progress and efficiency, and the 'lower world' of the printers, the machine-minders, talking in the uncouth accents of aggression, negativity, envy and distrust. And certainly it would have been possible for many viewers to see this division, as so often when we are presented with conflicts between two, utterly contrasting opposites, as simply a battle between 'white' and 'black', 'goodies' and 'baddies'.

But there was another aspect to this division, caught by the film, which again has much wider resonance to the more general state of Britain today – and that was the extent to which the management, with their new electronic technology clicking away on the third floorfi ready to go, represented a kind of computerized, dehumanized, West Coast future; while the printers, desperately trying to preserve with their clanking, oily old machines their notion of belonging to a 'craft', represented a past which, although undeniably inefficient, dirty and obsolete (like steam trains and Victorian city centres), still symbolized that style of life created by the first machine-age of the nineteenth century which, although it may have seemed in many ways horrible and inhuman at the time, has now in the computerized age of tower blocks, come to seem 'human', colourful and an almost universal object of nostalgia.

In this respect, there was one moment in the *Panorama* film more evocative than any other – when the printers went through their traditional ceremony known as 'banging out', by which they mark the retirement of one of their members. Everyone in the print shop rhythmically bangs the nearest piece of metal, producing a sound which for Wagner-lovers is irresistibly reminiscent of the hammerings of the anvils in the cave of the Nibelungen in *Das Rheingold*. And mention of the Nibelungen may remind us that the notion of a world irreparably and catastrophically divided into two warring realms, an 'upper' and a 'lower', long predates H. G. Wells or even the industrial society of the nineteenth century.

One of the most powerful, mythical images ever created is that of the conflict which runs all the way through the story of the Norse Eddas, between the upper, daylit world of the gods in Asgard, and their perpetual shadowy enemies, the giants and the dwarfs, who live below the earth and in the shadowy realms of Jotunheim. As one reads the Sagas today it is hard not to be reminded of our own society – and particularly by the giants, dependent on brute strength and cunning, deeply conservative, always causing trouble, racked with envy of the agreeable life they imagine is lived by the gods, constantly stirring in rebellious forays to seize gold or some other treasure from Asgard.

But not every literary reflection of a society divided into upper and lower halves is quite so catastrophic.

I do not believe it is wholly accidental that one of the most popular TV serials in the Britain of the Seventies has been that cosy, nostalgic evocation of life in an aristocratic Edwardian household, *Upstairs Downstairs*. Viewers have obviously derived some obscure comfort from this day-dream vision of a world in which the two realms, upper and lower, could still coexist in happy, interdependent harmony – such a striking contrast to the bleak, envious, divided, class-racked society of today. And the real point of how and why the world of *Upstairs Downstairs* did 'work', apart from the fact that 'everyone knew their place', was that, as in any large human organization which functions smoothly, such as an army at war or a ship at sea, this microcosmic society contained in effect not just two classes but three.

As I watched that *Panorama* film about Times Newspapers, the question I found myself asking more than any other was 'what has happened to the NCOs?' It seems to be a law of collective human nature that any efficient organization should be made up not of two, completely separate groups of people (who will only fall to battling with each other) but of two interlocking hierarchies, like two cones, placed one inside the other – and the senior members of the 'lower hierarchy', Hudson and Mrs Bridges of *Upstairs Downstairs*, the RSMs and Chief Petty Officers of the armed forces, are people of very considerable stature in their own right (held in awe, for instance, by junior members of the 'upper' hierarchy) whose loyalty, experience and wisdom are absolutely crucial to the whole operation functioning smoothly.

What has happened to the newspaper industry (as it has happened to a greater or lesser degree throughout our society) is that the old NCO class (Chief Printers and the like) whose pride in their job was a cornerstone of the whole organization, have been devalued – and replaced as chief spokesmen and representatives of the 'lower world' by shop stewards and trade union officials, who in old service language, are little more than 'barrack room lawyers', motivated by a love of power and the sound of their own voices, and incapable of exercising their function except in a perpetual trial of strength with the now completely split-off 'upper world' represented by the 'management'.

The real tragedy of what has happened to Britain today is that once this split between the lower and upper worlds has occurred, *everyone* becomes powerless, at least in any meaningful sense. The workers become mere 'giants', Morlocks, able to exercise their powers destructively, through envy and brute strength – which may give them the temporary illusion of self-importance and having more money in their pockets, but it is ultimately, because it is so negative, utterly soul-destroying. The management is reduced, Eloi-ike, to a kind of effete impotence, dreaming dreams of computerized efficiency – in effect, a world in which workers have been abolished altogether. And the ultimate irony is that no one has ever devised a world in which either workers *or* managers can be abolished. Even if the most extreme of the workers were to get their way, and bring the whole house of 'capitalism' (as they laughably describe the inevitable structure of technological industrial society) crashing down, they will only be faced with a new, much grimmer kind of 'management'. They will still find themselves playing the part of 'workers', at the bottom of a new, much more rigid, much more oppressive form of industrial hierarchy. And the new all-powerful state will presumaby not even let them see *Upstairs Downstairs* on the telly — so that they can at least dream, when they stagger home in the evenings, of a cosy, long-lost world in which Hudson and Mrs Bridges somehow kept the family together, and the whole show happily on the road.

23

1978–9 – Winter of Discontent

(25 January, 1979)

One of the more curious things about times like these is the way in which our national life becomes like a vast play, in which we are all simultaneously both actors and audience.

Day by day, we follow the unfolding of the drama, with its excitements, its miseries, its moments of suspense. We have not been told on the outside of the theatre whether it is a tragedy or a comedy, so we have no idea how it is going to end.

But as with any drama, one of the ways in which we naturally try to orient ourselves to what is happening, and to make sense of it, is by sorting out the actors into 'goodies' and 'baddies'.

Obviously there are differences of opinion in the audience as to which is which. When Sir Hector Laing, the biscuit king, comes on television to say that the country is going to the dogs, there are no doubt boos from the Left as well as cheers from the Right.

Similarly, even when Mr Bill Dunn of COHSE comes on to say, about ambulance men's plans to ignore 999 calls, 'if it means lives lost, that is how it must be ... we are fed up of being Cinderellas. This time we are going to the ball,' there are no doubt a few scattered claps and cries of 'right on' from the gallery – even though, through most of the house, these are drowned out by the almost unanimous chorus of catcalls and hisses.

In fact the remarkable thing about a drama like this is the way in which, like all the best plays, it in the end manages to convey the absolutely unchanging essence of human nature, morality and behaviour.

The one thing which all stage villains have had in common since the beginning of time is that they are fundamentally egocentric, and blinded by their egocentricity to the interest of others.

This is the age-old morality of stories, which has prevailed from the simplest pantomime or fairy story, to the most sophisticated Shakespearian tragedy. Religions and philosophies may rise and fall, but this is one fact about human nature which goes on for ever – that the character who is shown up as egocentric is not just deeply unattractive: his whole personality becomes distorted, by envy, hatred, violence, anger and every negative human quality.

Now clearly it is in such a general role that the great drama presently racking our national life has cast the strikers. TGWU pickets, NUPE spokesmen, callous ASLEF train drivers, heartless ambulance men, Alan Fisher, Alex Kitson and all – no group in the community has drawn such unanimous hostility from the public at large for years.

All this has long since ceased to have any connection with the strength or weakness of their particular economic 'case'. Like many a stage villain before them, they seem to have passed through the normal bounds of social behaviour into an unreal fantasy realm, where the only thing which governs their actions or behaviour is self-interest. Truth, generosity of spirit, a sense of common humanity, all seem to have flown out of the window.

There was a fine vignette of all this on television this week, when a lady in South Wales was berating some striking water workers for the fact that their arbitrary decisions to turn on and off the water had led to the flooding of her house.

To begin with they looked quite shifty, as if they knew they had been caught out – they were obviously thrown by the sheer force of her rage.

But suddenly a light came into the eyes of one of them (that same light which comes into the eyes of Clive Jenkins when he spots a weakness in the argument of one of his questioners that he sees he can turn to his advantage), and it was at her mention of her 'house'.

'So you're lucky enough to have a house,' he replied, in effect. 'Some of our members have to scratch and scrabble around . . .' You could actually see wild fantasies flooding into his head of how his members were so badly off that they had not slept under a roof for years. He could no doubt scarcely restrain himself from adding, 'Foxes have holes, the birds of the air have nests, but the members of NUPE have nowhere to lay their heads.'

Now the point is that we all have inbuilt in us such a deep awareness of what is objectively right and wrong, what is true and what is false, that prone though we all of us are to allow self-pity or rage or any other form of egocentricity to lull us into such 'one-sidedness' from time to time, we can all at bottom recognize it for what it is. It is that form of 'special pleading' which, even when we are guilty of it ourselves, makes us feel rather shifty and ashamed, because we know we have simply gone over the top in putting our own interests before those of others.

Similarly, it is for the same reason that most of us, as we watch the unfolding of this same great drama, instinctively recognize those qualities which characterize the 'goodies' – whether they be doctors and nurses battling to keep hospitals going against all the odds, soldiers trekking out to keep ambulances on the roads, or even those commuters who spare a cheerful word for the television cameras as they struggle into work after a five-hour journey. They are those who have somehow managed to transcend their own personal difficulties, in the name of some greater cause. It is very hard to make heroes in such a story out of any other mould.

When Mr Clive Jenkins claims that the only real villains of the present conflict are the 'media', who consistently present the strikers in a negative light, he forgets that men such as himself present *themselves* in a negative light, according to rules which were written into human nature long before there were any 'media' in existence.

Written into each of us is the knowledge that we are made up of a duality, between our own egocentric personality, and that infinitely deeper part which tells us that we are part of some much greater whole.

And as the present crisis shows so clearly, human nature has no more dangerous and alarming tendency than our ability to confuse the two – by abdicating sovereignty over our own individual moral kingdom to some external group, which then decides questions of right or wrong for us.

It is precisely in succumbing to that temptation that darkness falls over a man. He talks in bitter, negative terms, he becomes self-pitiful, aggressive, even violent – because deep down he is expressing self-contempt at the fact that he has abdicated responsibility for his own actions, his own life, his own soul.

That is why we see trade union spokesmen, when condoning some injury to other people, saying things like 'this is the last thing my members want to do', or 'I feel bloody sick about it, but there is no alternative.' Because they are shuffling off and externalizing a moral responsibility which can only ultimately lie within each individual. And that is why the most terrible challenge confronting mankind today is that of mindless collectivity, of any kind, whether Right or Left – because it renders human life meaningless, and prevents its victims from acting as anything but helpless puppets in that real drama in which every one of us has an absolutely full and equal part.

24

East, West, Is Home Best?

I hope you all enjoyed Christmas 1978 as much as I did –
but I must admit that the experience has left me in thoughtful mood. Three weeks ago I left you all behind in a country
which seemed to be falling apart. Garages were already
closing for the threatened petrol strike. Radio and television
programmes were in chaos and threatened with complete
closure. I arrived in Heathrow to find the airport almost
paralysed by an engineers' stoppage. A thick blanket of fog
settled outside the windows. Thousands of passengers
settled in for a seige which for some was to last more than
forty-eight hours. As discomfort and frustration multiplied,
and a sense of sheer, temper-fraying helplessness mounted,
it seemed an all too familiar vignette of life in Britain today.

Then, miraculously, our flight was abstracted from the
universal sea of 'Delayed', 'Cancelled', 'Non-Operational' on
the departures board, shot to the top of the list, and we
took off into a sun-drenched blue sky above the clouds,
which shrouded a grey Britain below. Two hours later we
were in a country where there are no strikes, no industrial
troubles, no trade union officials coming on television to
explain why it is essential that their members should incon-
venience everyone else's lives. For ten days we enjoyed one
of the happiest, most traditional Christmases imaginable –
singing carols, telling stories, lighting candles on the tree,
eating steaming bowls of carp – occasionally venturing forth

into a city where churches were packed for magnificent Christmas services. Trams, buses and public services were functioning efficiently. People warmly wrapped up, in fur hats, in the streets looked noticeably as cheerful, if not a great deal more so than their counterparts in Britain. No one gave any thought to the television or radio. It was altogether a model of how Christmas can be celebrated without recourse to outside resources – apart from the wonderful singing of the Christmas masses, or a box for *The Magic Flute* in a little eighteenth-century opera house at less than thirty shillings a head. But then, of course, I was behind the Iron Curtain, in the People's Republic of Czechoslovakia.

As we left this haven of light, warmth and jollity to return to Britain, a friend driving me along a freezing, snow-covered road to the airport, said, 'Of course you will be going back to a country where they would have put grit on roads like this by now.' We arrived back to a grey, depressed-looking London, headlines of 'Grit-spreaders' Dispute Brings Traffic Chaos', delays on the underground and the general bad temper of a traditional 'Britain Gets Back to Normal' – back in short to a scene not dissimilar to the one we had left, with news and conversation dominated by industrial troubles, petrol queues, lorry drivers on strike, food shortages, and an unending trail of further troubles stretching over the horizon into 1979, from the miners to the power workers. Somehow to cap it all was the spectacle of Clive Jenkins on television intoning one of those famous Jenkins litanies in which every sentence begins with the words 'I blame ...' almost everyone in the world other than his beloved, saintly self.

My first thoughts in reflecting on the contrast between these two experiences ran on the extraordinary sense of relief one now feels when given respite from the perpetual state of disintegration which prevails in Britain. There was a time, only a few years ago, when the main sense of relief one experienced going to Eastern Europe was the freedom from the more garish blandishments of consumer-capitalism – the constant, subliminal bombardment of advertising, of semi-pornography, of invitations to spend money, and of all those things which Solzhenitsyn in his Harvard speech last year summed up as 'the revolting invasion of publicity, TV stupor and intolerable music'. It is still a relief to get away from headlines about punk rock stars, corrupt football managers, unhappy heiresses and obsessive talk about last night's TV serial – but even greater is that which comes from escaping that perpetual blanket of psychic strain created by the awareness that on all sides one group of people or another is trying to disrupt the workings of society, by stopping newspapers, hospitals, trains, electricity, aeroplanes, docks or whatever little cog in the whole complex technological machine they happen to have their little bit of power over. It is only when one has been in a country where such things simply never happen that one really notices how depressing it is to the spirit to see night after night on television the faces of trade union leaders, distorted by that deadly combination of self-righteousness and negativity which is inseparable from their role. When did you last see Mr Alan Fisher, Mr David Basnett or Mr Sid Weighell looking open, warm, relaxed, in a word human? Such men are in the grip of a collective psychic condition which subconsciously depresses us all even more than we realize.

Of course not the least irony of the terrible price that has been paid for the absence of such disintegration in Eastern Europe is that it has been imposed by men by no means dissimilar in temperament or political background to our trade union leaders – their role in society suitably metamorphosed, but unmistakably wearing the same grey-faced, unhappy, negative look. With the hidden threat of power such as we can scarcely conceive of, they have lowered their grey pall of bureaucratic restriction, drabness, shortages over whole societies. Uniformed men are only too evident in the streets. The ever-present fear of stepping out of line so pervades everyday life that it is almost impossible for an outsider to appreciate. Private conversation continually harps on the success of this person in getting an exit visa for the West, the failure of that.

But in the interstices of this congealed authoritarianism, people manage to carve out their own warm, intensely private little worlds, preserving their own notions of what is true, what is false, what is important and what simply does not have to be bothered about. What to a Westerner is most lacking in Eastern Europe is the endless public hubbub of our own society – the din of publicity, of meaningless political argument, of whining and self-assertion, of sex, crime, discord, and shouting headlines. Life is so much *quieter*, more withdrawn, more isolated. One is no longer plugged in to that vast, all-pervasive, raucous *thing* which gives our society such a false sense of unity, by bombarding us through television and the newspapers with a constant stream of rubbish and trivia, in which politicians, singers, criminals, television personalities, sportsmen and other 'celebrities' are all blurred together as the supposed centre of our lives.

Never before on a visit to 'the Socialist world' have I felt more acutely the horrors of our own way of life as it has developed in the past decade or two, or been more ready to understand the shock described by Solzhenitsyn in his Harvard speech as he at last came face to face with the reality of life in the West. We have so much, and we make the worst of it. They, in some ways, have so little, and many of them make the best of it. Above all, as never before, both in East and West, I have found myself looking at how individuals react to their circumstances. I do not think I have ever more greatly valued cheerfulness, those people who regardless of circumstances refuse to look depressed, bad-tempered, self-pitiful, self-righteous, but preserve around them little islands of warmth and good humour. I think of an elderly lady tramdriver in Prague, cheerfully sweeping snow from the tracks at eighteen degrees below zero — or the smiling station-master on a Piccadilly Line station trying to keep up the spirits of a fractious, glum crowd of passengers who had just been turned off a train 'taken out of service' in mid-journey. Godfrey Winn I may sound like, but, by golly, if everyone behaved like Clive Jenkins where on earth would any of us be?

25

The Two Faces of Jeremy Thorpe

One of my earliest and most vivid memories of Jeremy Thorpe dates back to 1957. As a young barrister, he had come down to Dorset for the weekend after attending the most famous murder trial of the year – that of the South Coast doctor who was accused of killing off some of his elderly patients. On the evening of his arrival, Jeremy held a drawing-room full of people entranced with a blow-by-blow re-enactment of the high points of the trial. Striding about the floor, he brilliantly mimicked in turn each of the main actors, such as the chief prosecuting counsel, the Attorney General of the day, Sir Reginald Manningham-Buller. It was an astonishing tour-de-force by a young man, still in his twenties, who was already fast becoming the *beau idéal* of Liberals all over the country, a suitable Crown Prince to the Party's glamorous new leader, Jo Grimond. With the by-election triumphs of Rochdale and Torrington only months away, they were heady times for Liberals – and for Jeremy Thorpe in particular the future could scarcely have seemed more sunlit.

Most of those present in that Dorset drawing-room that evening would probably have predicted that in twenty-one years time Jeremy himself might well be Attorney General. The thought that he might be standing trial for conspiracy to murder would have seemed beyond the furthest reaches of fiction. And it is only because we have been inured by the shadows of rumour progressively lengthening over the past

two or three years that we are any of us, even today, prepared to contemplate anything so incredible. Even last
weekend, after those first, shattering evening newspaper
front pages – THORPE CHARGED – the media still
seemed fairly nonplussed as to quite how to cope with such
an earthquake at the centre of our cosy, familiar British
political scene. The television crews hung baffled round the
Thorpe cottage, trailed him in and out of Barnstaple, earned
themselves some familiar Thorpe satire at the Bishops
Nympton flower show. Thorpe himself peered grimly at the
pots of marrow jam, as if trying to pretend that it was just
any other Saturday in the constituency year. Perhaps the
full measure of just what an extraordinary thing it is that
has happened was caught by the *Sunday Telegraph* leader,
which claimed that Thorpe was facing 'one of the gravest
charges brought against any British politician in modern
times'. *One* of the gravest charges? What on earth was the
Sunday Telegraph suggesting could possibly be compared to
the gravity of a charge of conspiracy to murder? John Stonehouse's obtaining of passports under false pretences? Edward Short's receipt of £250 from T. Dan Smith? Hugh
Dalton's budget leak?

Undoubtedly the most perceptive and interesting press
reaction of recent days has been a two-page profile of
Thorpe in last Saturday's *Daily Mail*. Written by Peter Lewis,
under the title 'Man Behind the Actor's Mask', its theme
was the remarkably two-sided nature of Jeremy Thorpe's
personality. On the one hand, there is the familiar extrovert,
the 'Card in the Brown Bowler', the darling of the North
Devon Liberals and of constituency workers up and down
the land: the actor who can dress up as a Fleetwood fisher-
man, or a Nottingham milkman, or a West Country farmer:
the votewinner, with his 'amazing memory, leaping stiles
and walking village streets', who has a joke for every oc-

casion, and 'seems to know everyone's names, their cars, their dogs, their piglets'. On the other hand, one has to accept that there is another side to Thorpe, known to many of those who have worked with him most closely at Westminster – 'another face, sometimes seen, which is dark and sombre. His witty tongue also has a cutting edge, which workers at party headquarters have sometimes felt ... he can tear someone to shreds verbally. He can go on and on, then break off without giving you the chance to defend yourself. Among his favourite phrases is "a child of three would not have done what you have done".'

Certainly one of the more surprising things in recent months, as the net of fate has seemed to close round Thorpe, has been the *schadenfreude*, almost the vindictive glee, which normally quite sober and charitable people who have been Thorpe's senior colleagues in the past have shown at his discomfiture. One, with whom I had lunch a few months ago, said 'I cannot think of anyone I have ever worked with, or any one in public life, whom I would be more delighted to see brought down.' As someone who has on the whole seen only the 'public face' of Jeremy Thorpe, the charm and good humour, I was quite shaken by such vehemence – but as Peter Lewis's profile amply brings out, one must accept that Thorpe is a particularly dramatic example of that age-old psychological condition to which every one of us is prone in some degree or other: the split between what Jung called the *persona*, the outward personality that is turned towards the world, and the inner, hidden personality which, for the very reason that it is repressed, usually takes on a dark and negative (though of course not necessarily criminal) form. It is hard to think of any politician who does not suffer from the '*persona*-problem' in one respect or other – it is the occupational disease of politics, just as it is of any profession whose members are in some way in the public eye, whether they are television personalities, film stars, writers like Ernest Hemingway, or even doctors and clergymen.

The chief peril which arises from the growth of an elaborate *persona* is that the split between the two halves of the personality is likely to worsen. It may be vainly or temporarily repressed, by means of alcohol or other forms of escapism, but it may eventually become intolerable. In the worst cases, the 'dark side' may overwhelm the conscious personality altogether, as with Churchill's horrendous depressions, or even the suicides of such obvious '*persona* victims' as Marilyn Monroe, or Hemingway himself. While the split remains, such people are incapable of true depth, nor do they understand what is happening to them – because it is only when the two halves of the personality, 'outer' and 'inner', 'light' and 'dark', are consciously faced up to and reconciled that anyone can begin to reach real self-understanding.

However the Thorpe affair ends – even if he is eventually cleared of the charges which have been laid against him at Minehead – it seems certain that one of the most dazzling careers in post-war British politics has been brought to an end, and that the shadow of these past few years will continue to hang over him for the rest of his life. As it has so far been publicly presented to us, it is one of those real-life dramas which uncannily echo the dream-turning-to-nightmare pattern of tragedy.

Yet again we see a particularly vivid example of that great psychological conundrum of our age, the 'boy hero' who eventually comes unstuck, and many of whose inmost problems can be traced back to having a strong mother and a weak father (e.g. Jim Slater, David Frost, Harold Wilson, John Stonehouse). It may be that, as Freud puts it, 'a man who has been the indisputable favourite of his mother keeps for life the feeling of being a conqueror, that confidence of success which often induces real success'; but it may also present such a man with appalling difficulties in relating both to his own masculinity and to the opposite sex. Such 'boy heroes' may indeed conquer the world in terms of outward impact (as did Napoleon, one of the supreme examples in history). But such men are happiest when they can bask in the admiration of others, can 'show off' like precocious children without having to take real, grown-up responsibility – which is why so many of them are attracted to the glamorous world of show-business (e.g. Frost or Groucho Marx). They live in an infantile fantasy of masculinity (for example Groucho's behaviour in his films towards Margaret Dumont, Stonehouse's financial operations, Slater's likewise) which can cause no end of trouble.

Like Anthony Eden during the long years when he stood in the shadow of Churchill, such men are often seen to best advantage when they can play 'heir apparent' to some more obvious 'father figure', but come a terrible cropper when they have to succeed to the role of 'Father' or leader themselves – as did Eden, or that other prime example of the phenomenon, the late Duke of Windsor. Similarly Thorpe, with his 'show off' gifts of wit and mimicry, never shone to such advantage as during the years when he could play chief-lieutenant and 'heir apparent' to Jo Grimond. His succession to the leadership in 1967 coincided with his first marriage, and becoming a father – that brief sunlit period which was to end so tragically in his wife's death in 1970. But despite the Liberal Party's successes in the two general elections of 1974, Thorpe never seemed wholly at ease in the Liberal leadership. Even before his electoral 'triumphs' of 1974, his weakness on the 'masculine' side of his personality had led him to his foolish involvement with that very dubious financial operation, London and Counties Securities, the first of the 'fringe' banks to come crashing down in the post-November 1973 financial collapse. While his private world had already become shadowed by that growing nightmare which has now erupted into the open, first bringing him down from the leadership, then leading him to this present crisis, unimaginably the worst of his life. Until the outcome is clear little more can be said, except perhaps this. So long as he has the support of the two women who are close to him, his mother and his wife, both of whom have strong personalities, all will never seem lost. But at the same time, in the face of this horrendous public ordeal, it will be harder than ever for him to face up to that inner 'split'. The urge to preserve the *persona* to the last will be strong indeed, even though it becomes nothing more than an empty and lifeless mask. Truly has this been a tragedy of our times.

26

The Iron Lady

By the end of the Seventies, the British appeared to have taken with surprising equanimity to the fact that for the first time in history there was a woman presiding over their affairs at 10 Downing Street. Yet they were still puzzled by her as a politician, as a personality. They could not quite 'place her' – and this was indeed a consequence of her somewhat enigmatic gender.

From the moment Margaret Thatcher became leader of the Conservative Party in February 1975, a strange misconception grew up that, because she was a woman, she might somehow bring a 'female' influence to bear on the running of our national affairs. Just how this would express itself – in greater compassion, in showing the kind of housewifely prudence that led her to pile up her larder with tins during a food crisis – was never quite clear.

But what people who held this view failed to grasp was the simple psychological truth that women who get on in politics do so because it is the 'male' element in them which is hyperactive. What was ever truly 'feminine' about such raging viragoes as Mrs Barbara Castle or Mrs Judith Hart – let alone about Mrs Thatcher's prime-ministerial predecessors abroad, Golda Meir or Indira Gandhi?

Mrs Thatcher's driving force throughout her career has always been that masculine element in her, which led her to become a lawyer and an industrial chemist, which gave her such a careful, legalistic mind and her habit of always seeming, even in the most friendly interview, to be straining to make some over-insistent, contrary point. If there was any single achievement which convinced her fellow Conservative MPs in 1975 that she would make their best leader, it was her performance, just prior to the leadership election, in outdoing all the men at their own game as she fought the Labour Party's Capital Transfer Tax and other financial provisions, detail by detail, through a parliamentary committee. In her first year as leader, a lot of her success in the House of Commons and in the country at large was due to the fact that she seemed more of a 'man' than her opposite number, the wily, placatory, rather 'feminine' Harold Wilson. It was certainly not her own 'feminine' qualities which led the Russians in 1976 to dub her 'the Iron Lady', any more than they had given rise to her earlier political nickname, 'the Milksnatcher'. When she reached office as Prime Minister, she seemed more than ever to cut a forceful figure alongside most of the rather emasculated group of senior ministers, Keith Joseph, Willie Whitelaw, Jim Prior, who surrounded her. And on issues where compassion might have been called into play, such as immigration or the admission of the Vietnamese refugees in the summer of 1979, is was conspicuously Mrs Thatcher who appeared to take the tough, 'unfeminine' line, while some of her colleagues such as Lord Carrington were way ahead of her in urging a softer, more humane approach.

Nevertheless in the new mood which overcame Britain in the late Seventies, it was precisely this 'masculine' element in Mrs Thatcher, her insistence on financial rectitude and that people should be manly enough to stand on their own feet rather than rely for everything on the 'Nanny State', that was her chief strength. The chief fear was not that, once in office, she would behave in a 'weak, womanish' way, but that her attempt to take a tough, manly line would — as is usual when women are dominated by their masculine element, their *animus* — simply lead her to become 'bossy'; that she might antagonize the unions and others by attempting to play a man's role without that full weight of masculine authority which is necessary for true, persuasive leadership (and which, curiously enough, can only be effective when it is tempered by precisely those softer, more 'feminine' qualities, such as sympathy for others and a sense of humour, which the bossy woman so conspicuously lacks).

As the Seventies came to an end, these fears were still largely unresolved. Despite her determination in the face of a gathering economic storm, despite her apparently skilful opening moves in the international chess game over Zimbabwe-Rhodesia and her courage in flying to Ulster in the wake of the Mountbatten and Warrenpoint murders, she still had not really been put to the test. But as the Eighties began, there was perhaps a further fear which, although not widely expressed, ran even deeper than these — and it was one which stemmed from the whole of her philosophy and approach to politics.

At the heart of Mrs Thatcher's 'New Conservatism' was the belief that most of Britain's troubles stemmed from the fact that we had as a nation become soft, economically stagnant, over-reliant on the State — and that if only we could get production going again and produce more wealth, a large part of these problems would simply vanish. As a general diagnosis, this might have had some considerable truth — but in the climate of growing fears over the future of the world's resources, above all energy, was it any longer realistic to base a political prescription for the future of any country on the premiss of boundless economic growth? Even if, in the short run, Mrs Thatcher's drive for 'more private incentives, less public subsidies' *did* come off, sending a wave of new vitality coursing through the economy (which in itself seemed highly dubious), was it sensible to place all bets on such a proposition when it seemed that the real problem of the future might be to persuade, cajole and force people into *lowering* their expectations, in as fair and orderly a way as possible?

From one point of view, of course, it would have seemed the purest defeatism to talk in 1979 in this kind of language. For thirty years since the war, the whole of Britain's domestic politics had been centred on the promise of ever increasing growth, ever rising expectations. The two great ideological driving forces of the age, Socialism and Consumer-Capitalism, were so allied on this matter that they were indistinguishable, except in their prescriptions of how best to arrive at the common goal. And certainly the notion that there might simply not be the natural resources available to sustain unlimited growth throughout the world no more crept in to colour with caution the utterances of politicians, of any party, in 1979 than it had done in earlier election years.

In the short term it may well have been that Mrs Thatcher's policies were by far the more realistic of the two alternatives held out to the British people in the late Seventies. But in the long term it may prove that she was simply holding out yet another version of the unobtainable Holy Grail; indeed that in doing so in quite the way she did, she was ensuring that when real economic storms blew up, of a world-wide nature, she would be particularly ill-equipped to give the British people the kind of leadership that might help them to adjust to such cruel realities. In this respect, it might well be in the end that such feminine qualities as compassion and an intuitive insight into the deeper realities of the situation would have stood both her and Britain in better stead than the impressive, but rather too one-sided reliance on the 'masculine' that in May 1979 had carried her triumphantly to power.

27

Mountbatten: The Man and His Murderers

(1 September 1979)

In the wake of the news from County Sligo and County Down it is hard this week to write about anything else. When Airey Neave was killed earlier this year, one thought that the Irish troubles had claimed by far their most prominent victim since General Wilson in 1920 and the Phoenix Park murders of 1882. Now it is impossible to imagine how that terrible sickness could have reached higher in British public life, short perhaps of the Queen herself – in an event only made more shocking by its context, a peaceful fishing trip in that sunlit bay on the remote coast of western Ireland.

Indeed in a curious way it took the total shock of such an event to bring home just what an astonishing figure Lord Mountbatten was. As his golden career unfolded in the first-class obituary programme put together for BBC television by Ludovic Kennedy, it seemed as much a reminder of Britain's own glorious past, and of qualities and values we have lost, as a tribute to the man himself. It seemed almost unbelievable that one human being could have touched the history of our century at so many points, from the presence of Queen Victoria at his christening, through the resignation of his father as First Sea Lord in 1914; his friendship in the Twenties with the young Prince of Wales; staying in Hollywood with the Fairbankses and making a silent film with Charlie Chaplin; polo-playing in Valletta under the shadow of the battle-cruisers of the Mediterranean Fleet and being the man who brought the Royal Navy fully into the age of wireless; the Hornblower-style boy's adventure story of the *Kelly*; the South-East Asia campaign; the last Viceroy; being appointed First Sea Lord in 1955 by the same man, Winston Churchill, who had accepted the resignation of his father forty-three years before; having reluctantly to provide ships for the last ignominious imperial adventure of Suez. As we reached the period of Britain's decline into post-imperial seediness in the past twenty years, he seemed more than ever to be a last, sunlit link with that tradition of our national greatness which had run unbroken for hundreds of years, and which now seems so hard to connect with our present trivial age of small men. Was there a more telling contrast in the film than that between Clement Attlee calling in the First Sea Lord to tell him that Mountbatten was to be taken back by the Navy after his time as Viceroy ('I haven't called you in for your opinions – I'm giving you an order'), and the associations conjured up by the revelation near the end that in 1965 Harold Wilson had been toying with the idea of sending Mountbatten out to 'solve the Rhodesian problem'?

What emerged overall was a man who, within the framework of all the successive roles allotted to him in the public pageant of our time, developed a genuine and powerful sense of personal authority which stems not from mere personality but from character shaped over many decades by training, by self-discipline, by a developed and tested sense of self-reliance. He was a man who had learned how to relate fully and easily to his own masculinity, someone in whom all those human drives such as ambition and the desire to lead, which we have so often seen turned into immature self-parody by the lesser men of recent years, found proper expression. In the past two decades, for all sorts of reasons, we have been particularly ill at ease in this

country with the type of masculinity Mountbatten represented. We have lived in an age when it has been hard for
men to behave truly like men. We have seen endless displays of rather petulant pseudo-masculinity from men such
as Heath and Wilson.

But in Mountbatten (and in this he was perhaps fortunate
in the time he lived) we saw someone who had been able to
develop the 'larger-than-life' stature of true maturity, and
someone who, therefore, in that fundamental sense which
challenges and should inspire each one of us in the way we
conduct our own lives, was worthy of real respect.

What, on the other hand, can we say of the 'other side' of
this culminatory drama of Lord Mountbatten's life, of those
men who spent perhaps weeks or months carefully planning
his murder (and quite incidentally those of anyone else,
such as women, children and the rest of his family, who
happened to be around)? The other day I asked an analyst
friend of mine over dinner his definition of a psychopath.
He replied roughly as follows: 'He is a moral defective,
quite unable to share the "objective" view of morality. He
is so completely ego-centred that he interprets his own
needs, longings and desires as fundamental reality. Yet he is
sufficiently in touch with reality very often to carry others
along with him and to persuade them that he is right. He is
a pathological liar. He may be purely impulsive, or he may
be capable of long, obsessive planning to achieve his ends.
He does not learn from punishment or experience. He is
cold, unable to form close relationships, always ultimately
betrays trust. He is quite untreatable, because it is impossible to get through to him, and to put him in touch
with his own deeper self. He usually end up in prison.'

We tend to think of the psychopath as an individual, lone
figure – the Yorkshire Ripper, the Boston Strangler, possibly
with one or two accomplices, like Ian Brady. Indeed our

prisons are full of such, whether they are murderers or merely confidence tricksters. Nevertheless, far more dangerous than the mere individual mass murderer, as we have seen so often in our times, from Trotsky, Lenin and the Bolshevik revolutionaries, through to Hitler, Idi Amin or Pol Pot, is the psychopath who is created not just by his own psychic disintegration but by collective factors in society around him. These are the 'schizophrenic psychopaths' who may, in their private lives, be kind to women, children and animals (invariably with a heavy overlay of sentimentality), may even be 'devoutly religious', but who in their other personality 'justify' their psychopathic behaviour by reference to some collective cause — whether it be the 'party', some form of nationalism or merely that of a criminal gang.

In such a cause, the 'collective psychopath' behaves just like the individual psychopath, except that instead of interpreting his own, individual desires as fundamental reality, he merges his own ego into that of the group — and it is in the service of that collective ego that he is prepared to do all the things with which we are familiar, from the behaviour of the individual psychopath, such as lying, the obsessive planning of terrible crimes, the wanton killing of women and children, and in general the complete suspension of any normal moral sense.

Why should the Irish have developed a proneness to this particular form of collective psychopathology? One thing which strikes one about the phychological make-up of the Irish over the past century and a half is the way they have been inclined to fall into the familiar pattern of the 'boy hero who cannot grow up,' who is unconsciously dominated by 'Mother' (in this case 'Mother Ireland', 'Mother Church') and therefore remains frozen in permanent rebellion against the masculine world of 'Father', represented by authority, by the 'occupying British', above all by the British armed forces. Nothing could be more obviously reflective of the 'boy hero' acting out an infantile parody of masculinity than the spectacle of the IRA parading through Belfast with their black berets and sunglasses, playing at being 'men' (unconsciously looking for the approval of 'Mother' for their 'courage' in standing up to 'Father'). And of course the opposite, equally immature form of play-acting is that which affects the Paisleys, the ultra-loyalists, who identify with all the symbols of 'Father-masculinity', such as the 'flag', law and order, discipline – it was no accident that in his own tortured, lonely search for his own masculinity they should have attracted Enoch Powell.

It was perhaps ironic that, in so far as Lord Mountbatten was known to hold any view on the 'Irish problem', it was in favour of a 'federal solution' – in other words, the same as the declared policy of the Sinn Fein movement itself. But more important was that, as the most distinguished surviving member of the British armed forces, not to mention as a member of the hated Royal Family, Mountbatten was, as one now sees in retrospect, the ideal target for their particular form of psychopathology, and the fact that he presented himself, undefended and completely vulnerable, in a remote part of Ireland was, as we can now see, asking for trouble. Above all, perhaps, he represented precisely that which his killers most desperately lack and therefore resent most deeply of all – he was a 'real man'.

Part Four

Culture Heroes – Nostalgia and Self-deception

In the souvenir shops of London in the late Seventies there was on sale a postcard of peculiar poignancy. It showed a group of three politicians attending a Remembrance Day ceremony at the Cenotaph some years earlier — each with suitably solemn expressions, and clutching a large wreath. The three men were Jeremy Thorpe, Harold Wilson and Edward Heath — and the card was captioned, with I suspect wholly unconscious irony, 'Lest We Forget'.

By the end of the decade, of course, the rather foolish and fantastic period which these men had symbolized in Britain's public life, between the mid-Sixties when they had become leaders of the three major parties and the mid-Seventies when they departed, already seemed a long way away. Two of them had, for different reasons, passed under a very considerable cloud; the third, Edward Heath, still embittered by the circumstances of his removal from office, seemed more stubbornly than ever in the political wilderness.

But it was not only in politics that the great innovative wave which had thrown these men to the top of English life in the Sixties seemed exhausted and part of another age. For fifteen years from the mid-Fifties on, Britain's great social turmoil had thrown up an absolute plethora of new 'stars' and celebrities — playwrights, pop singers, television personalities, dress designers, film directors, novelists, artists. Now, in the Seventies, there was no more revealing symptom of the way that turbulence had run its course than the almost complete lack of new 'names'. With the exception of Mrs Thatcher, the odd lady news-reader (Angela Rippon, Anna Ford) and the inevitable crop of young sporting heroes (Jim Hunt, Sebastian Coe, Ian Botham), it was a decade when fewer 'stars' emerged from obscurity onto the national stage than any other of the century.

Indeed, both at home and abroad, the Seventies were a time when old reputations crumbled rather than new ones were made. From Richard Nixon to Jackie Onassis, from Marshall McLuhan to David Frost, from the Beatles to Muhammad Ali, there were few celebrities from those heady days of the Fifties and Sixties who commanded the same respect or exercised anything like the same glamorous sway by the end of the decade as they had at its beginning.

Under its general title 'Nostalgia and Self-deception', I do not wish to imply that the heterogeneous group of 'culture heroes' who are the subject of this section were all of equal significance, or had much in common — except that, in different ways and at different levels, they all reflected the general exhaustion and confusion of our culture in the Seventies.

The first essay, on David Frost, charts the career of the greatest 'superstar' ever to have been thrown up by television, in its Sixties heyday. In the ultimate emptiness of the 'Frost phenomenon', as it emerged in the Seventies, it is possible to read a reflection of the dwindling novelty of that essentially empty and superficial medium itself, which — though still obsessively watched, in 'living colour', by four-fifths of the population — turned out to have been perhaps the most over-rated of all the new toys twentieth-century man had devised for himself. The following essay, 'The Rise and Fall of the Super-Egotists', is a kind of footnote on the sort of fame Frost enjoyed.

The third essay is a more personal look at another very different 'TV personality' and culture-hero of the Seventies, Kenneth Clark.

Another inhabitant of the world of fashion whom, like Frost, we came to see in a somewhat changed perspective (as it emerged to what extent he had been as much a creation of the fantasy-bubble of the Sixties and early Seventies as its observer) was Tom Wolfe.

Two rather more substantial figures of our times have been John Betjeman and Arthur Koestler. Yet both in the Seventies could be seen as symbolizing in their own way the loss of confidence and direction of an age in which it had become easier to perceive the charms of the past and the follies of the present than to see a healthful way forward into the future.

The most tempting way out perhaps was simply to pin one's hopes to some utterly one-sided, distorted world-view, whereby the ancient archetype of the struggle towards some better, brighter future might somehow be kept alive. Here lay the path chosen by those two very different figures, Paul Johnson, the one-time Socialist, who decided that the only way forward to the golden future lay with Capitalism; and Germaine Greer, who looked forward to the distant day when the women of the world would usher in Utopia by rising up and throwing off their male oppressors.

Finally, not so much a hero as one of the most haunting books of the decade, there was *Watership Down* – which, as I argue, beyond its cosy, sunlit, innocent-seeming surface, was in reality an unconscious cry for help, a dream of escape from the growing nightmare engulfing mankind.

28

David Frost: The Man Who Rose Without Trace

(Adapted from an article written for the *Observer* in the week of the first Nixon–Frost television interview, May 1977)

Last Thursday evening, a curious thing happened. Millions of people in Britain turned on their television sets to watch what most of them knew was likely to be a spectacular media non-event. It was highly unlikely that any startling revelations would emerge from the lavishly-publicized interviews between David Frost and ex-President Nixon. Yet the very fact that they switched on was a last fading tribute to the man who was once the biggest superstar ever produced in the short history of television.

The real shock, as the two wraith-like figures from what seemed like another age hove into view, was the sheer stumbling, incoherent, sentimental, embarrassing amateurishness of it all. Was this really the man who was once President of the United States? Could this really be the man who was once known as 'the most ruthless TV interrogator of the Western world'?

Shortly before Christmas 1970, the entire Establishment of Nixon's America gathered at the White House, in full evening dress. For the best part of two hours, the President, John Mitchell, Billy Graham, H. R. Haldeman and the rest were held more or less enthralled by a selection of 'Christmas readings', interspersed with such ancient jokes as the notice supposedly seen outside 'a New York church' reading 'If you are tired of sin, come inside' – against which someone had pencilled 'If you are not, ring this number'.

Such chestnuts did not go down too well with all that

august audience (Billy Graham in particular was reported to have been fairly tight-lipped about the whole affair, despite the Bible readings thrown in), but for the show's star, David Frost, just thirty years of age, that evening at the White House in the high-noon of the Nixon Presidency was the peak of his astonishing career. A few months earlier an opinion poll in Britain had shown that he was better known than anyone except the Queen and Harold Wilson. In America, where his new five-nights-a-week chat show had swamped all opposition, he was described as 'the best-known Englishman since Winston Churchill'. Indeed his fame at that time was literally world-wide. In 1971, when Bangladesh became an independent nation, Frost was personally welcomed by Shaikh Abdul Rahman, the country's leader, in front of a crowd of 100,000 people. In New Zealand, when former Prime Minister Kirk was buried, Frost was reporter at the graveside with his arm round the premier's widow.

Yet in the past few years, something very strange has happened to the man who had travelled up through the frenzied, image-obsessed Sixties like a meteor. His appearances on television, though noticeably fewer, have by no means ceased. The company he has kept has on the whole been just as starry and cosmic as at the height of his fame. But he has become almost like a ghostly presence, totally unreal, so that one is no longer quite sure whether he is really there or not (I recall a particularly surreal moment in 1974 when no sooner had one channel shown a laughing Muhammad Ali, just after winning a world heavyweight fight in Zaire, with a seemingly diminutive Frost clutching a microphone on the edge of the screen shouting 'Super, Muhammad, super', than Frost appeared on another channel cosying up knee-to-knee with Senator Edward Kennedy, saying, 'It's a great joy to be with you again, Senator.').

Did the 'Frost phenomenon' ever have any reality? Or was it always something of an illusion? The answers to such questions, I believe, tell us a great deal about the curious nature of this freakish and unreal medium which in the past twenty years has passed into the centre of our public and private lives.

I first met David Frost nearly twenty years ago at Cambridge. It is hard to convey just how 'ordinary' he seemed in those days. Cambridge in the late Fifties was obsessed with 'success'. Undoubtedly the dominant personality among the undergraduates of the time was Peter Cook, whose funny voices and 'Goon' names (Pules, Rune) were imitated everywhere – and by no one more assiduously than the thin-faced young freshman from Beccles. When Cook introduced a 'Macmillan Press Conference' cabaret act, to wild acclaim, Frost quickly had a pale version of his own. Although he never produced anything very remarkable, Frost worked at it all so hard – at his sketches and little bits of journalism, at being everywhere and knowing everyone – that in that highly competitive world, he soon became a kind of affectionately regarded joke. He was so dogged and so open about his desire to 'get on' that despite his plagiarism (and despite such incidents as the time a group of his fellow cabaret arists arrived at Great Yarmouth to find posters announcing 'DAVID FROST presents The Cambridge Footlights' – of which he was at the time only a very junior member – he explained that he 'could not think' how such a poster had been printed), he was impossible to dislike.

By the time Frost came down in the summer of 1961 to work as a humble production trainee for a commercial television company, it seemed he might easily vanish into complete obscurity. For more than a year, while his contemporaries were winning fame in *Beyond the Fringe* and at the new 'Establishment Club', he was doing little more than make occasional £15-a-night cabaret appearances and being ruled by one of his TV company superiors as having 'the wrong face for television'.

The great turning point came on the night of 24 November 1962, when the BBC launched its new Saturday night 'satire show' *That Was The Week That Was*. Frost had come to be chosen as the show's 'anchorman' almost by a series of accidents (he was originally picked by producer Ned Sherrin as a supporting ad-lib comedian). But in the strange atmosphere of that winter, the twilight of Macmillan's England, *TW3* became overnight the most hypnotically watched TV series in history – and, as its chief star, Frost became, equally overnight, a national figure of a kind television had never produced before.

The transformation in him was remarkable. He even looked physically broader. Suddenly, at the age of just twenty-three, he had entered a magic new world – expensive restaurants, taxis (he helped to run up one of the BBC's largest ever taxi bills, by such devices as keeping drivers waiting for an hour while he underwent his twice-weekly grooming at the hairdresser), newspaper interviews – where every day was like a royal progress through a wash of compliments ('loved the show', 'super', 'bless you').

Frost was never by any stretch of the imagination a 'satirist' (indeed he scarcely held passionate views on anything) but there was one thing it was impossible not to be impressed by – his extraordinary, intuitive feel for television itself. In the studio, he was instantly, nervelessly at home, as if the very presence of cameras and lights gave him an extra charge of confidence and energy. Yet where could such astonishing ambition, unattached to any specific talent (other than his remarkable confidence on television), turn to next?

In January 1964 came a clue. We were together in New

York. Frost was in an unusual state of excitement. He had caught his first glimpse of the American TV 'chat show' – and, as he talked of Sullivan, Paar and Carson, he was more obviously star-struck than I had ever known him. He had at last spotted the Everest of his universe.

The following winter, he took at least a tiny step towards that immeasurably distant goal when, back in Britain, he worked himself (again not as originally intended) into the centre of the hugely ambitious attempt to follow *TW3* with a mixture of sketches and chat with modest celebrities, spread over three nights of each weekend, *Not So Much A Programme, More A Way Of Life*. But then came disaster. As the show's run came to a close amid a storm of public protests, the BBC chiefs panicked. There must be no more embarrassing satire. The chief cuckoo in the nest, Frost, must be sacked – and it was small consolation to him that, as their one concession to his 'image', they agreed it should merely be announced that he had 'resigned', as if of his own volition.

Through most of 1965 Frost was at a low ebb, unemployed and unnoticed. But he then pulled off the coup which was to be the hinge of his entire career. As Daniel Boorstin wrote in *The Image*, 'being well-known for their well-known-ness, celebrities intensify their celebrity-images simply by being well-known for relations amongst themselves. By a kind of symbiosis, celebrities live off each other.'

On 7 January 1966, gambling on a sudden hunch, Frost invited seventeen people to a champagne breakfast at the Connaught Hotel. They included newspaper tycoons, Fleet Street editors, such celebrities of the Sixties as Len Deighton and the Bishop of Woolwich – and the Prime Minister, Harold Wilson. Few of them had the slightest idea why they had been invited (let alone why they had accepted) – but Frost's intuitive sense of the power of television to blur all 'celebrities' into the same dream-like mass was unerring. They came – and from then on he was 'the man who invited the Prime Minister to breakfast'.

His career now took off like a rocket. Within months Frost had moved into an expensive house in Knightsbridge. He had built up his own team of advisers. By the autumn he had negotiated his own chat show on ITV, *The Frost Programme*, explicitly planned to associate him with 'big names' and headline-making coups, like the first TV interview with the rebel Rhodesian Prime Minister Ian Smith (which began 'Good evening, Ian'). The series ended some months later with the harrying before a specially invited audience of the fraudulent insurance chief Dr Savundra. As he left the studio to frenzied cheers, and shouts of 'good old Frostie', it was his most heroic moment.

In 1967, after setting up London Weekend Television, by a series of self-introductory telephone calls to prospective backers, such as Arnold Weinstock of GEC, he won a contract from the ITA for 'his own' television company. In October he made skilful use of a speech to 150 American TV executives at the Royal Garden Hotel (billed as 'Britain's Number One TV Personality') to win himself a million-dollar contract to interview all the following year's Presidential hopefuls on American TV. And by the end of 1968, after another carefully-timed telephone call to the head of the Westinghouse network (on hearing that their main 'talk-show host' was leaving), Frost was finally within sight of the goal he had set himself just four short years before.

There was just one last hurdle. When it was put to London Weekend's managing director, Michael Peacock, that his new company's star asset was contemplating a five-nights-a-week show in New York, in addition to three nights in London, Peacock was flabbergasted. It just could not be done. Eight nights a week on television was contrary to nature. Never was Frost's ambition so pushing, so insatiable. His biographer, Willi Frischauer, has described the extraordinary lobbying, negotiations and telephone calls that went on throughout a weekend. When Peacock finally caved in, as Frischauer relates, Frost ordered his chauffeur to drive him to Westminster Abbey, where he knew there was 'a special chapel set aside for private prayer'. It was closed, but, on the way back, St Columba's, Pont Street, sufficed for this unique moment of thanksgiving.

On 7 July 1969, after a coast-to-coast campaign of mysterious advertisements for 'The Great Briton', the 'David Frost Show' was finally unveiled (an interview with Prince Charles). Within months, the reports were coming back: 'David Frost is now a bigger success on American TV than he has ever been here.' In Britain that winter he interviewed Prince Philip, and Harold Wilson from Number Ten Downing Street. In New York he talked to Dean Acheson, Golda Meir, John Lennon and Yoko Ono. In the space of one week in June 1970 he was awarded the OBE in Britain, made Doctor of Laws in Boston, and given a 'Faith and Freedom' award by the 'Religious Heritage of America', for 'communicating the relevance of Judaeo–Christian ethics to twentieth-century America'. His agent let it be known that 'David' would be prepared to do a TV commercial for £100,000 ('he has always refused before . . . the commercial is now an international service in which he firmly believes').

In December, the ultimate accolade, Frost was invited by President Nixon to give his special White House Christmas Show (his mother Mona, flown over from Beccles to sit between Nixon and John Mitchell at dinner, told them, 'I had to give up a training session with the Women's Fellowship Choir to be here').

But the terrifying strain was beginning to show. In Britain that winter, Frost was running for the first time into heavy criticism. Noting that most of his guests on British screens were now American — Spiro Agnew, Woody Allen, Norman Mailer — Milton Shulman commented, 'Frost approaches them in the cooing, glutinous, chummy, ingratiating style which obviously appeals to American viewers ... one senses he has lost his instinctive grasp of what is going on in this country.'

Over the next two years, amid a clatter of falling ratings on both sides of the Atlantic, the whole thing collapsed with astonishing speed. In Britain he gradually vanished from the screen. In America, in a last desperate bid to retain his image, on 12 January 1972 he flew sixty guests to Bermuda for lunch, including Professors Galbraith and Schlesinger, John and Yoko, Sergent Shriver and Bobby Fischer. All in vain. On 6 May came the headline 'FROST SHOW CANCELLED'. The cancellation, according to Frost, was 'at my request. I felt the time had come to move on to something new.'

In Frost's cuttings file there are certain quotations which recur. One, used often in the Sixties, and ascribed to a sermon heard in childhood, was 'Happiness is a by-product of doing what you like.' In 1971 the remark appeared with a significant alteration: 'Money is a by-product of doing what you like.'

Frost was already a millionaire, and had for some years been building up a whole network of TV production companies, some registered in the Bahamas and Curaçao. But in 1971 his fascination with money began to show a new intensity. There was a night-club deal with Bass Charrington, an interest in a two-million-dollar scheme to sell replicas of the Liberty Bell to America, another in a Japanese–US steak house chain ('an all-important attraction is the ballet-like manner in which the chef serves and cuts the food').

Then in February 1972 it was announced that financier Jim Slater had bought a company called Equity Enterprises, as 'a sort of investment piggy-bank for 33-year-old David and other friends'. Over the next year or two it became clear that Frost had at last found a new world which had almost as much glamour for him as television. In particular his admiration for Slater became a wonder to behold.

I once met David around this time at a party. He came out into the garden, where he saw a senior executive of the *Sunday Times*, which had recently been running some hostile articles about Slater. 'Very good articles, Ron,' he began. 'I've no complaint about that. But if you're going to write about merchant bankers, why do you just pick on one?' He went on to suggest that, when 'all this is over', 'Ron' should invite Slater to lunch. 'You would be absolutely fascinated by his mind.' For dramatic effect, David pointed in the fading light to a nearby rosebush. 'I mean Jim is as interested in why that rose should wither and die as he is in a balance sheet.'

It was an eerie moment. David was addressing a small group of friends and acquaintances as if it were some shadowy television audience. It was as if, after years of living in the television bubble, he had passed permanently through into the looking-glass world.

In the past three years, although he is far from bankrupt, many of Frost's more grandiose financial projects have come unstuck. The shares of Equity Enterprises, in the wake of the Slater debacle, still stand suspended. And it is hardly surprising that, as a kind of last grand throw, he has returned to television, and to those two retired political 'stars' of the Sixties and early Seventies with whom in a curious way his own career has been so closely linked. Almost everything now hangs for Frost on the success of his two vast international collaborative operations with Richard Nixon and

Harold Wilson (as indeed, like three drunks leaning on one another, they depend on him).

What made Frostie run? For nearly twenty years I have been haunted by that question. He is so completely unlike any other human being I have ever met that I have even sometimes come to think of him as hardly 'human' at all, simply as a 'phenomenon'.

I once recognized the puzzlement of H. R. Haldeman when, in an interview, he was asked to assess Richard Nixon 'as a man'. He just could not place Nixon in normal human terms. And I have often felt over the years that Nixon and Frost (and indeed Wilson himself) had an extraordinary quality in common. It was as if, as people, they had no 'centre', as if they had become so completely absorbed and submerged by the demands of their public image, and by the whole shadowy realm of receding mirrors they inhabited, that in any other terms they had virtually ceased to exist.

Despite his universal geniality, from Cambridge on, David's most obvious quality was ambition of an all-consuming and extraordinary kind. With most people it is possible to localize their ambition – they want to be Prime Minister, or write a great novel, or make a million pounds. But David's ambition had a kind of distilled purity. He simply wanted to be amazingly famous for being David Frost. All the guises he adopted along the way – cabaret artist, satirist, fearless interviewer, cosy intimate of the stars – were merely passing means to that one all-consuming end.

Of course he could never have done it except in the age of television. He never had the specific ability as a writer or actor to achieve such unique fame through journalism or the films (he had very little ability, in fact, as either). Only television was sufficiently ill-defined (in McLuhan terms 'cool') to allow Frost to become famous simply for being himself – which is why he remains perhaps the supreme symbol of that curious, unreal period, the 'McLuhan Age'.

Nevertheless it would be a mistake (though one often made) to see David just as an ordinary person blown up large by the media. In fact he has unusual gifts – super-human energy, compelling charm, an extraordinary memory for faces, great personal generosity. In all these respects, his eulogists, such as Bernard Levin, are completely right. What they forget to add is that the bad fairy who came late to the christening decreed that all these gifts should be used only to serve one end, David's peculiar ambition to be world-famous simply for the sake of being world-famous. That is why, once that ambition finally began to crystallize round one specific goal, it could only be to head for the very heart of the furnace where, in the 1960s at least, 'celebrity-fame' was manufactured – the American TV chat show. In the context of real fame, of course, it is an astonishingly limited little goal (I remember once, when Frost's celebrity was at its height, asking a Nobel prize-winner who spent much time in both Britain and America what he thought of David Frost: he replied 'Frost? Who? I've never heard of this man'). But in prospect, for the minister's son from Beccles, whose world-view had been shaped by the *Reader's Digest* and *Time*, it seemed a goal transcending everything else in the world, worth seven years of astonishing energy and will to achieve. Only when it was realized, did it in-evitably turn to dust. Because in the end there has to be more to ambition than just the desire to become famous, to whatever superhuman limits it is felt and pursued. That is why the most fitting epitaph on Frost's career remains, alas, that coined as long ago as 1967 by Kitty Muggeridge, when she said, 'Frost has risen without trace.'

29

The Rise and Fall of the Super-Egotists

Without wishing to add further to the verbiage already lavished on the multi-million-dollar Drool-In between David Frost and Richard Nixon, I would just like to offer a kind of extended footnote to my observation last week that, as public figures, Frost, Nixon and Harold Wilson have certain remarkable qualities in common. I believe that we have here a type of man, or rather phenomenon, which, while seeming in some ways to be so contemporary, so much a product of the unreal, image-conscious television age, has in fact occurred many times before in history, and cries out for some kind of identification.

What are the qualities which distinguish such men? In fact it is of the essence of what we are trying to describe that such men are very *hard* to define in normal human terms. They seem to exist almost entirely in terms of their relentless upward drive, their almost unnatural ability to manipulate others into accepting them at their own self-valuation. They seem to transcend almost all the normal canons of what is acceptable and expected. They seem in a curious way (without necessarily being in any obvious way immoral) to be detached from morality. They display colossal cheek, and get away with it.

First, that curious personal elusiveness. Professor Daniel Boorstin touches on this, when he writes in *The Image* about 'the celebrity' – 'his qualities – or rather lack of them – illustrate our peculiar problem. He is neither good nor

bad, great nor petty. He is the human pseudo-event ...
made by all of us who willingly read about him, watch him
on television ... his relation to morality and even reality is
highly ambiguous.'

We can see how this applies to Frost, and the extraordinary way in which it was impossible ever to pin Frost
down to any of the various 'roles' he played during his
career – comedian, actor, satirist, fearless interviewer, cosy
intimate of the stars, big businessman. Was he ever really
any of these things? If so, he was never much good at being
any of them specifically – but what he was always superbly
good at was using those various passing roles to play himself, heading relentlessly on towards some mysterious 'place
in the sun', simply for being David Frost.

The same was true in political terms of Wilson and Nixon.
What did either of them ever actually *stand* for? Certainly
no identifiable point of principle, no philosophy, no fixed
position on anything. Like Frost, they played their various
passing roles, for or against the Common Market, for or
against détente with the Russians, like a succession of
costumes, chosen in accordance with the mood of the times,
simply to serve the supreme end of getting to the top and
staying there.

Secondly, there is the element of cheek or *chutzpah*, of
always doing the thing which no one would have thought
that even they would try to get away with, as if the normal
criteria of expected behaviour just did not apply. One of
the most revealing episodes I recall from my years working
closely with Frost was a visit to his hotel when we were
together in New York in 1964, shortly after Kennedy's
death. His room was almost papered with drafts of two
letters, one to David Ormsby Gore, our Ambassador in
Washington, the other to President Johnson. Their purpose
was to secure for Frost the first, exclusive BBC interview

with the new President. It was an extraordinary thing to try on. As a mere twenty-four-year-old member of the *TW3* team, Frost had no official status whatever (indeed Robin Day and a visiting *Panorama* team, seeking the same interview, were absolutely enraged to find that, whatever 'usual channel' they tried to get into the White House, the jumped-up young unknown had been there first).

Of course this colossal nerve was characteristic of Frost's career at many points on his upward climb – the outrageous 'plagiarism' of his early days, the embarrassing awfulness of his cabaret acts and his endless repetition of the same old terrible jokes, above all perhaps that astonishing breakfast at the Connaught Hotel in 1966, when Harold Wilson, David Astor, Cecil King and a whole crowd of celebrities turned up to drink champagne with a mere 'TV satirist' simply because they had been so taken in by his total self-confidence that they never paused until afterwards to realize what an extraordinary self-publicity stunt they had all un-wittingly given their support to.

Exactly the same suspension of disbelief has attended Harold Wilson's career at every stage – to the point where a sense of reality was almost eroded. Even when he ap-pointed Marcia Williams to the peerage, barely a month after the squalid 'land deals' affair, no one really knew how to react except with bemused acceptance. He 'got away with it' just as he had got away with a thousand lesser absurdities before, from his ludicrous *volte face* over the 'Bank Rate Leak' of 1957, to his dreadful pop-cultural name-dropping (I shall always recall one interview when, apropos nothing at all, he mentioned his constituency X – 'where the Z Cars come from, y'know').

Yet however embarrassing such things are to those who know their perpetrators closely, and are not under the spell, the extraordinary thing is just how potent and durable the spell is for millions of others. And here we may see a historical parallel. In Sir Lewis Namier's essay on Napoleon III, he describes the astonishment of those who knew Louis Napoleon well, that such a completely ordinary, mediocre little man should be the Emperor of France. But away from the court, away from Paris, Louis assumed, like the TV superstar of today, an almost divine stature – the millions, looking up, invested him with superhuman qualities which existed solely in their own minds.

Above all, so total is their ambition, these Super-Egotists seem to have missing from their mental make-up that X-Factor which for most of us preserves some sense of our place in society, and in the hierarchy of talent or birth or proper expectation. Like Balzac's de Rastignac, they see society simply laid out before them as a series of stepping stones, enabling them to hurtle 'upwards' without any in-hibition. There is no place so 'high' that they cannot in-stantly aspire to it, simply because in the end their own ambition is the only criterion of value they know. The only limit to their ambition is the limitations imposed by their own imagination as to how far they can climb.

Obviously one of the greatest examples of such Super-Egotism in history, hurtling up from nowhere in the social shambles that succeeded the French Revolution, was Napo-leon I. The way in which, in barely ten years, Napoleon Bonaparte rose from complete obscurity as a young gunnery officer to being first the ruler of France, and then the Emperor of half Europe, has much in common on a grander social and political scale with the meteoric climb of a Frost or other celebrity of our own day. Although Napoleon may have seemed to have more obvious talents, such as his generalship, he still had that same curiously elusive quality as a human being. His incredible climb to the top, even his military successes, were all ultimately achieved by colossal nerve and self-confidence, magnified into a seemingly irres-istible force of nature. And when I read of Napoleon en-throned at Erfurt in 1808, giving audience to the crowned heads of Europe, I always think of him as a kind of Super-Frost, sitting with all those celebrities at the centre of a kind of Super TV chat show.

Yet, like Groucho Marx not wanting to be a member of any club that would let him in, there is in the hour of triumph of all these men a kind of cosmic frustration, that in having achieved their supreme goals so easily they have in fact rendered meaningless the whole structure and hier-archy of the world they have conquered. So Frost, having become the ultimate TV superstar, sitting on his Everest in 1970, suddenly finds that he has lost his incredible inner drive, becomes inwardly tired and flabby, and finds the whole thing has turned to dust. Wilson and Nixon, having achieved supreme political power, find that they have not got the slightest idea what to do with it (except indulge in public relations exercises, and occasionally lash out by in-vading Cambodia or Anguilla), eventually fading away into nothing more than ghostly caricatures of their former selves. Napoleon III is eventually blown away by the first serious puff of wind, and all his grandiose make-believe 'Second Empire' with him. Napoleon I sits on St Helena, boring Las Casas and the few other wretched survivors of his court to death with his meaningless platitudes about power and life and 'fortune', endlessly wondering 'what happened?', as mystified as Nixon showed himself to be last Thursday night as to why the whole fantasy had mysteri-ously evaporated.

Finally there is one last, supreme example of the pheno-menon who must be considered – the most appalling and destructive of all – Adolf Hitler. Once again we see many of the same characteristics – the utter banality of 'the real

Hitler', the continuing mystification as to what he was 'really like', the astonishing 'nerve' by which he 'got away' with things which no one else would have dreamed of attempting, right up to the invasion of Russia. Once the spark had ignited, his upward drive was unstoppable, his manipulation of others incomparable – but at the heart of the phenomenon which had all Europe in its thrall and left tens of millions of corpses was a little man whom not a lifetime's-worth of home movies of the terrace at Obersalzburg can show as personally anything other than extremely ordinary and boring. Obviously Hitler left a huge legacy in terms of destruction, as in his lesser way did Napoleon (who also left the Code Napoleon and a few triumphal arches scattered about). But ultimately the astonishing thing is how little positive any of these men leave behind. They have all, in Mrs Muggeridge's immortal words, 'risen without trace', even if they eventually fade away without trace as well.

Their last legacy perhaps is that each in his different way has left a void of meaning where he has passed. Wilson and Nixon both emptied politics and political language of significance. Frost emptied television of significance (in so far as it ever had any). Hitler and Napoleon left a dark void which puzzled succeeding generations have desperately tried to fill, with their endless reconstructions of the great stirring days of Napoleonic Europe, or of the Nazi Empire and the Second World War. But having sucked the world into the black holes of their egos, the Super-Egotists eventually leave behind nothing but a series of rather depressing enigmas. For true achievement, for substance and for meaning, you have to look at quite other kinds of historical figure altogether.

30

Kenneth Clark: The Aesthete as Hero

(A review of Clark's autobiography, published November 1977)

Just before the Seventies began, as I described in Chapter 3, 'On Dover Beach', Kenneth Clark's television series *Civilisation* enjoyed a success unique in television history. Millions of people looked on the series with an almost superstitious reverence. It was as if, out of the dark night of the late Sixties, with all its frenzied contemporaneity and hideous confusion, people saw in the urbane figure of Clark and the magnificent array of agreeable images he presented, a kind of icon – an emblem of stability and eternity in a world which had become a nightmare.

Yet the most remarkable thing of all was that almost no one seemed to be listening to what Clark was actually saying (a small indication of this was the number of quite elementary mistakes which survived right through to the publication of the book, such as giving the date of the fall of the Bastille as 1792). Had they done so (as I argued in Chapter 3) they would have seen that far from providing reassurance, Clark was in fact quite unconsciously presenting the evidence for an astonishing pessimistic view of the past thousand years of European history – the 'centred' certainty of the medieval world view disintegrating, step by step, to an all but total state of catastrophe at the present day. There was almost no sign that Clark himself realized that this was what he was doing. He consciously ended the series, in fact, on a note of somewhat unconvincing optimism (as he puts it in *The Other Half*, 'I walked into my library, patted a wooden figure by Henry Moore, as if to imply that there was still hope, and it was all over'). But beneath the agreeable dream-like surface there unmistakably lurked a quite appalling nightmare.

Lord Clark has done precisely the same thing with his autobiography. In the first volume, he showed us an intensely lonely little boy, born into a rich, loveless, philistine Edwardian household, finding his escape into the 'secret garden' of Art – the magical frozen world of pictures and beautiful forms. We left him, in his late thirties, as Director of the National Gallery, having transformed his entire life into such a work of art: its foreground, the brightly-lit world of pre-war fashionable London, in which famous names shimmered around the central figure and his wife Jane like exquisite *objets* – while beyond the pool of light a vast, threatening darkness was ruthlessly shut out.

We take up the story in the second volume in September 1939. Having stuffed away the National Gallery's treasures like a Nibelungen hoard into a Welsh cave, he then presents an extraordinarily detached view of the war. The cataclysmic events rocking civilization are reduced to little more than noises off (one feels that Clark would scarcely have been aware of the Battle of Britain, had not Air Chief Marshal Sir Cyril Newall been a 'close friend' who kept him informed), while we move through a series of carefully composed scenes, from Myra Hess playing Mozart concertos in the empty Gallery, to Clark telling John Betjeman to watch out for a 'ravishing' girl in the Ministry of Information canteen called 'Miss Joan Hunter Dunn'. If Clark sits out an air raid in a cellar, it *has* to be with Arthur Waley, talking of Chinese poetry. He even manages two trips to Sweden, to talk about ceramics with that 'human masterpiece', the Crown Prince. While if occasional, disagreeable forays do have to be made into the darkness, like his abortive trips to provincial cities to persuade them to show works from the National's reserve collection, 'these well-meant expeditions gave me an insight into industrial England which I would never have enjoyed otherwise, and Jane, who always accompanied me, dressed in exquisite Lanvin clothes, gave immense pleasure to the local mayors'.

In May 1945 Clark seems barely aware the war has ended ('we were lunching with Mr Bevin that day, and the subject was scarcely mentioned'). The magic pageant floats onward, as Clark moves effortlessly from Ruskin Lectures in Oxford and his books (*The Nude*, *Landscape Into Art*, *Piero della Francesca*) to the chairmanship of the Arts Council, Sadlers Wells, the chairmanship of the ITA, Covent Garden. The sets continue relentlessly exquisite – his medieval castle Saltwood, Japanese temple gardens, cool green rooms in the Louvre, furnished with 'Maya carvings and Islamic pots'. The actors remain relentlessly famous – Picasso, Keynes, the Menuhins, Edith Sitwell, Vivien Leigh, Berenson, Gulbenkian, de Gaulle. Even at the very moment when Churchill has his famous stroke in 1953, it is Jane whose hand he clutches for support. It all seems too perfect to be true – and curiously empty, like a dream. Just occasionally the famous names are misspelt – 'de Gaspari', 'Monteverde', 'Parmigiano', Lawrence Olivier' – as if to show that what we are watching is a kind of eerie masque, below the polished surface of which something is mysteriously, fatally wrong.

In fact 'eerie' is precisely the word for this book; this chilling portrait of the 'incurable aesthete' as hero, desperately trying to keep out any hint of reality from the succession of waxwork animated *tableaux*. Where is the underside of all this glittering, dead surface? A feeling of terrible claustrophobia begins to mount. Every glimmering of life trying to break in is so rigorously excluded. There is even an extraordinary passage on page 108 (which must be read in full) where Clark describes an obviously genuine and powerful mystical experience ('my whole being was irradiated by a kind of heavenly joy, far more intense than anything I had known before') the implications of which he decides are far too embarrassing to face up to, so like everything else it is stuffed ruthlessly back into the darkness.

Then, like an idea whose time has come, Clark makes *Civilisation*: he is transformed in the late Sixties into one of the most celebrated men in the world. He goes to Washington, and amid near-riotous scenes, he is mobbed at the National Gallery by a huge crowd. He felt 'like some visitor to a plague-ridden country, who has been mistaken for a doctor but is not a doctor'. He rushes off to the lavatory where he 'sobbed and howled for quarter of an hour'. He knows that he is 'a hoax', that he has seemed to be offering what he cannot deliver, that beneath the marble surface is nothing but a deadly void.

This must be one of the most unconsciously self-revealing books ever written. What comes through is the self-portrait of a man who, by a steely effort of will, has subordinated everything in his life to the preservation of an almost flawless mask or *persona*; who has remorselessly fought off every temptation to self-analysis (as he says 'I cannot go very far in that direction'), to the point where he can no longer even endure going for a walk on his own because his thoughts 'are now so melancholy that I cannot face them'.

Of course the price that must be paid for such one-sidedness is always colossal. Throughout these pages there is never any doubt as to where the shadow from all this relentless artificial sunlight was falling – on his wife Jane. Again and again she is said to be suffering from mysterious illnesses. Finally, after an almost *Götterdämmerung*-like scene in Palermo (where the book becomes remarkably like some major tragic novel), Jane collapses altogether. For three years, while she is barely conscious, Clark keeps a lonely vigil by her bedside. After an evening when her mind had suddenly cleared ('We looked through a new volume of photographs of *quattrocento* art and she identified every one'), she dies. As the picture of a man who to the end has never dared face up to 'the other half' of himself this is a spine-chilling book, which ends up by casting fatal doubt even on those things where Clark's external reputation has always rested most strongly. Even the magnificent paintings, you realize, were only experienced as backdrops to a stage set (how could anyone speak of Piero's 'Baptism' in terms of 'good taste'?) — and when the lights went out, there was nothing left but a very lonely and silent darkness.

31

Tom Wolfe: Sage or Victim?

(A review of *Mauve Gloves and Madmen, Clutter and Vine*, published September 1977)

I vividly recall my first encounter with the writings of Tom Wolfe. It was in 1965, the year when that curious mania known as the 'Swinging Sixties' was at its height. I was deeply puzzled by this outbreak of cultural hysteria which seemed to be engulfing the Western world — the insane fashion-consciousness, the demand for bright colours and loud rhythmic noise, the worship of certain key figures, 'dream heroes', whose role was to provide imagery for the collective dream-state — pop singers, pop artists, photographers, model girls, dress designers. And not the least extraordinary thing about it seemed to be the extent to which almost everyone (in the media at least) seemed to be quite bewitched by what was happening. There seemed to be no one standing outside the bubble, and observing just how odd and shallow and egocentric and even rather horrible it all was.

Then one day there fell into my hands a new book from America called *The Kandy-Kolored Tangerine-Flake Streamline Baby* (1965), by a young journalist then in his mid-thirties (Tom Wolfe was born in 1931). From the moment I opened it, I was transfixed. Here at last seemed the very man I had been waiting for — the detached observer who not only saw that something very odd indeed was happening to the Western world, but had also (quite a problem) discovered the right style in which to write about it.

In his introduction, Tom Wolfe described how it happened. He had been sent out to California by *Esquire* to write an article on the 'custom car cult' – the backyard craze for building automobiles shaped like alligators and fish and heaven knows what, in extraordinary designs and colours. He had come back to New York, tried to describe this strange, surreal little world in his usual condescending 'totem prose' – and found it simply could not be done. Eventually *Esquire*, with 'a two-page wide colour picture for the story locked into the presses', told him in desperation just to type up his notes and send them over for someone else to write the article. Wolfe sat down that evening at 8 p.m., turned up the rock'n roll on the radio, and tried to put down every scrap of an impression he could recall, in a kind of stream of consciousness. Forget about main verbs ... finishing sentences ... if you're still groping for a word, just ... leave dots! By 6.15 next morning he had written forty-nine pages – and *Esquire* ran the story exactly as he had put it down.

Over the next eighteen months, in 1963 and 1964, Wolfe used the same vivid, breathless, epithet-drunk prose style to describe Billy the K., the disc jockey who became known as the 'Fifth Beatle', and Cassius Clay and Las Vegas (the 'new-style-town' *par excellence*) and Baby Jane Holzer, the 'girl of the year', who mixed with the Stones and Hockney and all those incredible new pop swingers from Britain ('They're all young and they're taking over, it's like a whole revolution, I mean it's exciting, they're all from the lower classes, East End sort of thing'). And at last there it all was on the page – the whole frenetic, nervous, crazy, egocentric, self-destructive, nightmarish *danse macabre* of the 'New Culture'! The 'Swinging Sixties' to the life!

But then came the nagging question. For all his extraordinary perception and ruthless eye for the sham and the egocentricity and the nightmarishness – to what extent *was*

Wolfe actually 'outside' what he was writing about? How *deeply* did he see — or was he still really inside the bubble, just another brilliantly gifted part of the charade he dissected so mercilessly? Did it matter?

Three years later, when his second collection of essays was published (in this country as *The Mid-Atlantic Man*), the questions still nagged. The book contained some of the most ruthless profiles Wolfe has ever written, such as that of Bob and Spike Scull, a couple of new-rich New York socialites who had made it big in the Sixties 'art scene' on money from his cab fleet. This culminated in a party of truly Inferno-esque quality out at Flushing, for Jasper Johns and Rauschenburg and 'Poonsy' and 'Andy' and everyone, the climax of which was a Warhol-type film showing the view from underside up into a lavatory pan, with a huge turd crashing in full colour into the audience's faces. There was an almost equally horrible portrait of Hugh Hefner, the pasty-faced Masturbation King, sitting at the heart of his horrible Chicago mansion on an enormous round bed, surrounded not so much by beautiful girls as by a mass of dials and video screens and electronic equipment, so that he can watch himself on the Ampex while the bed turns ... and turns ... and turns. There was a poignant description of Carol Doda, the San Francisco stripper, who had become the city's biggest tourist attraction by blowing up her breasts with silicone to grotesque size, until ... well, what would happen when the thrill and the silicone wore off, and poor Carol was alone with her withered balloons and no one to treat her even as human any more?

But for all his apparent searchlight eye for the grotesque fantasies by which people seek to make themselves rich and famous and popular and special (until one day they wake up and find themselves miserably alone), Wolfe did not bother to hide his admiration for some of the values and heroes of the strange 'New Culture' he was charting. He seemed to have an obsession, for instance, with physical description, and in particular with the difference between glorious, energetic, sexy youth ('beautiful little high-school buds in their buttocks-decolletage stretch pants') and the hideous deformations of advancing age ('old veiny white ankles, which lead up like a senile cone to a fudge of tallowy, edematous flesh'). Perhaps still more revealing was the essay on Marshal McLuhan which, while appearing to portray him as a kind of wonderful, absurd confidence trickster, could never actually bring itself to the point of denying that perhaps McLuhan was right! Perhaps, after all, he *was* the sage who, alone, had grasped the impenetrable truth about this strange madness which had seized the post-TV, Sixties world?

About the time *The Mid-Atlantic Man* (1968) was published, Wolfe wrote what is probably still his most famous essay, 'Radical Chic' — the horrific snapshot of a party given by the Leonard Bernsteins for a mixture of New York smart-set and the leaders of the 'Black Panther' movement, which more than anything else captured that insane blur in late-Sixties America between violence and glamour. In 1975 came that brilliant long article (or short book) *The Painted Word*, showing how the whole crazy fantasy-edifice of the New York 'modern art world' ultimately rests just on two or three critics, whose word alone decides whether a pile of garbage poured on the floor is just a pile of garbage, or the most wonderful new art sensation, worth twenty thousand dollars. And now we have Wolfe's first new collection for seven years, *Mauve Gloves and Madmen, Clutter and Vine*.

At first sight it seems to be much the mixture as before, although with rather more fiction and less straight reportage. The title story gets inside the mind of a successful

Jewish writer who has become so carried away by all the externals of his new role as a successful writer – the Lobb shoes (to think, his father had come over from Russia with nothing!), the Martha's Vineyard beach house, the smart literary party in their Manhattan apartment, with flowers by 'Mauve Gloves' and catering by 'Madmen, Clutter and Vine' – that he has virtually forgotten how to be a writer. There is another story about a black baseball player who is conned into making a dreadful TV commercial for after-shave. There are one of two rather jaded little essays on 'the pornography of violence' and the survival in America of give-away upper- and lower-class accents ('Honks and Wonks'). And by far the best piece of reporting in the book has nothing to do with the fashionable world at all, but is a portrait of American pilots flying off carriers into North Vietnam ('The Truest Sport: Jousting with Sam and Charlie'). This completely dispels (certainly as far as I was concerned) any view that those fliers were safely cocooned in a kind of air-conditioned, electronic bubble, murdering in comfort by remote control. Thanks to the unprecedented concentration of flak and super-sophisticated SAM missiles which were thrown up against them whenever they stuck a nose in off the Gulf of Tonkin, their survival rate compared unfavourably with almost anything in the Second World War.

The longest essay in the book, called 'The Me Decade: The Third Great Awakening' (already published over here in *Harper's-Queen*) begins with a description of a girl at a 'let-it-all-hang-out' therapy session in the Ambassador Hotel, Los Angeles. Everyone has to shout out the thing which deep down most worries them about themselves, and in her case it is ... haemorrhoids. From here the essay modulates somewhat improbably into an analysis of the great 'religious revival' which has overtaken America in the past ten years, from Hare Krishna and LSD to 'born-again' Jimmy Carter. Wolfe compares this ('the third great awakening') with the previous explosions of popular religious fervour in the 1740s (Wesley-ism) and 1825–50 (Camp meetings and Mormonism). And his thesis is that at the heart of this religious revival lies an obsession with 'Me' – that the ultimate fruit of post-war money and prosperity is that everyone has been liberated to concentrate on themselves. So recklessly does he mix up soul and body, religion and sex, that almost any movement which has caught on in America in the past decade can be seen as essentially just part of the same mish-mash of egocentricity.

Now this is perhaps an arguable, interesting thesis—although the case would have to be put with a great deal more psychological and historical rigour than Wolfe brings to bear. As it stands, it is just a long, confused, breathless attempt to jumble together by sleight-of-hand anything from 'group-sex', Germaine Greer, 'honesty sessions' and *Suck* to Gnosticism, Methodism and Zen. In fact one feels that the pages of *Harper's-Queen* were exactly the right place for it. But in the end this essay brings us back to the question – just where does Tom Wolfe stand, and how serious is he?

Because there is no doubt that he sets out to be something much more ambitious than just a casual observer of the passing show. He is an analyst, a deep thinker, a man who can use words like *kairos* and *antanacasis*, consider the nature of ecstasy, talk about Zoroastrianism. He asks to be taken very seriously indeed – so let us try.

It was extremely revealing that the one intellectual charlatan against whom Tom Wolfe was reluctant to pronounce *anathema* was Marshall McLuhan. For the point about McLuhan is that once upon a time he was an ordinary, dull little Conservative Catholic intellectual, influenced by

Chesterton, hating the modern world, and hankering for the lost paradise of a pre-industrial, agrarian society. Then one magic day, some thirty years ago, he read Poe's story *The Maelstrom*, about the sailor who, caught in the notorious whirlpool, realizes that the only way to escape is not to fight the downward pull of the vortex, but to leap out of his ship and float — like the surrounding driftwood — UPWARDS, to safety! The lesson was not lost on the Canadian professor. He decided that no longer would he fight the whirlpool of modern culture — he would float with it. Instead of castigating the mindless stream of imagery of television or pop music, he would bless it. He would acclaim everything — 'the medium is the massage' — he would float with the random sensation flow of 'post-linear', 'post-verbal' culture — and everything would be OK! Thus, telling people what they wanted to hear in the crazy late Sixties, did McLuhan win his brief reputation as the prophet of the age.

The parallel to Wolfe himself is inescapable. If you go back to the introduction to *The Kandy-Kolored Tangerine-Flake Streamline Baby* (1965), the nearest thing to an explicit credo he has ever written, his moment of 'literary conversion' was when he realized that the only way to write about the pure sensation flow of Sixties culture was not to 'fight it' by trying to describe it in old-fashioned, condescending 'totem prose' but simply to flow with it — by creating, McLuhan-like, a prose-style which exactly matched it. Deep down, of course, Wolfe made no secret of the fact that, far from dismissing 'the New Culture', he was celebrating it — revelling in what he called:

the new sensibility — *Baby baby baby where did our love go?* — the new world, submerged so long, invisible and now arising, slippy, shiny, electric — Super Scuba-man! — out of the vinyl deeps.

In a revealing passage in that introduction, Wolfe for the first time gave his 'explanation' for why all these strange cultural phenomena had emerged in the Western world in the 1950s and 60s:

The war created money. It made massive infusions of money into every level of society. Suddenly classes of people whose styles of life had been practically invisible had the money to build monuments to their own styles. Among teenagers this took the form of custom cars, the twist, the jerk, the monkey, the shake, rock music generally, stretch pants, decal eyes — and all these things, these teenage styles of life, like Inigo Jones's classicism, have started having an influence on the whole country.

Like *what*? Like *Inigo Jones's classicism*? What on earth is the man talking about? It is part of Wolfe's sleight-of-hand technique to rush the reader on at such a breathtaking pace that one does not always notice the 'serious analysis' (usually by sweeping analogy) that he is trying to slip in along the way — and when it comes to deeper psychological or historical or sociological explanations, he certainly (like McLuhan) tries to pull some very fast ones.

Wolfe's basic thesis here (so often repeated since) is simply that money creates the opportunity for self-expression, and always has done — and that *all forms of expression are the same*. Take this sentence (from the title essay of *The Kandy-Kolored etc.*:

'I don't mind observing that it is this same combination — money plus slavish devotion to form — that accounts for Versailles or St Mark's Square.

Well, I suppose one can see what he is driving at — but if one is prepared to rest on the simple equation of any form of artistic or fashionable expression with any other, St Mark's Square with the 'custom car' or 'the shake' or 'decal eyes', then one is not running very deep in terms of analysis.

Why not include Giotto's Arena Chapel frescoes, or Mozart's *Requiem* or Chartres Cathedral for good measure? The Rolling Stones equals Leonardo da Vinci. *Q.E.D.!* Indeed, whenever Wolfe ventures into these sweeping historical parallels (as in 'The Me Decade' – John Wesley equals Germaine Greer) he is soon treading on very thin ice indeed, simply in terms of his own ignorance:

I don't have to dwell on the point that cars mean more to these kids than architecture did in Europe's great formal century, say, 1750 to 1850 [*sic!*]. They are freedom, style, sex, power, motion, colour – everything is right there!

It would be hard to conceive of a more utterly meaningless (and in the widest sense illiterate) string of words – and there in a nutshell is the very worst of Tom Wolfe.

Of course there is more to Wolfe than that. His real achievement (apart from providing a great deal of journalistic entertainment) has been to capture in words, and from the inside, some of the more bizarre cultural inanities of one of the most insane and fascinating decades in the history of the world. He has been able to see through 'radical chic' and Hugh Hefner and the nonsense of the New York art world like nobody's business. But in the end, outside the world of the wonderful, exploding, self-expressing ego – however nightmarish and self-destructive and horrible that world can be – what is left? So let's just flow with it, baby! Wolfe's is a pretty bleak, harsh, loveless view of the world. He is like a man sitting on a fairground roundabout, feeling desperately sick, but seeing no way to jump off. Or like a soul doomed to wander for eternity through a particularly nasty modern version of Dante's Inferno, without the faintest hope of escaping into Purgatory, let alone Paradise. In the end, after re-reading his collected works, I am afraid I just feel slightly sick myself. I don't think I shall want to read any more.

32

Arthur Koestler: Sci-Fi Sage

(A review of *Janus: A Summing Up*, published November 1978)

One of the most remarkable events of our time has been the way in which, after several centuries of apparently brilliant progress, the whole post-Renaissance attempt to escape from metaphysics, and to explain the world rationally in terms of the physical sciences, has petered out in a series of baffling dead ends. In 1899, the German biologist Haeckel could confidently claim that of the 'seven great riddles of the universe', six were now solved, while the seventh ('free will') was merely a subjective illusion anyway. Today, less than eighty years later, Haeckel's heirs on the frontiers of knowledge have not just been driven back into metaphysics (or what might often be more suitably described as simply a dogmatic irrationality); in fact their plight is infinitely worse than that of their medieval forbears; for at least the Christian world-view of the Middle Ages gave its adherents the conviction that everything in the universe had both unity and meaning, whereas our post-rational metaphysics of today can offer neither.

One man who has been quicker than most to catch a glimpse of some of the astonishing implications of what has happened is Arthur Koestler. Ever since a kind of agnostic 'mystical experience' in a Spanish prison in 1936 helped him to see Marxist materialism as the God that failed, he has been on a long quest for some deeper and more satisfactory explanation of man's existence. And over the past twenty-five years, in a series of best-sellers — *The*

Ghost in the Machine, The Roots of Coincidence – he has been reporting his findings.

No one has done more than Koestler to popularize an awareness of just what an extraordinary twilight world the physical sciences have been moving into in our century. He has reported at length, for instance, on how the biologists have staggered on from one futile hypothesis to the next in their search for an explanation of the mystery of evolution to the point where they either join the former Professor of Evolution at the Sorbonne, Grassé, in confessing that 'confronted with these problems, biology is helpless and must hand over to metaphysics'; or more ominously, they take refuge like Monod or Simpson of Harvard ('Man is the result of a purposeless and materialistic process') in a kind of neo-occultism, elevating their faith in 'chance' into unshakeable dogma, without even bothering any longer to provide a shred of evidence. Similarly the physicists have stumbled into immaterialism, at both ends of their spectrum: in the world of sub-atomic particles, where an electron can go through two holes simultaneously, where time itself seems to 'move backwards', and where the universe appears ultimately to be held together by something indefinable called 'charm', matter, time and space have all passed over into a kind of dematerialized blur; while the astrophysicists, faced with such a question as 'what happens to matter when it is sucked into a black hole?' can only reply 'it may come out again in a "white hole" in some other universe, operating in a different dimension altogether'. Then there are all those countless more mundane patterns of events which cannot be accounted for by any apparent laws of 'cause and effect' at all: why for instance does the number of people bitten by dogs in the New York area scarcely vary year by year (it is always around seventy-two)? When the atoms of a radioactive substance appear to disintegrate in a totally random way, what force dictates that exactly half of them will always collapse in an absolutely predictable period (the 'half-life' of Radium A, for instance, is always 3.825 days)? It is one thing to say, with Jung and Pauli, that there appears to be an 'acausal connecting principle' at work in the universe which is just as significant as 'cause and effect' (incidentally restating in Western terms one of the cardinal principles of Chinese philosophy) – but in doing so we are simply moving further from a rational, let alone material explanation than ever.

After years of exploring the fast-crumbling iceberg of post-Cartesian rationalism, Koestler has decided to summarize all his findings – and had *Janus: A Summing Up* merely been a recapitulation of the reportage in his previous books, it might have been a useful exercise. But, alas, Koestler cannot resist the temptation to stray from description into theorizing of his own – and here he exposes a contradiction so glaring as to call his whole world-view into question.

Consider, for instance, his opening proposition. Faced with the possibility of man's nuclear extinction, Koestler asks: why, of all the species on earth, is *homo sapiens* uniquely self-destructive? The answer, he suggests, is that, thanks to a trick of evolution, we have two brains, in uneasy coexistence. Firstly, we have inherited our 'instinctive', or 'animal brain'. Superimposed on this is our distinctively human 'neo-cortical brain', which gives us the power to reason. The trouble is that our 'reasoning brain' is unable to control our irrational, emotive 'instinctive brain' – and we thus behave like animals, killing each other. But since, as Koestler has pointed out a few pages earlier, the whole point is that animals do *not* on the whole kill each other, then even in terms of his own highly questionable terminology, the cause of our uniquely self-destructive behaviour cannot lie in our 'animal' but in our 'human brain'.

Mr Koestler's view of the human condition never recovers from this original crashing illogicality (perhaps his 'animal brain' got out of control?). Indeed he is shortly afterwards led to suggest that since it 'stands to reason' that 'a biological malfunction needs a biological corrective', then the answer to the problems caused by man's 'split nature' must come from the 'biological laboratories'.

What is staggering about this is not so much its flavour of cheap, *Sunday Express* sci-fi sensationalism (of a kind one might have thought outmoded in the Fifties), but that it comes from a man who is about to devote the second half of his book to a devastating critique of the whole reductionist, materialist position. What it shows, in fact, is that, far from being a wise old sage who has truly seen the limitations of the materialist view, Koestler is still absolutely trapped by it. He is a disillusioned fox, desperately longing to become a hedgehog – but he simply cannot get rid of that red, bushy tail. He recognizes, for instance, that everyone and everything in the universe is what he calls a 'holon' – that is, both an autonomous whole and simultaneously a part of a greater whole; but, revealingly, although he can take up this progression from, let us say, the particle to the atom to the cell to the human individual to the group to the species, he nowhere seems to recognize that, by the law of infinite regress, he must eventually confront the question as to whether there is a whole so all-embracing that it can no longer be said to be a part of anything (i.e. the 'One').

In short, no more than those he is criticizing can Koestler fundamentally change his perspective. As a civilization we have been hoping that reason *alone* will give us some ultimate illumination. Not only has it conspicuously failed to do so, but it ends up (like Koestler himself) by toppling over into howling unreason. Clearly, or so our reason *should* tell us, we may have been looking in the wrong place for the answer.

The most glaring omission from Koestler's chaotic jig-saw is any understanding of twentieth-century work on that very thing which lies at the heart of all our attempts to discern meaning in the universe – the human psyche. It is true that he includes an ill-digested sketch of Freud's Eros–Thanatos theory, for what it is worth. But of Jung, who wrote extensively and profoundly on so many of the problems which preoccupy Koestler, he appears to know virtually nothing. If he did, he might at least have been able to propound a somewhat more sophisticated account of the 'split' which has so strongly emerged in the psyche of Western man since the Renaissance: between the 'masculine', ordering, rational functions which have created modern science, and those 'feminine', intuitive functions which have increasingly dominated art. In the almost total bankruptcy of both science and art, we today see the futility of all attempts to find meaning 'one-sidedly'. The only road back to meaning lies through a reintegration of both 'halves' of the psyche. The poignancy of Koestler is that, for all his awareness of the limitations of reason, he knows nothing else; he is all *yang* and no *yin* – as shows nowhere more painfully than in his pitiful chapters 'analysing' art and humour, full of such sentences as: ' "matrices" are mental holons ... controlled by canonical rules, but guided by feedbacks from the outer and inner environment ... ordered into "vertical" abstractive hierarchies which interlace in "horizontal" networks and cross-references (cf. "arborization" and 'reticulation")'. Here is a poor little fox, baying at the moon, and talking pure gibberish.

33

John Betjeman: The Lonely Teddy Bear

(Written on his seventieth birthday, 28 August 1977)

I have often wondered what English life would have been like over the past thirty years without the contribution of a very small group of remarkable men who were born within a few years of each other at the beginning of this century.

Perhaps to refer to such diverse figures as Evelyn Waugh, George Orwell, Malcolm Muggeridge and Kenneth Clark (all born in 1903), Graham Greene (1904), John Betjeman (1906), W. H. Auden (1907) and Osbert Lancaster (1908) as in any way constituting a 'group' may seem fanciful – although few would dispute how immeasurably the poorer we should all have been through the past few gloomy decades without them.

But two things I believe they have in common. The first is that (particularly as they grew older, which slightly excepts Orwell) they have all established in the public mind personalities so much 'larger than life' as almost to verge on self-caricature. And secondly, they have all in their different ways betrayed an intense strain of melancholy, both about the world and about themselves.

Indeed one almost feels that the outer *personae* these men have developed over the years – Waugh's crusty old Catholic reactionary, the ice-cool urbanity of Clark's aesthete, Muggeridge's world-weariness ('As I grow older, dear boy, I more and more see the whole show as finished'), Osbert Lancaster's moustached White's Clubman – have been almost deliberately erected as shells against the outer world, to protect the unusually sensitive and vulnerable personalities within.

Only very occasionally (as in Waugh's Gilbert Pinfold) have any of them allowed the full tension between their outer and inner lives to show — with one major exception, and that ironically in the case of the man who seems to have grown into his own outward self-caricature more than any. I refer to the man whose seventieth birthday we are celebrating today, John Betjeman.

The newspaper tributes showered on Sir John this week have presented him almost entirely in the light of his caricature — the bumbling, cardiganed, decrepit old teddy bear, shuffling amiably through life with a 'golly' and a 'gosh' and an 'isn't it fun?', interspersed with lovable mockery of the horrors of the modern world, and a few extracts from the better-known poems about property developers, the suburbs and the brains of the senior civil servant like 'sweetbreads on the road today'.

Of course in a way it is understandable. I have had perhaps even more cause than most people to be grateful to the jolly, 'outer' Betjeman — ever since the day twenty-seven years ago when, as an eleven-year-old school friend of his son Paul, I was first invited out for the day to the old rectory where the family then lived near Wantage.

Betjeman was a marvellous host to two small boys (I remember we always received, with complete impartiality, the princely sum of half-a-crown apiece when we returned to the Dragon School). We spent a memorable day visiting some people on a painted barge, and then William Morris's rather derelict house at Kelmscott by the Thames, while John bubbled with high spirits along the way (he had a phrase on the brain that afternoon about 'caiffs and koisks the world over').

Since then I have always felt more cheerful at the prospect of seeing him, whether at some elegant country house, or walking down a scruffy street in Soho ('Look at that Novello building by Pearson, isn't it wonderful?'), right up to the most recent occasion a few months ago, when he was attending the christening of his latest grandchild, in a house which seemed to be full of large and distinguished red-faced racing men. He seemed somewhat out of place, and a little while later, as card-playing began, we came across him sitting all alone in the lunch room, reading a copy of *The Well of Loneliness*, which he must have brought in some capacious pocket. 'Isn't it a wonderful book?'

Like others, I have been endlessly grateful too over the years for the more public activities of the 'outer' Betjeman — his 'City and Suburban' column in the *Spectator* in the Fifties, his masterly introduction to *The Parish Churches of England* (with its semi-satirical account of what each succeeding century has given to the parish church), his television programmes (of which the best of all, *Metroland*, was shown again last Tuesday), and above all perhaps, his role as the patron saint of the architectural conservation movement, dating back to that first forlorn struggle in 1956 to save Colcutt's Imperial Institute from the insatiable barbarism of London University.

But of course the one unmistakable thing about all the battles of the past twenty years against the final rape and desecration of Britain, despite the occasional seeming victory, has been just how forlorn they have all been. They have been Mrs Partington-like battles against an insuperable tide, for an England already lost — as Betjeman himself seemed implicitly to recognize a year or two back, when he finally abandoned his little oasis at Cloth Fair, to leave the City to the curtain walls and the motorways.

Turn then to the poems, still popularly supposed to be little more than jolly romps with Miss Hunter Dunn and amusingly outrageous invitations to lovely bombs to fall on Slough – and at last you are face to face with the real, inner Betjeman.

What hits you above all is what the late Lord Birkenhead, in his very perceptive preface to the *Collected Poems*, called 'the abysmal depression', the absolutely shattering melancholy, the desperate sense of lost innocence, departed pleasures, dissolution and decay.

Is there any poem in the English language more heart-rending than the 'Lament for Moira McCavendish'? Are there lines more bleak than the conclusion of 'Norfolk'?

> The peace, before the dreadful daylight starts,
> Of unkept promises and broken hearts.

The truth is that, for all the fun and jokes and mannerisms John Betjeman has all along – later even than Hardy, or Lawrence, or Eliot – been the last poet of the last days of a civilization. He has lived his inward life in that twilight on the edge of the abyss, where it is hard for men to remember that they are part of anything larger or more lasting than themselves, and where they are therefore terribly alone.

The despair is overwhelming. And therefore, while we offer him conventional thanks for all the amusement along the way, one ends simply by wanting to send him some small sign of love across the dark gulf.

34

Paul Johnson: The Convert Who Went over the Top

(Written at the time of the Conservative Party Conference, 21 October 1978)

As we consider the recent startling political and journalistic career of Mr Paul Johnson, an image which may spring irresistibly to mind is that of a river crossing a great waterfall. Such a familiar fluminous proceeding may be said to go through three distinct stages. The first, as the distant cataract approaches, is that in which the whole flow of the river seems mysteriously to develop a new, purposeful energy. The current appears to speed up, the surface becomes increasingly flecked with angry eddies, to the point where the river even seems at times to be fighting against itself. Then comes the great moment of release when, with a great roar, the torrent moves all at once from one level to another quite different. The third stage, immediately following the change, is that where the river is left boiling in a great maelstrom of froth – from which eventually, one hopes, it recovers, to resume a much more placid and reflective course towards the sea.

Mr Johnson, it might be said, is at present very obviously in the froth stage. It was two or three years ago that it first became apparent that something politically very remarkable was beginning to happen to the most brilliant left-wing journalist in Britain. As he launched with increasing fervour, particularly in the *New Statesman*, into a series of highly impressive articles excoriating the growing drift of the Labour Party into a mindless, collectivist brutality, spellbound by the greed and power-lust of the trade unions,

Johnson's journalism took on an energy, force and depth it had never shown before. So long as he continued to proclaim his loyalty to the ideals of Socialism, it was inevitable that eddies of apparent self-contradiction would continue to bubble up to the surface. One of the more conspicuous was the curious moment he chose to declare that only Tony Benn could save the soul of the Labour Party – in almost exactly the same week that he published a book called *Enemies of Society*, savaging long-haired students, trendy theologians, modern playwrights, and generally, as I remarked at the time, proclaim a view on the major political, social, moral, artistic and philosophical issues of our day 'indistinguishable from that taken for the past forty years by the *Sunday Express*'.

Finally Johnson went over the top. In September 1977, the ex-editor of the *New Statesman* declared his new-found allegiance to the Conservative Party in a roar of steam and spray reported on the front page of every serious daily in the land. And in recent months, in huge articles for the *Sunday Telegraph*, in lectures to American bankers and addresses at the Conservative Party Conference, he has churned away at his new political credo, in a vast, bubbling, mass of white foam which, as yet, shows little sign of abating.

Many people have been so nonplussed by the apparent conversion of one-time fiery, radical, Socialist Paul into tub-thumping apologist for Mrs Thatcher that they have actually missed the real point of the change which has come over him. There *has* in recent years been a fundamental change in Johnson's viewpoint, but it is by no means so simple and straightforward as various commentators, and particularly saddened Socialists like Mr Peter Jenkins of the *Guardian*, have tried to argue.

Some thirteen years ago, in more frivolous days, I once

began an anonymous profile of Mr Johnson with the following:

> The fashionable drawing rooms of London have always been happy to welcome outsiders – if only on their own, albeit undemanding terms. That is to say artists, so long as they are not too talented, men of humble birth, so long as they have since amassed several million pounds, and Socialists, so long as they are Tories. Such a man and such a Socialist is elegant, cynical, red-haired Mr Paul Johnson, newly-appointed Editor of the *New Statesman*.

I went on to point out that one of the most interesting things Mr Johnson had ever written was his essay in a now totally forgotten book called *Conviction*, published in 1958, in which, along with several other fellow-sufferers such as Ken Tynan, he described how it was that he had come to be converted to a belief in Socialism and support for the left in politics. Johnson recalled how, as a young man, he had been a conventional, comparatively unthinking public school Conservative. Then, seated one day in 1954 outside an agreeable café on the Left Bank, he had witnessed to his horror the French police beating up some demonstrating students. From that moment, Johnson conceived that there were two great forces which might shape a man's political convictions – the first was a Love of Power, the second a Sense of Outrage.

Now, no one can doubt that it was a Sense of Outrage which led Johnson over the next ten or twelve years to become one of the most brilliant journalists in Britain, and indeed to his position in 1965 as editor of our leading left-wing weekly. It is indeed precisely that same Sense of Outrage (presumably to be seen as always in direct and deadly opposition to the Love of Power) which had led him on in more recent years to perceive with more acuity and greater passion than any other journalist the evils of unbridled trade union power and the drift of the Labour Party into an ever more marked collectivism. In all this it might well be argued that Johnson has shown a much greater degree of consistency to his principles than has the Labour Party itself — and equally it might be argued that there is no reason why a Sense of Outrage and a distrust of power in themselves should lead a man to be politically *left*-wing any more than they should make him right-wing.

Nevertheless, even in the days when his left-wing credentials were still fairly impeccable, there was another aspect to Johnson's Sense of Outrage which occasionally disconcerted the comrades no end, and which was at least one of the reasons why in that profile in 1965 I implied that he was already a certain kind of Tory. I was not thinking of his perfectly innocuous habit of dining with Lady Antonia Fraser, or even his alleged fondness for consuming more oysters at the Beefsteak Club than all the dukes of England put together, so much as those occasional outbursts which so used to upset the *New Statesman* readers, such as his apoplectic tirade on one occasion against the way that Europe's newly affluent proletariat had taken to blocking the roads to the French Riviera with their beastly little new-rich cars. An even more famous occasion was his celebrated attack in 1964 on Beatle-mania, in which he lashed out at the proletarian kiddies mesmerized by the Fabulous Foursome, their 'huge faces, bloated with cheap confectionery and smeared with chain-store make-up', their 'open sagging mouths and glazed eyes'. When Johnson himself had been sixteen, he recalled, 'I and my friends heard our first performance of Beethoven's Ninth Symphony. I can remember the excitement even today. We would not have wasted thirty seconds of our precious time on the Beatles and their ilk.'

Voiced as they appeared to be in the authentic accents

of Sir Herbert Gussett in a letter to the *Daily Telegraph*, the conclusion one might well have drawn from articles like these was that what really offended Mr Johnson about our contemporary cultural scene was the hideous, mindless, soulless materialism produced in no small measure by a decadent, consumer-oriented capitalism – the very engine, after all, responsible for all those cars, Beatles records, 'cheap confectionery and chain-store make-up' which had so debauched the proletariat that they no longer had precious time available for listening to Beethoven's Ninth Symphony. It was exactly the kind of contradiction which many old-fashioned Tories have found it hard to resolve.

The truly remarkable thing about the earthquake that has taken place in Johnson's view in recent years is not that he has suddenly decided to attack power-crazed trade union leaders, or the proliferation of non-democratic bureaucratic power in our society. Here, as observers still caught up in a mish-mash of 'social democratic' wishful thinking like Peter Jenkins cannot see, Johnson is quite right in proclaiming that he has only been inspired by precisely those same liberal, humane instincts which had once led himself and thousands of other intelligent, liberal, humane people into the Labour Party in the first place. What is remarkable about Johnson's change of heart is purely and simply his quite astonishing and blind new worship of the wonderful world of capitalism. As he first set out in that extraordinary book *Enemies of Society*, and recently repeated in an address to a convention of American Bankers (reprinted last week by *The Times*), it is here that Johnson has undergone an almost spiritual conversion, comparable to the power and suddenness of that Damascus moment at Les Deux Magots all those years ago.

No longer do we hear about the evils of an affluent proletariat having nothing better to do with their affluence than block the roads of the Riviera with their beastly motor cars, or the kids sitting glazed-eyed in front of their Japanese trannies. Now all human history must be seen as a mighty drama, which only has one hero — plucky little capitalism, which has brought such inestimable benefits to mankind, and yet today is beset by such terrible enemies that it may not survive. Why did the Roman Empire rise to its greatness? Because of Rome's capitalist middle class. Why did it fall? Because imperial bureaucracy and high taxation killed off the middle classes. Why did that miracle, the industrial revolution, take place? Because of wonderful capitalism, which rescued millions from 'rural poverty, which was deeper and more degrading than anything experienced in the cities' and plunged them, presumably, into the Utopian delights of nineteenth-century industrialism. Why is our civilization today under such threat of destruction? Because of the rise of the 'eco-lobby', a maniacal group of 'Christian Scientists, anti-vivisectionists, those who campaign fanatically against the fluoridation of water supplies' and others' who, with their 'hysterical' fantasies about over-population, the exhaustion of natural resources, pollution and the H-Bomb, stand almost alone in the way of the Johnsonian hope for the future of mankind — a Holy Vision of Capitalist-inspired Growth leading humanity on an asymptotic curve up into the Heaven of Total Consumption.

As one contemplates this lonely figure, dancing like a crazed savage round the totem of capitalism when even some of that faith's most devoted acolytes have long since begun to express the most profound doubts about the possibility of economic growth continuing for more than a few more decades, one cannot but be reminded of that familiar old dictum of Chesterton's that when a man ceases to believe in God, he believes not in nothing but in anything. It was ironic that in the very week when *The Times* was publishing the latest instalment of Johnson's Visions, the paper's Transport Correspondent should have soberly reported that in perhaps as little as fifteen years time, oil 'will have become far too scarce and expensive to be used in the ways that we use it today'. The article was based on an interview with the Director of Scientific and Technical Development of Renault – a man whose subsequent remarks showed that, even though his company is technically state-owned, he is precisely the kind of enlightened, liberal, forward-thinking, energetic capitalist whom Johnson should be regarding as among the high priests of his new religion.

I have already written in these columns of what I believe to be one of the saddest conclusions to be drawn from Johnson's spiritual tergiversations – that when a man speaks as often as he does of his own devotion to 'reason', and of the 'fanaticism' of his opponents, one may look to his own works with confidence for a conspicuous absence of the former, and an over-abundance of the latter. There is now another truth to which I fear he has borne scarifying witness. That when a man sees through the folly of one extreme and one-sided view of the world there is no greater danger and no greater likelihood than that he will rush to another, equally extreme and even more one-sided. As we have seen so often in our time, the other side of the journalist who has a particular gift for exposing the follies of mankind is always a desperate, unspoken need to believe in something positive as well. When that need comes to the surface, he must be extremely wary of where he chooses to place his new-found faith.

35

Germaine Greer: The Real Failure of Women's Lib

In recent years, it has become almost a commonplace to say that the trouble with our civilization is that it has become over-dominated by masculine values, has lost touch with and undervalued the feminine. Certainly it was scarcely surprising that, at the end of the 'Swinging Sixties' in particular, there should have been something of a violent reaction to the 'degradation' of women. For ten years, our machine-based culture had publicly debased the image of womanhood as never before in history. In millions of pornographic magazines, women had been portrayed as mere functions of onanistic male fantasies. Dressed up in mini-skirts and shiny PVC macs, given such impersonal names as 'dolly birds', girls had been transformed into throwaway plastic objects. In books like *Last Exit to Brooklyn*, with its horrific mass-rape, women had been treated with more violent contempt than in the fantasies of the Marquis de Sade. Even on the more 'respectable' outer surface of our culture, in the TV commercials and colour supplement ads, the bikini-clad girl had been used as the single most exploited stereotype to sell anything from drink to motor cars, deodorants to Spanish holidays — a mere 'marketing tool' of the consumer boom. And then, at the end of the Sixties, came Women's Lib — bra-burning, defacing the pornographic advertisements and all the rest.

Was this, as claimed, the moment when women 'hit back' on behalf of the values of their sex, the re-assertion

of the 'feminine' in our culture? Or was it the manifesta-
tion of something else, in its own way just as alarming as
the degradation of the feminine which had set it off?

One of the most popular and articulate of all the books
produced by the 'feminist' movement was Germaine Greer's
The Female Eunuch, first published in 1970, but best known
to most readers in the paperback version brought out the
following year, with its eye-catching cover of a plastic female 'torso-cover' swinging from a rail.

At the heart of Miss Greer's book was a savagely con-
temptuous attempt to contrast the public image of womanhood usually presented in our culture with what she saw
as the reality of most women's lives. On the one hand, we
have the Dream of the TV ads, the romantic novels, the
Sunday Times women's page profiles of successful millionaire's wives, running smart dinner parties and being re-
warded with all the jewels and expensive clothes they can
wear; on the other hand, we have the Nightmare Reality –
millions of bored, lonely, frustrated, exploited women,
chained to screaming children, to 'little boy' husbands
whose only interests are sport, drink and sex, driven to pills
and alcoholism, ceaselessly mocked by the utter unreality
of the Dream dancing over their TV screens. In fact, argued
Miss Greer, 'women have very little idea how much men
hate them.' Even the best qualities of women are cruelly
traded upon and exploited. Nurses, for instance, in an
example she uses twice, kidded into 'feeling good because
they are relieving pain', underpaid and overworked, are
almost invariably 'tired, resentful and harried'. Women, in
short, are 'the only true proletariat left'.

So what is the answer, where lies liberation? As one
might expect when talk of the 'proletariat' is flying around,
Miss Greer's prescription was that women should rise up
against their exploiters, should bring about a 'revolution'.

But before we go on to the nature of that revolution, we might perhaps look a little more closely at the nature of that suppressed femininity in whose name the revolution was to be carried out.

One of the first things which strikes one about *The Female Eunuch* (even more perhaps, in the changed perspective of the past ten years, on re-reading it) is Germaine Greer's anxiety to show how very similar women are, physically and psychologically, to the hated men. She begins by pointing out that the only difference in genetic make-up between the two sexes derives from one tiny chromosome out of forty-eight. Later she compares the mental abilities of the two sexes, with such statements as: 'non-verbal cognitive abilities like counting, mathematical reasoning, spatial cognition, abstract reasoning, set-breaking and restructuring, perceptual speed, manual, mechanic and scientific skills have all been tested, and no significant pattern of difference has emerged, except this slight pre-eminence of the girls'. Like many Women's Lib thinkers of the time, in heavily labouring the physical aspects of womanhood, she seemed to have a preoccupation with what is known as 'the clitoral orgasm', i.e. that sexual gratification which is derived from the female's nearest vestige to a male sexual organ. And in one of the most poignant passages of the book, she lists some of the 'success stories' of women who have made careers for themselves, including 'Asha Radoti' who 'is now Portfolio Manager for the Castle Britannia Unit Trust Group', 'Miss Isabel Webster' who after 'twelve years working as a depilator in the Tao Clinic' has 'now patented her own formula for an aerosol depilator called "Spray Away"' and a former housemaid from Camden Town who became 'a director of Acme, Britain's largest firm of industrial cleaners'.

In other words, the values by which Miss Greer measured

the success, the capabilities, even the physical make-up of women, were as near as possible those by which men supposedly value themselves. Now, when we talk about 'masculine' and 'feminine' functions in the human psyche (those functions *all* of which have to be realized and brought into balance if any of us is to become truly 'whole' and mature) what precisely do we mean? The chief 'masculine' functions are physical power and sensation — those things which pertain to the body — and rationality, the organizing principle of the mind. The chief 'feminine' functions, which are absolutely crucial to give the male functions balance, are sympathetic and protective feeling, and intuition, that enormously important function which, rooted in the unconscious, gives us a sense of the spiritual, of the hidden connections between things.

The one thing which hits one between the eyes about Miss Greer's book is how completely lacking it is in appreciation of 'feminine' functions, how astonishingly unbalanced it is in its reverence for the 'masculine'. As for intuition, Miss Greer simply writes it off as 'only a faculty for observing tiny insignificant aspects of behaviour and forming an empirical conclusion which cannot be syllogistically examined'. As for feeling, compassion, there is nothing so striking about the book as what an utterly bleak, loveless, tortured, hard view of the world and people it conjures up — it is almost totally lacking in real feeling throughout.

Now the question which arises is — why should Miss Greer have got into this state where she so undervalues the feminine in herself, in what seems almost like a parody of the masculine one-sidedness she is rebelling against? Like many of the leading figures in the Women's Lib movement, she makes no secret of the fact that she had a deeply unhappy childhood, 'unspeakably dreary teens'. She describes her domineering, unfeeling virago of a mother, constantly trying to emasculate her father, bullying the children, pouring contempt on their softer or finer feelings. To a psychologist, in short, Miss Greer presents an absolutely classic study of a girl who is the victim of the 'Terrible Mother', without any proper model on which to develop her own femininity, her compassion, her intuition. The result, as in millions of other cases, is a girl who grows up, desperately over-compensating by her flight into masculine rational activity, but fundamentally hating the feminine, and unable to relate properly either to feminine or masculine — a girl, to use the jargon, possessed by her *animus*, that hard, masculine part of herself which is asserted against the world in a continual rant of often pyrotechnic mental brilliance, but almost completely without feminine softness or intuitive feel for the true 'nature' of things.

It is scarcely surprising that Miss Greer came out of such a background with such a fierce, *animus*-ridden desire to avenge her own repressed feminine by proving that she, and her kind, could do just as well in a man's world as men — be successful, be intellectual, even enjoy 'clitoral orgasms'. She has hazy visions of a lost 'Golden Age' when things might not have been so — a Calabrian village full of poor but happy 'extended families' (though even here she cannot resist adding that the menfolk of the village were mainly away 'working in Germany' — even this Utopia could basically do without men). She has an even hazier fantasy of her own personal Utopia — a kind of commune, again in Italy, where her own child need not know who her 'womb-mother' was. But in general, collectively, the great revolution is to be achieved by a rising up of the 'last proletariat' — of women like 'Abby Rockefeller' who has a green belt in karate and the 'Tufnell Park Liberation Workshop' with their magazine *Shrew* — who must assert themselves, not in the case of true femininity, but in the name of some shadow of precisely that unbalanced and therefore infantile masculinity they affect to despise.

Looking back after ten years, in other words, the real tragedy of Women's Lib was not that it expressed a reassertion of the feminine, so much, as the final victory of our culture's overdevelopment of the masculine (as the Women's Libbers unconsciously demonstrate, nowhere more clearly than in their passionate obsession with abortion – the ultimate denial of the feminine role). The catastrophic loss of the positive aspects of femininity in our culture is something which has been going on, not just for twenty years, but for centuries – certainly as far back as that overvaluation of the masculine reflected in the Reformation, and the hysterical hatred of the witch-burning new Puritans for everything that was symbolized by the Virgin Mary. The growing one-sided rationality of European culture, through the age of Descartes and Newton, reached a first peak in the obsession with order of the 'Age of Reason', then developed further into the love of technological power, the suffocating 'masculine' respectability of the Victorian era. Meanwhile the loss of the feminine was unconsciously reflected with desperate poignancy in so many romantic stories of the nineteenth century – as we see in the consumptive heroines, the 'persecuted maidens', the 'elusive anima-figures' who suffer or flit bewitchingly through so many operas, novels and poems of that time. In the plight of the heroines of the age of romanticism – from Gretchen to Mimi, from La Belle Dame Sans Merci and the victims of de Sade to Tolstoy's Anna and Hardy's Tess – we see the most explicit record imaginable of a civilization which was literally 'losing its soul'. The real task which confronts us today is to do precisely what Women's Lib set out not to do – to rescue the 'lost feminine' in all of us, men and women alike.

36

Watership Down: Rabbits and Reality

Arguably the most successful piece of fiction produced in the Seventies (certainly by a Western author) was Richard Adams's mini-epic about the adventures of a group of rabbits in the Berkshire countryside, *Watership Down*. The story of the book's origins will probably be familiar – how it evolved from tales told to his two young daughters by a then obscure, middle-aged civil servant, working in the clean air and pollution section of the Department of the Environment, on their journeys up to Stratford-on-Avon. When the book was first published in 1972 it was given only a modest reception. The next year, after considerable trepidation and talk of extensive re-writing, Puffin put out a paperback edition. Within twelve months it had become one of the best sellers of the age. Its total sales to date, in the Puffin and Penguin editions alone, are around three million – and its world-wide sales are several times that.

Why should a fiction about rabbits, studded with somewhat portentous-looking chapter headings from Shakespeare, the Earl of Chesterfield, *Così Fan Tutte*, Xenophon, Yeats, Tennyson, Napoleon and the South Sea Bubble company prospectus, have caught on in this way? The touching of what deep chord in the public imagination has led *Watership Down* to be accepted within such a brief space of time as one of those classics of children's literature which speak to readers of all ages, fit to be mentioned in the same breath as, say, *The Wind in the Willows*, *The Lord of the Rings*, or even *Gulliver's Travels*?

The story of *Watership Down* centres round that age-old theme in the literature of the world, a Quest. It begins with a group of rabbits receiving the intuitive warning that some appalling fate is about to overtake their warren. Like so many fields on the outskirts of English villages in the early Seventies, the rabbits' home has in fact been earmarked by a rapacious property company as the site for a 'high-class' housing development. The little group of rabbits, who become the book's heroes, just manage to get away in time, before their *confrères* are hideously gassed and bull-dozed to death. The rest of the story tells how they make their way, through all sorts of perils, across the countryside to Watership Down, where they eventually manage to establish a flourishing new warren.

In all of these respects, the story is remarkably similar in outline to other, more celebrated Quest stories, such as the *Aeneid*, describing how Aeneas and his friends leave the burning city of Troy to found their new city in distant Italy, that of the Children of Israel escaping from bondage and threatened destruction in Egypt to set up a new home in the Promised Land, or Christian in *Pilgrim's Progress* leaving the 'city of destruction' (which he has a premonition is about to be engulfed by fire) to set off on his perilous journey to the distant Celestial City.

In fact the parallels between *Watership Down* and other stories formed by the Quest archetype run even deeper. It is a misconception, for instance, that the essence of Quest stories is that they simply describe a long journey towards a distant goal. In almost all the best-known stories of this type, the journey itself only accounts for a part of the tale. The worst ordeals of all await the hero and his companions when they have already come within sight of the goal, and face the obstacles which still stand in their way of winning it and securing it for the future. The whole of the second half of the *Aeneid* is taken up with Aeneas's battle to secure his new home in Italy against the tribes who already live there. The same is true of the Jewish Exodus (the Battle of Jericho, etc). Jason's fiercest tests await him when he has already arrived in the neighbourhood of the Golden Fleece in Colchis, just as Odysseus's arrival in Ithaca before the final great battle with the suitors occurs exactly half way through the *Odyssey*. And it is here that we can see, in almost every instance, what is the real nature of the goal of the Quest story. What matters is not mere arrival at a goal, the winning of a treasure, or whatever, so much as the securing or establishing of a Kingdom, and usually, simultaneously, the winning of a Princess into the bargain.

In this respect, *Watership Down* is absolutely true to its underlying archetype – to an extent which I suspect even Richard Adams, for all his background in Jungian analysis, was not fully aware of. The journey across country to the new home only takes up a comparatively small amount of the story. The rest describes the great struggle which faces the little group of male rabbits when they get there, first to win a group of rabbit 'Princesses' from the hostile warren of Efrafa and then to make their new kingdom secure against the avenging depredations of the 'monster' General Woundwort. Only then, after their final victory, is the future of the new kingdom secured, and can 'King' Hazel die in peace, knowing that the union of 'masculine' and 'feminine' has assured future generations of little rabbits to carry the kingdom on into the future.

But at this point, having moved in the lofty realms of comparison between a children's book of our own time and some of the greatest stories in the history of the world, we come down to earth with a bump. It is all very well to descry these heady similarities with the *Odyssey* or the *Aeneid* but the fact remains that *Watership Down* is not about great mythic heroes, cosmic enlargements of our own human nature. It is about bunny rabbits – and in the very nature of the somewhat sentimental association that conjures up, not to mention the diminution rather than magnification of scale it implies, I believe we have a further very important indication as to the reasons for *Watership Down*'s success.

One of the book's most appealing qualities is the way it transforms a stretch of our own familiar, Home Counties countryside into a vast, seemingly mythic, realm. Just a few miles of fields, woods and downland have been magnified into an almost boundless kingdom. The English Channel, as visited by the black-headed gull Kehaar, seems unimaginably far away. Crossing a railway line or a tiny stream becomes for the rabbits a gigantic ordeal, comparable with Odysseus evading the clutches of Scylla and Charybdis. Now, as we all know, the trouble with the modern world as seen on a human scale, or through human eyes, is that it is no longer like that. There are virtually no more 'boundless, unknown realms' left. The world has shrunk to a tiny, over-populated, over-explored, over-mechanized backyard. It takes a great feat of the imagination to transmogrify the contemporary English countryside, with its broiler farms, barbed wire fences, motorways and housing estates, back into a 'faery-realm' of romance and high adventure. But by diminishing his heroes to mere rabbit-size, it is that which Adams has achieved – thus creating the most successful 'pseudo-mythic' landscape since the imaginary world conjured up by Tolkien.

Similarly – and ironically – one of the great advantages of having animals as your heroes, rather than human beings, is that you can invest them with purely *human* qualities, as opposed to all those dehumanizing distortions of human qualities which are unavoidable when you set an adventure story in our modern world of motor cars, aero-planes, space rockets, telephones and all the rest of the gadgetry. With James Bond, *Star Wars* and the rest, the 'dehumanizing' of the epic hero, by placing him perpetually in the shadow of machinery and technology, has gone just about as far as it can. With the rabbits of *Watership Down*, however, we are firmly back in a pre-mechanical world, where the hero and his friends can only survive by their direct exercise of a balance of our primary, innate functions – physical strength, intuition, a courageous heart and all the rest.

And herein, I believe, lies the real clue to *Watership Down*. The very fact that in order to conjure up a fully human story, according to the age-old pattern of the Quest, the author has had in effect to escape from our modern technological world altogether, is the most reveal-ing comment of all on the nature of the book's appeal. It is no accident that men, with their cars, trains, bulldozers, traps and gassing devices, are by and large seen in the book as 'enemies', as the greatest 'monster' of all in the natural world of the bunnies. Equally it is no accident that the rabbits' adventure is set in motion in the first place as an attempt to escape from that supreme symbol of the steady advance of an alien, dehumanizing future, a development scheme – nor at a deeper level still that the whole book should be about an attempt to escape from these man-made horrors into some place of distant, happy, innocent security.

As may be apparent, I have great admiration for Adams's book. I find it gripping, moving and in many ways profound. But let us not at the same time overlook the horrific mes-sage which is implicit in the book's success. At the deepest level, it is yet another of those countless fantasies of escape thrown up by the unconscious of modern man –

escape from the unspeakable, inhuman world we are creating for ourselves by technology, shot through with every
kind of premonition of some ultimate disaster. It is all very
well to dream of getting back to a simpler, more natural
world where we might once again become fully human. But
in the conscious, outward world, the truth is that we are
still doing almost everything we can to ensure that we are
travelling self-destructively in the opposite direction. On
that level, alas, *Watership Down* must be seen as nothing
more than a charming piece of nostalgic wishful-thinking –
as was demonstrated for me by nothing more clearly than
a copy of the local Newbury paper which I saw a year or
two after *Watership Down* had raced to the top of the best-
seller list. The front-page headline announced that there
was such a 'plague of rabbits' on the nearby Berkshire
Downs (the very place where Watership Down is situated)
that £20,000 was to be spent on a 'massive extermination
programme'. It is one thing to dream of that purer, simpler
world, where we are once again at one with nature and with
our own nature. But if, in the tiniest respect, such dreams
conflict with our drive to subject nature to our own use
and comfort, it becomes a different matter altogether. Then
is our sentimentality as a species shown up in its true
colours as nothing more than the most appalling double-
think – if not as the expression of our potentially quite
catastrophic self-deception.

Part Five

Cultural Collapse

Of all the views expressed in this book, none is likely to meet with more resistance than the suggestion that, in the past ten years, our culture in the widest sense — architectural, artistic, scientific, philosophical — has reached the most dramatic dead end in the entire history of mankind. Like the estate agent who assures you that the old house he is trying to sell you is 'in absolutely sound condition — needs nothing more than a lick of paint and it will stand for another three hundred years' (when in fact it is so riddled with dry rot that it would collapse into a pile of dust at the press of a finger), the professional boosters of our culture — TV impresarios, saleroom directors, the publishers of coffee table books, newspaper critics — will tell us that it has never been in a more thriving state. They will point to expensive television series bringing artistic riches and philosophical debate to a wider audience than ever before in history; to lavish art exhibitions; to the feast of music available on the airwaves and in our concert halls, the almost unprecedentedly high standard of performance; the world-wide ferment of scientific research; the record flow of books from the presses. Thanks to the omnipresence of our modern image-conveying apparatus, we have been able to blur all the world's 'culture' together and to keep it constantly before our eyes and minds in such a way that we scarcely notice how much we are simply feeding on the stored-up vitality of the past. By an ingenious sleight of mind, we are able to convince ourselves, through the frenzy of cultural activity that constantly surrounds us, that we are still adding to that store. And if anyone dares for a moment to question such a comforting notion, no one will come down on him more like a ton of bricks than those diehard 'Old Believers' who are still conditioned by the ideology of the Modern Movement to believe that the less something is liked and understood today, the more certainly will its genius be recognized tomorrow – without noticing the fact that, in the past decade, the Modern Movement itself has finally disintegrated.

In fact the whole of post-Renaissance Western culture has suddenly become nothing more than a vast, fascinating museum-piece – a huge, rickety memorial to a civilization which simply lost its way. Of course along that way there were many brilliant achievements. The artists, scientists and philosophers of the past few hundred years have made astonishing advances, carried human experience and observation into realms undreamed of. But suddenly, standing at the end of that great adventure, we can see with appalling clarity where it was all leading – to the eventual complete loss of *meaning*. First in the aftermath of the Renaissance, even more since the simultaneous rise of Industrialism and Romanticism two hundred years ago, a great split has opened up in the Western psyche: on the one hand, the scientists have accumulated more and more facts and 'knowledge', the philosophers have subjected language to ever more minute and rigorous examination; on the other, artists have more and more pursued effects, sensations, illusion; and as that gap has opened ever wider, so, almost without our noticing it, has meaning gently been sliding further and further out of view – to the point where, confronted with the gaping void, the cosmic despair which lies at the heart of our contemporary culture in all directions (except where we can paper it over by rushing back for consolation into those embodiments of meaning which survive from the past), we do not even recognize the fact.

But part of the extraordinary importance of the past ten years has been the fact that, despite all the whistling in the dark, the din of self-congratulatory reassurance from the media, the bankruptcy of our culture has intruded more inescapably and prominently than ever before. This section in fact continues in more general vein the theme of the last, 'Nostalgia and Self-deception' – and it opens with two essays on the deeper significance of our sudden astonishing passion for conserving the past in architecture. The first consists of thoughts inspired by the campaign in 1977 to preserve Mentmore House in Hertfordshire, complete with its bizarre collection of *objets d'art* (the campaign was, of course, unsuccessful, the art objects were sold off in an undignified scramble, and the shell of the house rather suitably became a centre for that vacuous vestige of man's search for spirituality, the Transcendental Meditation movement, run by the old megalomaniac whom *Private Eye* once nicknamed the Veririshi Lotsamoney). The second essay, 'Something Old, Something New', takes a somewhat deeper and broader view of the growing 'conservation craze' of the past hundred years, showing how the final collapse of architectural self-confidence in the Seventies marked the end of a cycle that had begun at the time of the Renaissance.

A third essay examines that other phenomenon of our times, the great craze for 'nature'. The two which follow examine aspects of the way we have more and more desperately and confusedly tried to sustain our faith in 'science' as the way to truth and a better life. The pieces on the collapse of the Modern Movement and on latter-day philosophy are, I fear, little more than jottings on subjects worthy of deeper and more detailed consideration else-where. There are notes on the psychology of modern archi-tecture, and the theatre. Finally, in rather different vein, there is an analysis of the various attitudes commonly held today towards the possibility that our civilization may be facing some ultimate catastrophe.

37

Mad for Conservation

(Written during the controversy over the future of Mentmore,
12 February 1977)

In the past few days the press has been filled with news of
yet another 'conservation battle' – one which I believe
casts particular light on one of the most profoundly revealing dilemmas facing our late-twentieth-century civilization.
I am referring to the debate over the future of Mentmore
Towers, the great mysterious Rothschild treasure house
which stands in 'Jacobean' splendour in the countryside
near Luton. Years ago, reading Robert Rhodes James's *Life
of Lord Rosebery*, I was haunted by the photographs of the
Liberal Prime Minister's four houses: Barnbougle, a bleak
little Scottish baronial box standing by the Firth of Forth;
Dalmeny, a huge, almost equally bleak four-square Scottish
mansion; the Durdans, a cosy, low, ivy-covered Victorian
house near Epsom; and finally, by far the most impressive,
the misty towers and pinnacles of Mentmore (which came
to Rosebery as a result of his marriage to Hannah de Rothschild).

The little-known story of this fabulous Aladdin's Cave
of a house, built by Joseph Paxton for the Baron Meyer
Amschel de Rothschild between 1851 and 1854, has been
so superbly set out by that admirable organization SAVE
in their new pamphlet 'Save Mentmore for the Nation' that
I cannot but recommend anyone who is remotely interested
to send for a copy. With the aid of an astonishing set
of hitherto unpublished photographs, Marcus Binney of
Country Life and a small team of experts have for the first

time in this century brought to light one of the most
extraordinary houses in Europe. Inside, Mentmore is a cross
between the 'Italian Palazzo' style of Barry's Reform Club
(the great Hall and Staircase), and a series of 'French Versailles' rooms – crammed with one of the greatest treasure
troves ever amassed in private hands. For page after page,
Binney and his colleagues lovingly unveil one glittering
assemblage after another – Gobelin and Flemish tapestries,
gilt lanterns from the Venetian state barge, the *Bucintoro*,
curtains of Genoese velvet and others worked on by Marie
Antoinette, a mass of magnificent clocks, the great
chimneypiece designed by Rubens for his house in Antwerp,
an untold wealth of furniture, ranging from loot from the
Doge's Palace to a vast rococo cabinet made for Augustus
III of Poland in the 1750s, Sèvres porcelain, jewels and
objets de vertu, paintings by Titian, Rembrandt, Greuze,
Boucher, a unique sporting scene by Gainsborough, two fine
Turners – it is a haul of 'world importance'.

Even in the crudest economic terms, the SAVE team's
case that Mentmore should be bought for the nation is unanswerable. The house and its entire contents have been
offered to the government for a laughable £2 million (in lieu
of death duties which would be payable anyway on the 6th
Earl of Rosebery's estate). If the contents of the house go
to auction in May, as seems likely, Sotheby's alone may
well make more than half that sum, just in commission
fees. As Marcus Binney suggests, it would be quite absurd
of the government not to accept the offer, at least for
two years, while a 'permanent solution' to the endowment
of the house can be explored – at the end of which time,
if the search is unsuccessful, the entire £2 million investment could be recouped just by selling off half a dozen or
so of the chief treasures.

It was only when the SAVE team goes on to outline

what a 'permanent solution' for Mentmore might be that certain deeper questions begin to intrude themselves. Undoubtedly, they argue, such a house standing just half an hour up the M1 from London could become a major national tourist attraction. Even if it drew only 100,000 visitors a year, spending £1 a head on tickets, souvenirs, postcards and ice-creams, that would yield the greater part of the £100,000 needed annually to run it. While the house's grounds and other amenities would lend themselves admirably to such other profitable uses as a 'national equestrian centre', complete with three-day events, Princess Anne falling off her horse and all the rest.

Faced with this prospect of Mentmore transformed into a kind of 'cultural Longleat', the Scenicruisers nose to tail in the new asphalt car parks, the aimless mass of tourists wandering like bewildered sheep through those great, dead rooms, does not a terrible weariness of the soul set in? In some ways, the spectacle of any great house transformed into a museum is always depressing. Similarly, one of the most extraordinary cultural phenomena of our time is the spectacle of tens of thousands of tourists wheeling endlessly through any stately home (or art gallery, or museum) somehow seeking a sense of significance from mere contact with the artefacts of the past that, even when there is a guide to tell them the exact value of each item and the dates of the artist, they simply do not know how to find.

If this is true of a house which was once for centuries a home, how much truer would it be of Mentmore, which was actually built as a museum (or *kunstkammer*), and was therefore in a sense never truly alive in the first place. One of the more curious claims made on Mentmore's behalf in recent days was that of James Lees-Milne in a letter to *The Times* that it 'in the eyes of discriminating people, constitutes one of the glories of Britain's peak of greatness'.

The only 'British' thing (and indeed the only remotely 'creative' thing) about Mentmore is the house itself, designed by a Derbyshire gardener who was undoubtedly one of the most remarkable and gifted Englishmen of the nineteenth century. But even Paxton's design was unashamedly an imitation of other models. The house is a magnificent pastiche, a masterpiece of that eclecticism which was in itself so telling a clue to the underlying spiritual nullity of the Victorian age. As for Mentmore's contents — what are they but simply the accumulation by a rich Jewish banker, of Austrian stock, of a great magpie jumble of pretty things, pillaged with discriminating indiscrimination from three centuries of the culture of post-Renaissance Europe? In a way nothing has reflected the spiritual decline of Europe more surely over the past five centuries than the different stages whereby supremely rich and powerful men have in succeeding centuries managed to build up these great treasure hordes — the Dukes of Mantua, the Hapsburgs, Charles I, the 'Grand Tour' collectors of the eighteenth century, Beckford and George IV, then the nineteenth-century commercial and industrial magnates, from the Rothschilds to the Vanderbilts, finally shading off in our own time into the ultimate absurdities of the Citizen Kanes, the clients of Duveen, Hitler and Goering. At every stage the distance between the collector and the spiritual roots of the art and craftsmanship that was the object of his desire has yawned ever wider (at least the Gonzagas patronized Mantegna, Charles V befriended Titian, Charles I employed Rubens and Van Dyck). While today we see the final *reductio ad absurdum* in the pillaging of Western culture for trinkets and toys by the oil sheiks of Arabia, or Impressionist-hungry Japanese transistor billionaires. The severing of cultural roots is complete.

That is why, while I applaud the SAVE campaign for

Mentmore (*sic et non*) the prospect also fills me with a great melancholy – at the thought of that great, dead house as yet another tombstone to our rootless, disintegrated civilization. We should wander round it (if it were saved), not with the joy of new life in our souls, but with little more than an increasingly oppressive sense of looking back to a life that has gone. This raises questions about the whole cultural significance of the great mania for conservation presently sweeping the world to which I would like to return.

38

Something Old, Something New

(19 February 1977)

In the first programme of his *Civilisation* series, Kenneth Clark quoted Ruskin as saying, 'Great nations write their autobiographies in three manuscripts. The book of their deeds, the book of their words and the book of their art ... of the three, the only trustworthy one is the last.' Clark went on to add, 'If I had to say which was telling the truth about society, a speech by the Minister of Housing, or the actual buildings put up in his time, I should believe the buildings.' But what are we to make of a society like our own, which, for the first time in history, has virtually lost faith in its ability to put up new buildings at all?

To see this extraordinary fact in its proper perspective, let us begin by taking a historical excursion through one of the most fascinating cultural pendulum swings of the past five hundred years.

In the autumn of 1503, the dashing and cultured Cardinal Giuliano della Rovere became Pope Julius II. As the supreme embodiment of High Renaissance self-confidence, one of Julius's first actions was to plan for himself a magnificent tomb. The work was to be carried out, of course, by the most distinguished sculptor of the day, Michelangelo. But the more Julius considered his monument, the more ambitious he became that it should be seen to the very best advantage. It was thus there came into his head what Lord Clark has described as 'a project so audacious, so extravagant, that the thought of it to this day makes me slightly jumpy'.

For more than a thousand years, the vast basilica of St Peter's, begun by the Emperor Constantine in 326, had been the largest and most venerable building in Christendom. Julius's plan was simple as it was breathtaking. St Peter's must be swept away — and replaced with a new building, by the most distinguished architect of the day, Bramante, which would without question be even larger and more magnificent. By 1506 so much of the ancient cathedral had already been razed to the ground that Bramante became known as 'the ruinous architect'.

In a sense, to appreciate the full measure of Julius's incredible audacity has been reserved for us who live at the end of the twentieth century. For even though his particular act of daring remained the supreme example of its kind (it is, for instance, a remarkable fact that, apart from fires, not one of Europe's great Gothic cathedrals was pulled down during three centuries when their style of architecture was largely scorned as barbarous and 'mean in spirit'), men all over the West continued until well into the nineteenth century to demolish and replace ancient buildings simply as need arose. In the eighteenth century, fine Elizabethan and Jacobean houses were destroyed by the score, to make way for more sumptuous mansions in the modern style. In the nineteenth century, of course, the havoc wrought to medieval churches in the name of 'restoration' was untold. But from Wyatt to Scott, it never for a moment crossed the minds of the architects (or their clients) that what they were doing was anything other than by way of that great keyword of Victorian culture, an 'improvement'. What was old might be good. But what was new was still without question better.

The first portents of a great shift in cultural attitudes came quite suddenly, in the seventh and eighth decades of the nineteenth century. In 1865, the Metropolitan Board of Works conceived a plan to drive through a new road from Trafalgar Square to Bazalgette's new Victorian Embankment. The scheme would require the demolition of Northumberland House, the large Jacobean palace standing on the south-east corner of the square. But when plans for the compulsory purchase of the house became known, it was not only the Duke of Northumberland who was enraged. There was also a howl of protest against the pulling down of this fine old building from the public at large.

It was a profoundly significant moment. In fact, after a fire in 1868, the scheme for the new Northumberland Avenue did eventually go through, and the house was demolished in 1875. But in the same year, the destruction of the Oxford Arms, a galleried sixteenth-century coaching inn near St Paul's, prompted the foundation of a Society for the Photographing of Old Buildings. In 1877, alarmed by the rate at which old churches were giving way under the onslaught of Victorian 'restoration', William Morris founded the Society for the Protection of Ancient Buildings. Sir John Lubbock began his annual attempts to bring in an Act for the preservation of ancient monuments which, when it was finally approved in 1882, laid the foundation for the whole of our elaborate structure for the legal protection of 'listed' buildings today. For the first time in history, in short, men were beginning to feel such an affection for old buildings, for their own sake, that they were actually prepared to battle to save them.

Even so, for nearly a century longer, despite the ever-growing nostalgia for old buildings, the conviction still remained that on the whole to pull buildings down to replace them with something 'better' was still quite natural and desirable. In the 1920s, Nash's Regent Street, one of the finest of nineteenth-century townscapes, was swept away almost without a thought. In the 1930s, only the coming of war prevented the similar destruction by Sir Reginald Blomfield of the Nash Terraces in the Mall. To today's reader, one of the most startling things about that celebrated book *The Face of London* by Harold Clunn (published in the 1930s) is the relentless way in which any large development of those times (the 'splendid' new Shell-Mex building, the 'magnificent' new ICI block on Millbank) was still automatically looked on as a mark of ever-onward, ever-upward progress.

In fact this underlying sense of confidence survived until remarkably lately. Certainly through the first two decades after the Second World War, despite the steady growth in legislative protection of outstanding gems, despite the odd public furore over an Imperial Institute or a Euston Arch, we embarked on the greatest transformation our cities had ever known, with tower blocks and 'comprehensive re-development schemes' and the new technological style in architecture, with a confident abandon that would almost have done justice to Julius II himself.

Then suddenly, in the 1970s, came the collapse. Within just a few years, the great conservation movement mush-roomed into one of the most powerful social forces of the age. For the first time we had seen the future, and it did not work. Our architectural and cultural self-confidence disintegrated with quite astonishing speed. From Michelan-gelo's Rome to Britain in the late 1970s, the pendulum has finally swung its full arc.

And so we arrive at the extraordinary dilemma we are in today. Firstly, far from believing that anything new is better, we are now (generally) convinced of almost exactly the reverse — that anything new is worse, and that almost any old building should be preserved at all costs. So total is our lack of confidence in our ability to design, to plan, even to build properly, that we are now prepared to revere almost any building from 'the past' — not just masterpieces, or Georgian terraces, but grim Victorian warehouses, factories, back-to-back jerry-built Victorian slums, even the serried ranks of suburban semis of the 1920s and 1930s.

But secondly, and here is the rub, as our society continues to change with great speed old buildings still continue to outlive their original uses. Churches, railway stations, warehouses, town halls, country houses continue to become redundant, or 'uneconomical' in ever greater numbers. But just as we can no longer bear to think of anything old being pulled down, so we desperately switch all our architectural skills, our resources and our cultural ingenuity to adapting these old structures to new uses. Churches become concert halls, warehouses become 'World Trade Centres', country houses become museums (or 'garden centres' or 'equestrian centres'), Cotswold tithe barns become trendy restaurants. Yet, in some mysterious way, almost every time the trick is performed, something of the essential spirit of the old building vanishes. As one wanders round the beautifully restored fragments of what survives of St Katharine Dock, the eighteenth-century timber-framed warehouse transformed into a trendy pub, across the twee little 'authentic' cobblestones, one is no longer in a grim survival of nineteenth-century commerce, but a sub-Williamsburg fantasy world. Even some of our great cathedrals which in the past twenty years have been lovingly restored, and cleaned and floodlit, have (for my taste at least) been transformed into little more than beautiful soulless film sets.

We are, in short, finally stuck, trapped in our wonderful, comfortable, late-twentieth-century material prison. We can neither build anew with faith in the future nor can we preserve the past that we love by artificial means, and yet preserve that intangible thing about it which we feel our civilization has mysteriously lost. But here I believe we are confronted with the heart of the cultural crisis which in the past few years has finally crept up on our civilization without our being fully aware of it — and it is something which runs much deeper and wider than mere considerations of architecture.

39

Back to Nature?

(1 July 1978)

What are we to make of the great nature craze presently sweeping our civilization? Thirty years ago, when I first began looking at birds and butterflies, the 'botanist' or 'entomologist', roaming the countryside with his butterfly net and specimen box, was still generally considered a pretty odd sort of cove. Today, when 'natural history' has been transformed into 'environmental studies', scarcely a middle-class British family does not have its copy of Keble Martin on the back seat of the car. Not a month goes by without some new Guide to Fungi or Complete Book of Waterplants racing up the best-seller charts (in the past ten years, more new nature books must have been published than in the whole of the previous five centuries since Gutenberg). Even for those whose interest is more casual, the television screens pump out an almost nightly diet of films on 'the vanishing Broads', the corncrakes of the Hebrides, the voles of Cumbria. For media exposure, the birds and the bees leave the World Cup nowhere.

It might seem a trifle ironic that this obsession with Wonderful Nature should coincide with the very moment in history when *homo sapiens* seems generally bent on the destruction of nature more ruthlessly and efficiently than ever before. But of course the two phenomena are hardly unconnected. It is true that, in a sense, the whole story of mankind has been written in our attempts to separate and emancipate ourselves from nature, to transform the world into a safe, tame, hygienic place, in which we can live out our lives in the maximum of material comfort. Nevertheless, the more we have managed to insulate ourselves from nature, the more do we seem to feel that something important is missing. Living in our cosy little technological prison, the more do we seem to be afflicted by a terrible yearning for that lost sense of wholeness with the rest of creation of which we are still, like it or not, a part; the more desperately do we seek our lost souls in that very thing from which we have become so estranged – the free, untamed world of birds, flowers, animals and the few remaining uncontaminated places of the earth.

In short, we are utterly bewildered by our attitude towards nature. We are unable to make up our minds whether it is simply an object, to be probed, taxonomized, despoiled, polluted and generally put to our egocentric use; or the last relic of a beautiful, free, instinctive world which mirrors our own lost harmony. But it would be a mistake to think that this ambivalence is a new thing. Take, for instance, what is perhaps the most famous nature book ever written, Gilbert White's *Natural History of Selborne*. In the late twentieth century, the earthly paradise conjured up by the obscure Hampshire curate is usually presented to us as the very picture of lost innocence. Nothing could seem further, we think, from that other more terrible world which was coming to birth elsewhere in England in precisely the years White was writing (1767–88) – the age of steam and iron and rampant technology, whose bemused heirs we are today.

Re-read White more carefully, however, and we may recognize that the difference was not so great. The exact observation which led White to become the first man to distinguish scientifically between a chiff-chaff and a willow warbler sprang from that same restless, inquiring eighteenth-century mind which was contemporaneously producing Watt's steam engine, or Abraham Darby's iron bridge in Coalbrookdale. White's measure of value for all his industrious botanizing was not just that it might induce 'his readers to pay a more ready attention to the wonders of the Creation', but utility ('he would be the best commonwealth's man that could occasion the growth of "two blades of grass where one alone had grown before" '). Although we think of White as inspired by a deep love and sympathy for the creatures he described, we may note that, if he wished to examine a bird more closely (particularly if it was rare), he never hesitated to shoot it. In fact it was only because White and his eighteenth-century contemporaries, such as Linnaeus, were becoming even *more* separated from nature than their predecessors – as man's self-consciousness increased, and the duality between observer and observed opened up in such spectacular post-Cartesian manner – that they were able to describe and catalogue the natural world so memorably.

One consequence of the fact that it was European civilization which led the way in this estrangement from nature was that it was in Europe before anywhere else that men first reached that point of eleventh-hour shock which has led them to take measures to prevent the actual disappearance of fellow-species threatened by human aggrandizement. Not the least of the many fascinating facts in Jeremy Mallinson's efficient memoir of thirty-three species of European mammal currently faced with extinction is that, of the thirty-six species which have already disappeared from the face of the earth since 1600, only one was native to Europe (the aurochs, which died out around 1627). Populations of such once-widespread species as the wolf, lynx and brown bear, may have been reduced to only tiny, isolated fractions

in the wilder parts of Europe — but in recent decades, conservation measures have resulted in small but significant
increases. The European bison was actually exterminated in
its wild state, when the 737 animals living in the Bialowieza
Forest in Poland were killed during the First World War —
but thanks to the fact that sixty-six bison from Bialowieza
survived in captivity, enough could be released back into
the wild over the next forty years for the total population
(wild and captive) to have risen by 1973 to the total of
1,514 animals.

In a sense, in fact, the title of Mr Mallinson's excellent
little book, *The Shadow of Extinction*, is misleading, in that
quite a number of the species he describes (with, in each
case, a profile of the animal's characteristics, distribution
and prospects for survival) seem not only to be surviving
fairly well, but even to be multiplying quite rapidly (e.g. the
wild cat, the European beaver, the pine marten). The species
which seem to be most seriously under threat tend to be
those which are too small and elusive to command dramatic national conservation programmes, such as the poor
little Pyrenean Desman, a furry creature of mountain
streamsides, which is threatened by hydro-electric schemes;
or of the Greater Horseshoe Bat, whose numbers have declined in England by an estimated 90 per cent in the past
thirty years, due to a variety of factors ranging from
insecticides (responsible for a general catastrophic collapse
in European bat populations) to 'the trade in cave-dwelling
bats for museums, schools and research'.

Such discrimination might confirm the suspicion that we
really today have less of a true kinship than ever with the
millions of species with whom we share the earth. Whenever they stand in the way of our comfort, or our imagined
quest for 'knowledge' (e.g. those wretched, vivisected bats),
we still have remarkably little compunction in consigning

them to destruction. I shall always recall a few years ago meeting a group of schoolboys on the Berkshire Downs, each clutching a jam jar packed with dead and dying butterflies. The insects were all of the same two species – Meadow Browns and Small Whites. I asked them what they were up to and they said that they were on an 'environment project'. Their biology master had told them to go out to collect as many butterflies as they could find. Of course this is only a microcosm of the way in which, finally separated from nature as we are, our civilization is in effect waging ruthless war on the rest of creation in almost everything it sets its hand to – usually quite unconsciously (for every feathered victim of the *Amoco Cadiz* disaster depicted struggling in its death throes on *News at Ten*, millions die unremarked so that we can go on driving our motor cars). Perhaps the sickest thing of all, as we engage in this ubiquitous, round-the-clock carnage, is the way we finally turn round to sentimentalize that which we are destroying – congratulating ourselves, as we go off to gawp at our victims in those unspeakable safari parks and dolphinariums, or flip over 'shock' colour supplement articles about 'the doomed forests of Amazonia', that we are actually doing something to help 'nature survive'.

40

Faust without the Hellfire

(27 September 1975)

There is usually no more sure-fire contributor to the silly season than the annual proceedings of the British Association for the Advancement of Science.

There was, for instance, the year not long ago when an American biologist described how he had injected an unfortunate rabbit with meat-tenderizer, only to find that its ears 'flopped like those of a spaniel'.

In another paper, a psychiatrist solemnly reported his finding that 'in general fat people do not go to university'. Best of all, a professor of geology announced his discovery that rocks brought back from the moon showed certain properties which are only to be found on earth in Cheddar and Emmenthaler cheese.

These farragos of improbable pseudery, reminiscent of Swift's projectors who sought to extract the sunlight from cucumbers, tend to be prefaced by an enormously portentous address from whatever *savant* happens to be President of the Association, in which he invariably states that science is morally neutral, and that it is time the rest of the human race caught up with the scientists, by developing the ethical framework whereby science can be used to benefit mankind rather than destroy it.

This year's presidential address, delivered in Guildford Cathedral on Wednesday night by Sir Bernard Lovell, was no exception. 'SCIENCE NEEDS ETHICAL BASIS' was one headline. 'Science itself' proclaimed the proprietor of the Great Dish, 'is neither a magic wand nor a poisoned arrow' – but unless we find that dear old 'ethical basis and moral purpose' soon, man might not 'long survive the consequences' of the scientists' probings.

Decked out with impressive quotations from Carlyle, about man being a fumbling midget at the 'centre of mysterious immensities', Sir Bernard seemed to be particularly worried about the consequences of the search for life on other planets – although it wasn't quite clear whether the mysterious dangers he spoke of would come from invasions of Quatermass-like cacti from Jupiter, Venusian plagues or just that we might soon find the universe so incomprehensible that we should all simply go off our heads.

Isn't it really time that this ludicrous argument over the 'moral neutrality' of science, and whether it is a 'magic wand', a 'poisoned arrow' or neither, was knocked on the head? The answer is, of course, that science is both – and since the rise of the philosophy of experimental science with Bacon and Descartes in the seventeenth century, particularly with respect to the development of its handmaiden technology, our Western attitude to science has been a moral issue in the most profound sense.

Implicit in the great Western 'scientific experiment' of the past 300 years have been two assumptions.

The first is that the purpose of scientific technology is to ensure for the human race an ever greater degree of material comfort by controlling and dominating the rest of nature.

The second is that by the mere accumulation of scientifically observed facts we shall eventually come to some kind of superior illumination about the nature of the universe and of ourselves.

It is now abundantly clear that the pursuit of each of these two assumptions has produced a host of unforeseen and unpleasing consequences. The more we attempt to subdue the rest of creation to our own immediate advantage, the more we become separated from nature, and the more we store up for ourselves a host of appalling side-effects — ranging from over-population and pollution to the prospect of the exhaustion of natural resources, and nuclear destruction.

Similarly the more we seek to replace our old mythical frame for existence with an infinite series of apparently unconnected material facts, the more we become disoriented, rootless and confused.

All these things are precisely implicit in the Mephistophelean bargain.

There is almost no belief more firmly rooted in the mythology of the human race than that which holds that man is part of the natural order which he can only interfere with at his peril.

It was the ancient Chinese view. It was the Greek view, expressed through the legends of Prometheus and Icarus. It was what Horace touched on when he wrote that if you chuck out nature with a pitchfork, it will come back some other way. It was an awareness of the terrible dangers implicit in the pursuit of science which led Pythagoras and his followers to designate philosophy as a 'sacred mystery', only to be divulged to those who had undergone the proper moral initiation. It was a desire for 'new experience of the uninhabited world behind the sun' which, in the Divine Comedy, led Ulysses to self-destruction.

And as for the spiritual and mental confusion which follows from the scientific exploration of the universe, when Sir Bernard Lovell spoke on Wednesday of 'the mind of man' being 'adrift', he had advanced not one jot from Donne's tragic version in the heyday of Bacon, Descartes, Kepler and Galileo:

> The sun is lost and the earth and no man's wit
> Can well direct him where to look for it.
> And freely men confess that this world's spent
> When in the Planets and the Firmament
> They seek so many anew; then see that this
> Is crumbled out again to his Atomies.

In fact all that Sir Bernard and Lord Todd and all the others mean when they say that we must develop the 'ethical base' to allow us to control the destructive power of science is that they want the human race to enjoy the benefits of scientific advance without its inevitable consequences — an ever uglier, more dangerous, more sterile world, leading to spiritual death and probable physical destruction into the bargain. They want the fruits of the Faustian pact, without having to pay the price — as did Faust himself.

It really is time that, as the heirs of Pythagoras, they began to take a more truly 'scientific' view.

41

Round in Scientific Circles

(9 November 1978)

Two of my favourite minor characters in the surreal Commedia dell'Arte of our times are that Tweedledum and Tweedledee-like pair, David Wilson and Peter Fairley, whose job it is to come on the BBC and ITN television screens to tell us about the latest 'exciting scientific breakthroughs'.

We usually see these comfortably rotund men, with strained concerned looks on their faces, standing in white coats by models of satellite solar panels, or machines for getting energy out of waves – and their essential role is to reassure us, as a great black wall of evidence to the contrary mounts up on all sides, that everything is going to be all right.

Don't worry. The good old scientists are still there, working away at breakthroughs for mankind – test-tube babies, energy from winds, two grains of rice growing where one grew before. Technological man is still in control of his destiny.

A rather grander version of Dum and Dee is someone called John Maddox, who first hit the headlines a few years ago, during a particularly nasty outbreak of 'eco-panic', when he was editor of the scientific magazine *Nature*.

Maddox would have none of this talk about exhaustion of energy sources, or pollution, or fears of over-population. This wild scaremongering was simply a passing phase, as mankind headed upwards into an ever brighter future, where there was no problem which could not be solved by our inexhaustible scientific ingenuity.

Now the important thing about all these men — Maddox, Dum, Dee and Co. — is that they are not really connected with science at all. They are in a more literal than strict sense of the word the soothsayers of our time, soothing our fears with constant promises of unlimited energy, health, and scientifically-produced happiness which is always just round the corner in the future.

In order to understand their role properly, it is necessary to look below the surface at the very simple message they are constantly repeating — and at what it indicates as to their view of man.

A good example of what I am talking about came on Wednesday night when, on Radio Three, John Maddox was again addressing himself to one of his favourite themes — the belief that has grown up in recent years, among certain doctors, that mental illness, and in particular that series of conditions generally described under the heading of schizophrenia, may have purely physical or chemical causes.

What these doctors have discovered is that, in the brains of schizophrenic patients, there appear to be deficiencies or over-supplies of certain chemical substances which transmit messages from one brain cell to another.

If this is the case (and the evidence appears to be strong that it is so) then what more tempting, you might think, than to argue that these chemical malfunctions are in themselves the *causes* of schizophrenia. Because of course the corollary is that if mental illness has purely physical causes, then we can envisage that it may have a purely physical *cure*.

This is such an enticing vision that it is tempting to overlook altogether the possibility that the chemical changes might be merely by-products of psychic malfunctioning which stems from altogether deeper, more complex and therefore less tractable causes. As man has become increasingly bewildered by his inability to understand or to cope with the problems that are caused by his own advancing consciousness, few dreams have haunted him more than this one – that somehow, one day, a magic pill might be discovered that would put an end to all the mental and spiritual ills our flesh is heir to.

Never mind that Aldous Huxley viciously satirized this dream in his zombie-like *Brave New World*, dependent on the 'happiness drug' soma, or that the LSD-generation of the Sixties pursued their hallucinatory visions of 'oneness', only to find that in many cases it led to an even greater psychic confusion than before.

The dream dies hard – and earlier this year even Arthur Koestler (one of the poshest of all the Dums and Dees) was peddling in his book *Janus* the idea that somehow, in the chemical laboratories, might lie the answer to wars, crimes and all the other psychic disorders which appear to be so uniquely endemic to mankind.

Now the most important thing of all is to recognize the view of man which underlies all these fantasies and wishful thoughts.

We often hear it said that we live in a materialistic civilization – and the image this usually conjures up is of supermarkets and colour television sets and everyone wanting to go on strike all the time for more money.

But the real sense in which our civilization has become materialistic goes so much deeper that it is almost impossible for us any longer to 'stand outside ourselves' and see what it does mean.

It means that by imperceptible stages, over aeons of time, our whole level of consciousness about the world and our existence within it has changed, to the point where we see just one part of ourselves as infinitely important – and that part is our bodies.

Of course we still talk blithely about other 'bits' of ourselves – our hearts, our minds, even on sentimental occasions of something called our 'souls'. But most people have simply no conception just what an astonishing change has come over us in the extent to which we now see the highest end of life and civilization as being to achieve physical comfort for our bodies, and to prolong the life of those bodies for as long as possible.

The other 'bits' have become mere appendages, to be soothed, stimulated, suppressed or stilled.

What is existence? The very term itself has come to mean mere *physical* existence and that is why there is such a deep yearning in our collapsing, spiritually and mentally bankrupt, nightmarish civilization to cling on to any last, vain hope that somehow this attempt wholly to re-interpret ourselves and the universe in purely physical terms is going to work.

It is not – and it is one of the saddest commentaries of all on the pitiful state science has reached that, in its closing stages, it has become so totally *unscientific*. The truly scientific, 'whole' view would be based on trying to appreciate *all* the evidence – and that means seeing physical explanations for phenomena in their true perspective as part of a whole hierarchy of other relationships.

The true lesson is that once men lose their sense of the whole, and concentrate their view on one part of the picture, they always end up trying to put together a jigsaw that simply does not fit any more. And inevitably, as an iron law of the human psyche, they collapse into nothing more than vapid and fundamentally ego-centred wishful thinking.

42

The Collapse of 'The Modern Movement'

(24 May 1977)

My eye was recently caught by a phrase in a new book by Paul Johnson, in which he referred to Harold Pinter as 'a major tragic writer in the tradition of Ibsen'.

The odd thing was how ludicrously hollow this claim for Pinter now seemed. At a debate at the Cambridge Union, a month or two ago, I heard a visiting speaker completely dismissing Pinter and Beckett as having absolutely nothing of importance or interest to say. The fascinating thing is that there was not even the slightest murmur of dissent from the audience – the remark was simply accepted, in a way which even five years ago would have been unthinkable.

Lying behind this shift of opinion is, I believe, one of the most important things to have happened in our culture in the past decade.

I refer to the sudden and almost complete collapse of what has so far been the most important artistic force in twentieth-century Western civilization – what may be called, in the broadest sense, 'The Modern Movement'.

Just consider how many of the artistic giants of our century have died in the past ten or fifteen years. In painting, the modern movement was symbolized above all by those twin geniuses of post-Cubism, Braque (died 1963) and Picasso (died 1973). In architecture the giants were Le Corbusier (died 1965), Gropius (died 1969) and Mies van der Rohe (died 1969). In poetry, there were Eliot (died

1965), Pound (died 1972) and possibly Auden (died 1973). In music, Stravinsky (died 1971), Shostakovich (died 1975), and possibly Britten (died 1976) and Kodaly (died 1967).

With the exception perhaps of Solzhenitsyn and Beckett (both of whom I shall refer to later) and of one or two curiosities like Salvador Dali, most of those international stars who remain, Stockhausen, Pinter, Henze, Hockney, are pretty thin stuff by comparison.

Lying behind the physical departure of these towering figures, however, has been something even more revealing in recent years – and that is an increasingly general sense that most of the ideas which lay behind that great explosion of creativity that was 'the Modern Movement' have reached a point of almost complete exhaustion.

On all sides one can see signs large and small of a great reaction to what the Modern Movement stood for. One of the most glaring examples is the revolt against 'modern architecture' – the complete reaction against tower blocks, and all the forces which made such a nightmare wilderness of our cities in the Fifties and Sixties.

In painting there is the remarkable resurgence of interest in the United States and elsewhere in the sort of academic painters of the nineteenth century, for decades laughed to scorn – who are now back in vogue simply because people can 'understand' them.

In music, after sixty years of modernism, the popularity of composers of almost any century but our own has never been higher.

What was the Modern Movement about? Clearly it produced many artists of astonishing talent. But what did they use their talent to express?

For a start they were in revolt against the past – they were seeking liberation from all the old forms and conventions. In poetry this led to 'free verse', in painting to ab-

stractionism, in music to atonality, in achitecture to a kind
of individualism run riot, so that every building had to be
conceived anew and from 'first principles'.

For the first twenty or thirty years of this century, while
they were still in the first flush of revolt, and being derided
and 'misunderstood' by conventional society, the modern-
ists gloried in being an avant-garde minority.

By the Fifties and Sixties, 'modernism' had swept into
triumphant acceptance as the orthodoxy of the age. No
longer would anyone deny that Picasso or Le Corbusier
were towering artists, fit to rank with the greatest names
of the past.

But built into the whole modernist adventure was a kind
of self-destruct. At the end of every line of liberation there
appeared to be a black hole of meaninglessness. The
painters reached the blank canvas, the composers reached
random, uncontrolled noise, the writers pushed through
the final frontiers of meaning to the point where, like
Beckett, they claimed that they had nothing left to say
except that there was nothing left to say.

That is the point we have reached today. And suddenly
we can look back over the Western art of the past five centuries and see with dazzling clarity that what has been laid
out before us is a perfect model of the psyche of man, and
a beautiful demonstration of what art is all about.

We can see that what has happened is that Western man
has progressively lost touch with the very centre of his
being, the sense of union with the divine. The more he has
explored the by-paths of his material consciousness, the
more the artist has come to see himself as an isolated
figure expressing his own individuality – rather than drawing that strength from the sense of belonging to some infinite, spiritual 'whole' which gives him universality.

Of course along the path of the past five hundred years

there have been many great artists who (against the general trend) have still managed to make that return to the 'centre' — Titian and Rembrandt, Bach and Beethoven, Dostoievsky and Tolstoy, and many others. Even in our own disintegrated times, many of the leading artists (Eliot, Britten, Stravinsky, Auden) have burned with a 'low blue flame', as Edmund Wilson called it, of that religious sense which must lie at the heart of all true creativity.

And today it is no accident that one of the few remaining artists with a claim to universality and real meaning is Solzhenitsyn, who through the purging away of all material irrelevance in the horrors of totalitarian Russia, has been brought back into contact with spiritual reality.

But the final lesson of the story is that it is only in recognizing our divine centre that we can in fact be fully human, and flow with the creative stream of the universe, what Dante called 'the love that moves the sun and other stars'. Once leave that, and inevitably at the end of the day you will end up with the blank canvas, the play that is just a despairing silence and the inhuman moonscapes of modern architecture. If we are to regain our sense of meaning and life, we simply have to learn and accept once again who we truly are — divine sparks, floating in a beautifully-ordered, living universe. Then, and only then, will the well-springs of art once again put forth living water.

43

The Death of Philosophy

(28 January 1978)

There was something deeply melancholy last week about the sight of Sir Isaiah Berlin and Bryan Magee sitting on a large green club sofa in a television studio, opening BBC-2's monster series of fifteen discussions which will give the intelligent layman some idea of the state of modern philosophy.

Magee could scarcely have done better than to introduce his series with Sir Isaiah, who is not only one of the most intelligent men in Britain, but also beats George Steiner and A. J. P. Taylor by a short head as the best academic music hall turn in the Western world.

Yet even this first episode seemed somehow pervaded by an air of weariness. Sir Isaiah once again rehearsed the familiar distinction between the two kinds of statement which philosophers will allow as possible to settle – statements which are empirically verifiable, and those, like the propositions of mathematics, which relate to a set of formal rules.

But between them, as the proper province of philosophy, lie all those other questions to which inquiring men have sought answers since time immemorial – what is the purpose of my life, what is good, what is God? – and upon which modern philosophers find it almost impossible any longer to pronounce.

Although it is early days yet – Magee promises a grand tour through almost every conceivable byway of modern philosophy, from Marx to Marcuse and Wittgenstein to Chomsky — I think one can safely make two predictions about this series.

The first is that it will attract a surprisingly large audience. The second, I suspect, is that at the end of the series, many of those viewers who last the course will feel somehow profoundly cheated and let down.

For more than fifty years it has seemed that the history of Western philosophy was rather like a man climbing up a tree. He begins with the solid trunk (as philosophy began with the central mysteries of human existence); as he climbs higher and higher, the branches get thinner and thinner, until finally he is perched on a tiny twig at the top of the tree. He then prepares to saw it off.

In fact the evolution of philosophy conjures up an inescapable parallel with that of modern art. Every new development has seemed in retrospect a logical progression from the last. Yet, at the end of the day, there is nothing left but a hubbub of chattering voices, trying by their babbling to cover up a desperate void of meaning.

It was as long ago as 1922 that, at the end of the *Tractatus*, Wittgenstein wrote what is probably the only widely familiar utterance of any modern philosopher — 'of those things of which he cannot speak, man must remain silent' (in other words, more or less all those questions which older philosophers took as their starting point). It is only lately that the artists have consciously arrived at the same position, as in Samuel Beckett's statement, 'I have nothing to say, and I can only say to what extent I have nothing to say.'

It is a general rule of human affairs that, when the end of one road of development has been reached, the next great source of life and spirit-renewing inspiration will come from some quite unexpected quarter, which for a long time is not recognized by orthodox opinion.

My own view is that the one really promising road towards an entirely new philosophical perspective on human existence has in fact been opening up now for some fifty years – since almost the exact moment when, in those closing lines of the *Tractatus*, Wittgenstein in effect sawed off the last twig on which rationalist philosophy rested.

I believe that, over the next fifty years (if mankind survives), the most startling philosophic development will be the move right into the centre of philosophic concern of the workings of that very instrument from which all philosophy stems in the first place – the human psyche.

I believe that the reason why the philosophers have apparently led themselves up a mental cul-de-sac is that, by pursuing the rationalistic road to its logical conclusion, they have lost their overall perspective on the different functions of the psyche.

The depth psychology pioneered by Jung is still only in its infancy as a scientific discipline – but in a curious way, Jung began his researches into the way we actually look at the world at precisely the point where the Wittgenstein of the *Tractatus* left off.

Just when the philosophers were saying, 'we cannot say anything meaningful about ideas such as God', the depth psychologists were saying 'quite right – of course we cannot say anything meaningful about these things in themselves. But what we can observe are the ways in which the human psyche seems at its deepest levels to work naturally around precisely the forms and patterns which have given rise to these ideas. The patterns whereby we find a sense of meaning and purpose in life seem to be imprinted in us, in almost exactly the way that an acorn is imprinted with the coding which will transform it into a mighty oak tree. This is what we should be looking at – and it is this which we ignore at our peril.'

I am more convinced than I am of anything that this is the way through which (without for one moment veering off into leaps of faith, or onto paths which contradict reason), science will one day lead us back to an entirely new dimension of self-understanding and to that proper pre-occupation of philosophy which is wisdom. Then one day we shall perhaps be able to look back on the terrible sterility of twentieth-century philosophy as simply part of 'a long dark night of the soul' through which humanity had to pass in order to re-integrate its view of itself, and once again to find the spiritual meaning which lies behind the extraordinary mystery of our existence.

44

Collectivism by design

(24 February 1979)

A good many *Daily Telegraph* readers may have sat up to
watch at least part of *City of Towers*, my mammoth BBC-2
documentary on the destruction and rebuilding of our
cities in the past twenty years, last Monday night. The film
had to be as long as it was because the purpose of my
exercise was not, as a number of feather-brained critics
seem to have thought, just to pass a few random prejudiced
opinions on modern architecture.

I was trying to tell, for the first time, the full story of a
certain image of the city. I tried to show how that image, of
collossal buildings and restless traffic, first came to haunt a
number of science-fiction writers and architects more than
fifty years ago – and how eventually their ideas became
the orthodox, which hovered over the wholesale reconstruction of many of Britain's cities in the Sixties and early
Seventies.

It is indisputable that, in the great revolt against tower
blocks, 'concrete jungles' and comprehensive redevelopment, those dreams have in recent years ended up the most
bitter disillusionment.

But one of the more predictable criticisms made of my
film is that, in the course of this gigantic story, I was 'un-
fair' to modern architecture. I failed to put the case for all
the *good* buildings put up in Britain in the past thirty
years.

Such critics need only have waited a few days for Patrick

Nuttgens's film *Architecture for Everyman* and they would have seen just what they were waiting for — a sympathetic account of the brighter side of the great modern architectural experiment, an anthology of some of the new buildings we really can admire, ranging from the Festival Hall to the Regent's Park bird cage, from an office block in Ipswich to the Byker housing estate in Newcastle.

My overall reaction to Mr Nuttgens's film was that he had made just about as neat a job of defending modern British architecture as anyone could want.

The kernel of his case was that the best modern architecture uses technology to create spacious, uncluttered, 'free-flowing' environments, full of light and air — as his title implied, a truly 'democratic' architecture in which 'Everyman' and 'Everywoman' can wander expansively through halls of metal and reflecting glass, in which all conventional distinctions are broken down (even those between the outside and inside of the building).

Yet it was precisely here, as I watched, that I began to see forming yet again the deepest reservation of all I have about modern architecture — which is that it cannot allow anyone to have an *individual* identity.

No one in his right mind would deny that modern architecture has created many visually stunning buildings, admirably fitted to serve the needs of a technologically based mass society. But its overriding message (and all architecture *has* a message) is that you can only join in this fantasy world of happy consumers, or office workers, or airline travellers, so long as you submerge your individual identity in the collective.

When I say that all architecture has a message, I mean that all architecture, whether it be a medieval cathedral, a thatched cottage, or a thirty-storey tower block, makes an

implicit statement about the nature of man and his relations to himself and the universe.

Architecture is ultimately about human identity – it is
one of the most important external things which help to
tell us who we are. There is no clearer book in which to
read the changes in the prevailing view of who we are and
what is most important to us than in the kinds of building which our civilization has raised over the past 800
years.

In the soaring verticals of the great Gothic cathedrals we
see the reflection of a society ultimately centred on its
sense of the transcendent. In the harmoniously proportioned
horizontals of the Renaissance or the eighteenth-century
terraces of Bath, we see a society becoming more materialistic and 'man-centred', but for which the highest values
were still aesthetic and intellectual.

In the hideous sprawl of the nineteenth-century factories,
railways and slums, we see a society for which the highest
value was becoming man's material power to transform
nature. In the surburban semis of the first half of the
twentieth century, we see the true architecture of democracy, everyone an individual in his own individual (though
almost identical) box.

Finally, in the neogargantuan architecture of the past
thirty years, the great office blocks and housing estates,
shopping centres and multi-storey car parks, we see the full
visible reflection of a society whose highest values are
material comfort for the greatest number, and the re-
submergence of the individual in a new kind of collectivism,
based on subservience to the all-providing machine.

What really worries me about almost all modern architecture, both 'good' and 'bad', is the extraordinary ambiva-

lence, the ease with which it seems to pass from 'dream' to 'nightmare'.

Almost the entire theme of my film on Monday was the contrast between the architect's vision, the dreamworld, and the hideous, de-humanizing nightmare which has so often succeeded it.

Mr Nuttgens, not unnaturally, was at pains only to show the 'dream' – the vision of 'Everyman' strolling happily through his technologically-shaped fantasy world. But even here the dark underside of the dream of man liberated rather than trapped by his technology could not help showing through.

One of the more haunting images in his film was of a West Indian steel band playing for the swimmers in a municipal 'leisure pool'. Compare the dead, sad expressions on their faces with the gaiety of almost any group of folk-musicians in the pre-technological world, and you have the whole story in a nutshell.

Human beings do not find their inmost identity, that thing which tells them who they truly are, in any submergence in the collective, however lavishly and agreeably it is packaged. The dreamworld created and held out by modern technology is one of the most beguiling men have ever created for themselves – forget who you are, runs the message, surrender to your material appetites and to these free-flowing fantasies, and you will be happy, liberated, a child of the future.

It does not work for the simple reason that such illusions contradict the very structure of our human nature. There is always a terrible price to be paid for such dreams, and if it is not just some of the grimmer of the concrete wildernesses and anthills I showed on Monday, it may well be lurking in the missile silos of Nebraska and the Urals.

If we insist on turning mankind into an infinite mass of

de-humanized, de-spiritualized children, we may unconsciously be led to doing away with ourselves precisely because we shall have finally lost sight of that which not only
tells us who we are, but which alone tells us why life is
really worth living.

45

Dreams That Crack Like Concrete

(22 November 1976)

The other day I had one of the most familiar experiences of the late twentieth century. It came in the course of a visit to one of the most admired modern buildings in England – a block of flats built in East London in the early Fifties by that currently most fashionable of all British architects, Sir Denys Lasdun.

Over the past twenty years, Lasdun's celebrated 'cluster block' has appeared in many a handbook of modern architecture, invariably photographed under blue skies, with its concrete gleaming white in the sun.

Today, as I discovered when I turned down the little Bethnal Green side street, it is hard to imagine that you are looking at the same building.

The fifteen-storey tower block stands tatty and forlorn, its concrete cracked and discolouring, the metal reinforcement rusting through the surface, every available inch covered with graffiti – 'Manchester United Rules, O.K.' Inside there is a stench of urine. Piles of old cigarette packets and broken bottles fill every corner, while the wretched, glum-looking tenants shuffle past to wait for the only lift that is still working.

When I say the experience is familiar – that of the contrast between the dreamworld of the architect's drawing and the grim, inhuman result that only too often emerges – I am not, however, referring just to architecture alone.

The bright, anticipated dream followed by a seedy, nightmarish reality has of course been the dominant pattern of much of our schizophrenic century – whether the dream has been of the bright new city centre, the Socialist Utopia, the technological paradise or whatever.

We are witnessing the process of disillusionment over another dream with which Sir Denys Lasdun has been associated, the National Theatre. In recent weeks it has seemed curiously appropriate that the chief architectural inspiration for the pile of concrete blocks on the South Bank appears to have been a cross between Speer's Atlantic Wall and the Führerbunker.

As the beleaguered Peter Hall has been subjected to ever more thunderous bombardment on all fronts, the sad truth has slowly dawned on an increasing number of people that the new National Theatre is an almost unqualified disaster.

As a building, despite the quite feverish wave of eulogy when it was opened, Lasdun's £16 million complex is, both outside and even more inside, a neurotic mess. As its chief administrator, Hall seems to be presiding over a kind of parody of bureaucratic chaos and extravagance run riot. The plays put on have been dreary beyond belief. And the actors, despite their vast salaries, appear to yearn (like many of the more discerning members of the audience) for nothing more than the good old days of that agreeable little theatre, the Old Vic.

On Thursday night, BBC-1's *Omnibus* programme showed a remarkable little film-essay by Peter West on the state of the subsidized stage (the force of which was in no way diminished by the rather embarrassed comments at beginning and end from Humphrey Burton). Entitled 'A Stately Pleasure Dome?', the film took a look at three theatres.

First was The National. Second was the Clwyd Theatre

at Mold, which forms part of the vast new 'cultural complex' for North Wales, looking like a nuclear power station, and merging appropriately with the even vaster new council headquarters dominating the town. Third was a little travelling theatre group (also subsidized) which drums up plays on burning local issues, like the closure of the Shotton steel works, and takes them round village halls to the accompaniment of loud pop music.

As Burton said, the film was deeply 'depressing'. The overwhelming impression was of vast technological structures, full of grey bureaucrats and Quango men on huge salaries, spouting meaningless jargon about 'excellence' and 'the quality of life' and 'investing for the future' (this last was a reference to Mold's new 'educational technology centre', next to the theatre, in which local school children can plug into machines from the 'media resources library', playing back strip cartoons of fairy stories).

I rather suspect from the fact that Lindsay Anderson was performing the commentary that we were meant to look on the travelling Grass Roots Theatre as the only genuine, democratic thespian enterprise of the three (although I fear that for my money this cross between a wartime ENSA show and early Seventies 'pub theatre' made me long for the local amateur dramatic society's performance of *The Mousetrap*).

What has gone wrong with the theatre? The answer of course is – nothing more than has gone wrong with our civilization. One of the most ironic quotations in the *Omnibus* film was a piece of guff from Bernard Levin (admittedly written when the South Bank project was still in its 'dream stage') claiming that this vast project would once again make of a theatre building what the theatre was 'two thousand years ago' – 'a temple'.

The reason why Greek theatres were akin to temples,

and their tragedies forms of religious celebration, was that Greek culture was still sufficiently integrated with itself and with nature to look on these great semi-mythical patterns enacted on stage as observations of the mysterious way in which the world actually works. *Hubris* was succeeded by nemesis. The world was a thing to be understood, rather than changed.

But today, in the last stages of disintegration of our post-Renaissance culture, the world is only to be changed. The idea of *hubris* has been abolished, because we are all part of the most hubristic experiment in man's history.

And nothing in the twentieth century has more characterized our cultural disintegration than two inevitable consequences. On the one hand, as with ever more desperation we have sought salvation through 'welfarism' and technology, has been the proliferation of a vast, dead structure of bureaucracy, and bureaucratic ways of thought. The other has been the natural reaction of poor bewildered human beings who cease to see any structure at all in the universe, and take refuge in all the neurotic chaos of rebellion, protest, 'individualism' run riot and escape from all forms.

These two manifestations of collective neurosis are seen in almost every aspect of our culture. It is hardly surprising therefore that they are reflected also in our theatre, and that there, as in architecture, politics, science and everything else, we are doomed to an ever more rapid succession of feverishly anticipated dreams leading to such absurd and dead results as the National Theatre. But I cannot help thinking that what has happened on the South Bank would make a wonderful subject for a good old-fashioned drama on the theme of *hubris* and nemesis.

46

Facing the Catastrophe?

(June 1977)

I recently reviewed a book by Mr Paul Johnson, called *Enemies of Society*. I am afraid that, like one or two other reviewers, I was not very friendly to the book. Considering Mr Johnson's continued public declarations of total devotion to Socialism (*pace* his recent 'open letter' to Tony Benn, imploring him, as the one just man left in the government, to save the Labour Party's soul), the book's most remarkable characteristic seemed to be the fact that on almost all the most important issues of the day – political, social, moral, artistic, philosophical – Mr Johnson has arrived at a view indistinguishable from that taken for the past forty years by the *Sunday Express*. Perhaps he draws comfort from Scott Fitzgerald's remark in *The Crack-Up* that 'the test of a first-rate intelligence is the ability to hold two opposed ideas in the mind at the same time and still continue to function'.

Nevertheless Mr Johnson was not pleased that anyone should venture to oppose his thesis. And two weeks ago, readers of the *Daily Telegraph* must have been somewhat startled when he devoted a whole column to an explosion of rage against all those, such as myself, who dared to disagree with him.

The particular point on which Johnson was infuriated was the response to just one chapter in his book, which he called 'Ecological Panic'. He pours infinite scorn on those people who in recent years have expressed concern that our civilization might be facing a grave crisis, from such things as over-population, the exhaustion of natural resources, pollution or the H-bomb. Protesting his own total devotion to reason, and calm pursuit of the truth, Johnson describes all such doom-talk as insane alarmism, the creation of an 'eco-lobby' of members of the middle classes, who mostly live in 'pleasant rural suburbia'. The kindest thing he can say about these people is that they are 'the respectable end of a spectrum of middle-class cranks which embraces such sects as the Christian Scientists, the anti-vivisectionists and those who campaign fanatically against the fluoridation of water supplies'. Otherwise they are 'trendy', 'irrational' and 'hysterical'. In reaction to his book they rarely speak in tones other than 'snarls and shrieks of rage'. (I fear that I myself am 'a modern flat-earther' who would 'like us all to return to living in caves', living off 'marinated seaweed'.)

The destructive power of these cranks knows almost no bounds. 'The eco-lobby's most impressive triumph so far' has been the great world oil crisis since 1973, 'a disaster of the first magnitude for our civilization'. This was almost entirely brought about by the effect of the propaganda of the eco-lobby on the 'less sophisticated governments' of the OPEC countries (the Arab-Israeli War was 'merely a pretext' for the quadrupling of oil prices). 'The precise economic effects, in terms of misery and death, of the eco-lobby's coup will never be known.' In the West, by enforcing cuts in public spending on such things as education, hospitals and pensions, disaster has fallen on 'the innocent heads of the urban poor'. In the poorer countries of the world the catastrophe has been immeasurable. 'In spring 1976 more than 500 million people were near starvation level in the Third World.' In Africa, the 'economic climate' produced by the crisis pushed country after country near to totalitarianism. 'In Asia it brought down the world's largest democracy, India, which in 1975 abandoned free speech and the rule of law.' 'The only gainer was the archetype [*sic*] totalitarian state, the Soviet Union.' Quite an achievement for a handful of middle-class cranks in their comfortable 'rural suburbia' (who presumably want everybody to live off seaweed).

Why have I devoted so much space to Mr Johnson's views? Because I think that unconsciously he has here raised an extremely important point about this whole debate over whether our civilization is heading for eco-catastrophe or not. Mr Johnson, as I say, attaches great importance to the use of 'reason', to working 'from the facts to opinions' and not vice versa. But in the end, I do not believe that 'examination of the evidence' or the pursuit of reason, however rigorous, can in themselves lead us to any firm conclusion as to whether mankind is facing an unprecedented crisis today or not. Whether one takes population-curves, estimates of natural resources or any of the other possible statistical measures, there are simply too many variables and unpredictable factors to be fed into any equation, for the evidence to provide anything other than a rather shaky support for the case one has already chosen to put for quite other reasons.

Of course this does not mean that we should be anything other than extremely careful in our use of that evidence, when we do use it. There is no question that 'facts' and statistics are very often flung about by almost all parties to the argument as if they were nothing more than mud pies. No one can doubt that there has been a laughable degree of inconsistency among the eco-lobbyists (some, for instance, saying that we are all going to drown to death because the heating up of the atmosphere by carbon monoxide will melt the ice caps, others saying that we are all going to freeze to death because a new ice age is going to cover the earth). Equally there has been a widely irrational optimism among the 'growth lobby' that at whatever speed we continue to use natural resources, we shall always somehow find more, and that man is ultimately a rational creature who will manage to control his self-destructive urges.

Nevertheless, in the end, the evidence one chooses to look at and to believe is that which broadly supports one's preconceived position. Some years ago when I took part in a television discussion on this issue with three other people, it struck me that there are four possible general attitudes to the 'eco-crisis', each of which was represented by one of the speakers on the programme.

The first view (represented on that occasion by Bernard Levin, as it is today by Paul Johnson) argues that everything is fundamentally fine, and that the eco-lobbyists are just irresponsible neurotics. There will always be enough energy (if we run out of existing sources we shall find new ones). Forecasts of the exhaustion of other natural resources are ludicrously exaggerated. Population curves will flatten out. Man is rational and will not destroy himself.

The second view (perhaps represented today by Jimmy Carter) says – yes, there is a crisis. We have to accept that resources may be finite, that civilization cannot expect indefinite material growth for ever. We shall have to make certain sacrifices, certain changes in our way of life. But ultimately, by ingenuity, self-discipline and a little adjustment, we shall survive.

The third view is that we are facing a really major, unprecedented crisis, which can only be faced up to by taking unprecedented and drastic steps. In fifty years time, if we are to survive at all, we shall all (particularly in the West) be having to live a very different kind of life. We shall have to use natural resources at a much lower rate. We may have to accept compulsory birth control. We can make it, but only at a terrible price, which may involve serious disorders on the way.

The fourth view is entirely black: that we are bent on a course of self-destruction, that man is ultimately an irrational, greedy, aggressive creature who will find it impossible to make the sacrifices and changes which would be necessary to save him (in any physical sense), and that sooner or later we shall face a holocaust of destruction, from which something may survive or nothing – certainly nothing remotely recognizable in our present highly-sophisticated, growth-bent materialistic civilization.

I now believe that there is also a fifth view, which draws perhaps on a wider base altogether. This says that man is certainly heading for catastrophe, the way he is going, but that there is infinitely more to the great mystery of existence than just the material survival of one little civilization (or even, in the end, that of man himself). If there is to be a holocaust, it will merely be part of the endless cycle of death and rebirth. Something will survive, whether it is a new kind of man with a wider consciousness of himself and his place in creation, or just that spirit which Dante calls 'the love that moves the sun and other stars', which is in all of us and imperishable.

Such a view would clearly strike most people as so irrational as to be verging on the insane. But the fact remains that *whichever* view one takes is beyond the power of reason to decide. It is an entirely metaphysical question, reflecting the metaphysical view of each person who adopts an attitude towards it. If, at one end of the spectrum, one believes that man is essentially a good and rational creature, and that his material well-being is his highest good (as Paul Johnson does), then he will take the view that civilization can survive on its present course without much problem. If at the other end of the spectrum one believes that what is important about man is that he is merely a material expression of the spirit which moves in all creation, then one is likely to accept firstly that our present civilization is rooted in a denial of that truth and will probably destroy itself – but secondly that in doing so the world will in some sense be renewed, and whether man himself survives is in the most important sense irrelevant. As I say, which of the five positions along this spectrum that a man chooses says a great deal about the man who chooses it, and really nothing about what is actually going to happen. And certainly reason alone (while it must not be denied its proper place and use) will not tell us which of these positions should be ours.

Part Six

Re-appraisals

In the year before the Seventies began, 1969, two quite disparate happenings each cast fascinating light on the curious position mankind has reached in the late twentieth century. The first, as I have already described, was Kenneth Clark's enormously popular *Civilisation* series – on the face of it, a triumphant celebration of our civilization's most glorious achievements, yet underneath giving such an extraordinarily despondent picture of just where we have all got to in the 500 years since the Renaissance. In his autobiography, Clark recalled the astonishing scenes which had greeted him in America when the series had first been shown there. As he entered the National Gallery in Washington, 'all the galleries were crammed full of people who stood up and roared at me, waving their hands and stretching them out towards me'. With his remarkable gift for self-revelation, Clark describes how he felt 'like some visitor to a plague-ridden country, who has been mistaken for a doctor but is not a doctor', and how he then retired to the 'gents' where he 'sobbed and howled for quarter of an hour'.

The second event, in the same year, was America's first manned landing on the moon – in a sense the symbolic culminatory moment in the whole of man's post-Renaissance exploration and 'conquest' of the external world. Again, on the fact of it, this should have been a moment of unadulterated triumph – the supreme justifica-

tion for that road mankind has set out to travel when the
first late-medieval explorers had set out from Europe to
subdue the vast unknown realms of the earth beyond the
sea. Yet in fact, as I analyse in the opening essay of this
section, the whole event left us feeling, once the superficial excitement had died away, strangely baffled and flat.

In the ten years since those two strangely ambivalent
events there has been abundant evidence that the glorious
age created by post-Renaissance civilization, from the late
fifteenth century to the present day, may be nearing some
fundamental turning point. Behind the roar and clatter of
collapsing old ideologies, beliefs and illusions, amid mount-
ing pessimism, disillusionment and despair, we cannot possibly see with clarity what the future holds. But on the
other side of the great darkness which appears to be gathering over the human race, it may well be that some entirely
new era awaits the world – and that we are already living in
the seed time of that future epoch. Certainly in the Seventies
there were already countless embryonic signs of a great
change beginning to come over our human perspective on
ourselves and our place in the universe – and in this section
I refer to some of them.

One of the most interesting things to have happened in
the past decade or so has been the emergence of the so-
called 'ecology' movement. By the end of the Seventies,
scarcely a week went by without reference to some new
campaign to save seals, whales, eagles or other species from
extinction at the hands of man. Undoubtedly there was in
this eleventh-hour uprushing of compassion a considerable
element of sentimental confusion and double-think (as when
oil companies engaged in the wholesale unconscious extermination of wildlife through pollution ostentatiously
contributed funds to the 'saving of the tiger'). But beyond
the sentimental veneer, there was beginning to dawn, all

over the world, a new attitude to nature – an awareness that man is inextricably part of some great Whole, that he disturbs the balance of the Whole at his peril, and that somehow he must find the way to restore the harmony between himself and nature.

This attitude expressed itself in the Seventies in countless way, large and small: through the growing revulsion against modern technological farming methods, and the cult of 'organically' grown foods; through the increasing recognition by more thoughtful scientists of the inbuilt limitations of technology and the 'scientific method' itself; through the growing interest in Eastern philosophies and religions, centred on a more 'holistic' attitude to man in nature than the Judaeo-Christian tradition, which has only too easily been used to underpin man's illusion that he could and should somehow become the 'master' of nature.

It would of course be foolish to overestimate the importance of these signs and portents. The prevailing momentum of our civilization in the Seventies remained overwhelmingly, seemingly unstoppably, committed to the 'conquest' of nature, to technological 'progress' and to all that legacy of beliefs and assumptions which had grown up in the great era of 'scientific method' since the seventeenth century. But never before had the foundations of that mighty edifice seemed so shaky. Even many of those who still inhabited it, such as the philosopher Stuart Hampshire, whose lecture on 'The Future of Knowledge' makes the basis for my last two essays, were beginning to get an alarmed glimmering of just how worm-eaten the whole, rickety structure had become (though they could not as yet think their way outside it). Even here change was inescapably on the way.

47

Reaching for the Moon

(Written on the tenth anniversary of the first moon landing, 21 July 1979)

President Nixon called it 'the greatest week since the creation of the world'. Norman Mailer, in *Fire on the Moon*, was a little more modest, describing it only as 'the greatest week since Christ was born'. But the fact remains that, even when these hubristic claims were first uttered, they had a hollow ring. Despite the astonishing wave of world-wide excitement engendered by the event, the actual response of most of the human race to the news that on 21 July 1969 two of their kind had set foot on the Moon was, deep down, one of strange bafflement.

We watched the two figures in their diving suits slowly blundering about on the Moon desert. We listened to their euphoric clichés. We knew it was all terribly important, the greatest thing ever to happen, the greatest triumph of man's ingenuity since ... well, since ever ... and somehow, at that secret level deep within ourselves, we simply did not know how to relate to it at all. As some joker pointed out, and there was more truth in the jest than might have appeared, we actually had no evidence that the whole thing was not taking place in some television studio somewhere, was not an elaborate hoax. The problem with the Apollo Moon landing was that it was literally outside our frame of reference.

On the face of it, this might have seemed curious. After all, men had been dreaming of this moment for centuries. The literary history of men's imaginary journeys to the

Moon long pre-dated Jules Verne — stretching right back *via* Cyrano de Bergerac, Kepler, a seventeenth-century Bishop of Hereford and Ariosto's *Orlando Furioso* to the very dawn of the Renaissance. It was the symbolic culmination of the whole of that great adventure which the men of Western Europe had embarked on in the late Middle Ages when, in an entirely new way, they had begun to seek ultimate significance in the external world outside themselves.

They had discovered America, and that the earth was not flat. They had been through the colossal psychological upheaval of discovering that the earth was not even the centre of the universe. They had invented steam trains capable of travelling at eighty miles an hour, internal combustion engines which might actually lift them up above the surface of the earth, rockets which could soar up into the stratosphere. Step by step, over 600 years, they had totally readjusted their way of relating to the natural frame which had given them birth — as they subdued distance, calculation and everything else to their vaulting ambition, with radio, television, computers and all the rest. Finally all this mountain of knowledge and hardware had carried man up to the height where he was ready to make the most symbolic leap of all out of his original natural frame — actually to leave the earth behind, to set foot on another solar body, that 'pale Sister of the Night' which for tens of thousands of years had exercised a symbolic hold over the psyche of man second only to that of the life-giving Sun itself. It was the ultimate act of man's self-liberation, the moment when Apollo, the god of the Sun and human consciousness, was finally, once and for all, to ravish Diana, the goddess of unconscious night. And yet when this glorious act of emancipation took place, what happened?

We saw two men stumbling out of a metal prison, cocooned in plastic, still connected by umbilical cords with every single thing — even air — that was necessary to keep them alive. There was nothing they had not had to bring with them from the distant world they had supposedly left behind. They arrived on a completely dead lump of matter, more inconceivably dead than any square inch of the earth. And apart from dust and rock and an unearthly light, the only thing they could see which they could not have seen back on Earth, was the Earth itself floating unimaginably beautiful above them, the only home they knew, the only centre to the universe which really mattered.

It should hardly have been surprising that no one at that moment of shock could make sense of what had really happened, because almost everyone on earth had been so seduced into the point of view which gave rise to the experiment in the first place that almost no one at the time realized that it might be looked at from a totally different psychological perspective altogether.

It was some months before there was even the glimmering of an attempt to give what had happened some kind of deeper perspective, in Norman Mailer's book *Fire on the Moon* — a journalistic *tour-de-force* which at least tried to set that first Moon-journey back in some kind of metaphysical dimension. As, with enormous skill, Mailer reconstructed the whole awe-inspiring episode, right down to the technicalities of the nuts-and-bolts (for which he had been surprisingly well equipped by his early training as an aeronautical engineer), seeing it as the ultimate triumph of 'WASP culture', his constant theme was the question — 'Was God or the Devil at the helm?'

Looking again at Mailer's book nearly ten years later, I regret to have to report that it nevertheless now seems pretty thin stuff — strained, naive, sentimental — because ultimately, for all that he tried, even Mailer himself was still so awed by man's achievement that he could not escape the pull of that view which did see the Apollo mission as a divine act — and, for all his outsider's scepticism towards 'WASP culture', there was no doubt in Mailer's mind as to whom the responsible divinity was — *homo sapiens* himself.

But over the past ten years, almost without our being aware of it, perhaps we have been just beginning to change our perspective a little. As we look back on that astonishing episode, we can see that it certainly *was* a supreme symbolic moment in the history of mankind. By the most titanic concentration of effort, in developing just one part of himself, man *had* managed to 'break free' from nature as never before. It *was* the supreme achievement of his wonderful, separating consciousness, centred as all consciousness must be on the *ego*.

But the whole point of the way our minds, our psyches are ineradicably constructed is that, try as we might, we cannot find ultimate *meaning* by travelling such a road. As Romantics of every hue and permutation have endlessly demonstrated in the past two centuries, we may find every kind of thrill and sensation — even the tantalizing promise (*à la* Faust) of fathomless meaning. But we cannot find that sense of engagement with some 'ultimate reality' that alone brings real meaning into human existence, because that can only be found not in *separation* from nature but in rediscovering that other hidden centre of the psyche, the Self — that which alone gives us a sense of our participation in the totality of existence. The patterns made through the *ego* alone can never be ultimately resolved.

As we look back over the past ten years, it is hard not to be struck by what has happened to America, after working up through the Sixties to that concentration of energy (contemporaneous with America's rather more obviously 'dark' concentration of technological energy in

Vietnam). After those climactic efforts of the Sixties, America has more and more come to seem like an exhausted giant — the collapse in Vietnam, Watergate, the resignation of Nixon, the presidency of Jimmy Carter, and now the energy crisis itself.

Indeed, in the wake of the Moon shot, a strange new exhaustion has come over the whole of mankind's great post-Renaissance adventure. The 'mastering' of nature, the finding of new frontiers to cross, has all suddenly seemed to become much harder work. We may sometimes try to recapture the old thrills, as we acclaim the 'first balloon crossing of the Atlantic' or 'the first man-powered flight over the Channel' — but in fact the whole 'new frontiers' show is over, and deep down we know it.

When the ancient myths spoke of a Quest to some distant, immeasurably valuable goal they were ultimately speaking not of an outward journey to some material treasure, but of an inner journey — that journey which the hero must make in order to realize himself, to become fully a man, to discover who he really is. For 600 years, men have externalized that deep inner drive in what seemed like the greatest series of quests of all — those to explore, to 'conquer' the external world around us, the South Pole, Everest, the cures for diseases and all the rest. The Moon was the greatest example of all of such an external projection of the Questing drive. And when the goal was realized, we just could not perceive the true lesson which the whole experience should have taught us with beautiful, profound clarity. But there it was, as Armstrong and Aldrin stumbled about on that dead surface, looking back towards the infinitely beautiful, soft, blue planet 240,000 miles behind them. Their presence, as our representatives on that dead satellite, had made of the Moon nothing more than a symbol of man's dead *ego*, when separated from the lost life-giving totality of the Self. At that moment, if we had been heedful, we should have realized that the real goal of our Quest was not there at all. It was not out in the immeasurable, dead, silent emptiness of space that we should have been seeking our lost identity. That could only be found right here at home, where it had been all the time.

48

The Arrogance of Humanism

(26 May 1979)

As the Seventies come to an end, what is the most important thing happening in the world? The Middle East 'peace process'? The re-orientation of China? The gathering prospect of a world oil shortage? The development of the neutron bomb? I believe there is one thing which runs much deeper than any of these. As yet it is only in such early stages that most people are scarcely aware of it. But what I am referring to amounts to the dawning of one of the most profound shifts in human self-awareness that has ever taken place – and this book, *The Arrogance of Humanism*, by David Ehrenfeld, is just one of its growing multitude of symptoms.

Its author is the Professor of Biology at Rutgers University. In recent years, like more people than he is aware of, he has found himself beginning to look at the whole great 'experiment' on which Western man has been engaged in recent centuries from an entirely new perspective. He perceives that the driving force of that experiment has been what he calls 'the religion of humanism' (something far transcending mere political ideologies, like communism or capitalism) – a psychological perspective which has led men to believe that they can understand the world by reason alone, and that they can thus take control of their destinies in a way which to our ancestors would have seemed inconceivable. The essence of this humanism, as Professor Ehrenfeld puts it, is that for rational mankind 'all problems are soluble'. By the use of technology and applied science, it is within our grasp to produce a perfectly-ordered, problem-free, materially comfortable world. We may seem at present still to be faced by serious problems, but 'when the chips are down, we shall apply ourselves, and work for a solution before it is too late'. 'Human civilization will survive.'

What is interesting about Professor Ehrenfeld is not that he has lost his faith in these incantations – so, to a greater or lesser extent, have many people. It is the manner in which he has done so. He begins, conventionally enough, with a chapter entitled 'Myth', in which he details a whole range of the boasts and achievements which might underpin an optimistically 'humanist' view of the world, such as our astonishing advances in conquering diseases like cancer, in learning to monitor human behaviour through such statistical devices as 'castastrophe theory', in obtaining an unprecedentedly accurate view of the historical past through the science of 'cliometrics'. He describes schemes to bring deserts into flower through damming rivers, our hopes of obtaining 'clean', unlimited power through nuclear fusion, our plans to build whole new artificial 'worlds', fit for human occupation, in space. There is almost nothing we think we cannot do, from devising machines to pick the tender shoots of asparagus to saving the windows of Chartres Cathedral by coating them in plastic.

In the succeeding chapter, 'Reality', Professor Ehrenfeld examines each of these boasts again, in the light either of how they have already proved empty, or how they are based on so inadequate an appraisal of evidence and probabilities that they amount to pure wishful thinking. For every acclaimed 'advance' in curing cancer, the 'fundamental breakthrough' remains as elusive as ever, while the figures of deaths continue to rise. Mathematical attempts to 'monitor' human behaviour are shown to be based on so pitiful a choice of variables as to be meaningless. 'The 'cliometric' approach to history is exposed as so selective in its choice of evidence as to be mere charlatanry. The damming of the Nile, far from solving Egypt's problems, brings such a host of unforeseen ecological disasters in its wake that it might have been better if the Aswan Dam had never been built. Calculations of the benefits to be derived from the still unrealized dream of 'clean' power from nuclear fusion demonstrably fail to take into account a further enormous range of ecologically catastrophic consequences which would inevitably follow simply from the use of that power. Almost wherever we look, wherever man is seeking to use his reason and his technology to give him greater 'mastery' over the mysterious world of nature (including his own nature), the story is the same. Even the asparagus-plucking machine proves to be so much useless metal, because it cannot distinguish between shoots that are ready to pick and those which are still immature – while a coating of Viacryl has already irreparably destroyed the sombre luminosity of three of the thirteenth-century windows of Chartres, by turning them into mere tinted glass.

It is at this point that Professor Ehrenfeld comes to the crux of his argument. Human rationality, he argues, however sophisticated it becomes, is simply not equipped to match up to the literally unimaginable complexities of nature. There will *always* be something that we have not foreseen. In words he quotes from the meteorologist Eric Kraus: 'all science involves simplifications. There is an inevitable discrepancy between our scientific models and the much more richly textured world of everyday experience ... this means that the model does not contain all the information which would be needed to simulate the process as it occurs.'

Now the importance of this realization – which is beginning to dawn these days on a wide variety of people, including a number of more thoughtful scientists in many different disciplines – can scarcely be over-estimated. For what it means is that what we have been trying to do in the past 400 years may, in essence, simply be something which cannot ultimately be done. With our conscious, rational minds we can only construct models, theories, approximations to the reality of nature which are inevitably over-simplifications, telling us only a fraction of the real story. And when, at the instigation of our collective ego-drive to re-shape the world to our own better material advantage, we carry those over-simplifications out into the infinitely complex world of nature by means of technology, we are faced with those now all-to-familiar chains of 'unforeseen consequences' which ultimately bring disaster, in seemingly direct ratio to the degree to which we sought to interfere with the patterns of nature in the first place. What is truly radical and revolutionary about the kind of attitude which Professor Ehrenfeld and his like represent is that they are saying the time has come when we have to start accepting these limitations on human reason and human capability as part of the unshakable constitution of the universe. This does not mean to say that we should have avoided travelling the route we have come – the roots of our one-sided love affair with reason go back so far into human development that it is simply a fact. Nor does it mean, as the human race seems hell-bent on turning the world into a technological wilderness, that we can necessarily do anything practical to avert the major catastrophe or series of catastrophes which are probably the only way in which our 'humanist' adventure can be checked.

What it does mean, however, is that at least individually (and preferably, of course, on as wide a scale as possible) we have to find an entirely new (ultimately spiritual) perspective on who we are and just how we relate to the nature which has given birth to us, and of which we are still inextricably a part. I say 'new' perspective advisedly, because for the first time in human experience, we have actually travelled right through the tunnel of rationality – and we are at last beginning to discover its limitations by the very method which is its own supreme value, by empirical verification.

Again and again while following Professor Ehrenfeld's argument I found myself thinking of another, very different, book which topped the American best-seller lists a year or two back, Fritjof Capra's *The Tao of Physics*. As a physicist, Capra showed the quite remarkable correspondences between the view of the world opened up by post-Heisenbergian physics and that underlying Chinese mystical philosophy – a world in which all the 'oppositions' and the rigid logic of cause-and-effect which lie at the heart of Western rationalism are seen for the very partial kinds of explanation of 'reality' they are. Capra concludes that 'the world-view implied by modern physics' is simply and utterly inconsistent with our present conventional thinking and forms of society, which do not 'reflect the harmonious inter-relatedness which we observe in nature'. He believes that the survival of our civilization depends ultimately on 'our ability to adopt some of the *yin* attitudes of Eastern civilization; to experience the wholeness of nature and the art of living with it in harmony'. As another scientist, Professor Ehrenfeld would agree. Perhaps the ultimate cosmic profundity of human existence we have to face up to, however, is that we could only be brought to the final 'scientific' realization of that truth by travelling the very path which may also destroy us.

49

The New Religions

(13 April, 1977)

This week I had a fascinating experience. I spent an afternoon at Olympia wandering around the so-called 'Festival of Mind and Body', a 'celebration of the New Age'.

The temptation to poke cynical fun at this strange assemblage of 'freaks and weirdos' under the unlikely setting of Olympia's vast Victorian cast-iron canopy is one which a number of journalists have found irresistible. The *Times* diarist, for instance, almost fell over himself with excitement when he was able to light upon 'the bio-activity translator which allows plants to talk to you', or the stall offering to 'photograph your aura for £1', or the 'pleasant young woman munching some nutty confection' with whom he fell into conversation at the (strictly vegetarian) snack bar.

The stands fall into four main groups. Firstly there are the health-food enthusiasts.

Then there are the eccentrics of an ageless nature, such as Mr J. Rutherford of 31 Station Road, Harpenden, who advertises his 'theory that the passages and chambers of the Great Pyramid depict in stone God's plan for mankind through the ages'.

Thirdly, there are the commercial stands, showing everything from frisbees to karate equipment (most incongruous of all is the stall which consists merely of a rather melancholy-looking character standing by a shiny kidney machine bristling with dials).

Lastly, there is the mass of stands occupied by more or less serious representatives of what, if you were being rude, you might call the 'New Religions' – taking forms which are sometimes Christian, sometimes Eastern (several gurus are on offer, via their smiling bearded photographs) and sometimes not particularly either.

One cannot escape the fact that the emergence of this new 'spiritual wave' across the West, in all its myriad manifestations, has been one of the most surprising and interesting developments of the past decade. Indeed, we forget just how unexpected it was when it began to break the surface (at the time the Sixties pop-culture 'madness' was at its height, in 1966 and 1967).

At that time, many of its more obvious, headline-worthy forms were so blatantly dubious or shallow – the great LSD craze, the instant mysticism of the Beatles and the dear old Maharishi, flower power and hippy bells – that it might have been easy to dismiss as just another passing fad.

But behind the craze for 'whole-food' and the smoke of a million joss sticks I believe that this sense of what many of its adherents describe as 'the dawning of the age of Aquarius' constitutes part of the most remarkable shift in Western consciousness for several hundred years.

What do the best of these new movements have in common? Firstly, a tremendous sense of liberation from the sterile deadweight of our collectivist, technological, materialist, rational culture (it can no longer lay claim to the title of 'civilization').

Secondly, they share a belief that we all of us initially (and particularly under the influence of the dominant orthodoxies of the age) tend to look at the world through a limited 'ego-consciousness' – but that if we learn to travel within ourselves, we become aware of a second, much deeper self within us which in some mysterious way is not only much more individual to us than our little ego-self, but universal.

Thirdly, they have re-found in everyday life a sense of the sacred, of the kind which has long since departed from our trivial, neurotic, rationalist society (not to mention from most established Churches).

Now all this bears an uncanny resemblance to the model of man's psyche discovered over fifty years of observation by the great Swiss psychologist Jung, and in any attempt to survey the re-emergence of this view of man in the twentieth-century West, Jung must obviously have a very important place.

I say 're-emergence' because of course, in its broad out-lines, this is a view of man which has been held many times before in history – by the neo-Platonists of the Renaissance, by many of the Ancient Greek philosophers, by the Eastern religions, by Christian mystics. Indeed, before the institutionalization of Christianity, it was the very essence of Christ's own message – which was always directed to individuals, that they should find 'the kingdom of Heaven within'.

But as Jung in his role as twentieth-century scientist continually emphasized, the battle to discover that 'deeper self' within us is no easy, instant thing.

It means becoming aware of all those hidden parts of our-selves (what Jung called our 'shadow') which, so long as we remain unconscious of them, remain to leap out and dominate our behaviour without our even being aware they are doing so.

The fact that this is so difficult means of course that many of the more modish, group-centred cults of recent years (all those instantly mystical pop singers, for instance) are really doing nothing more, in Jung's words, than show 'a positively morbid avidity to practise Indian yoga, observe a strict regimen of diet, learn theosophy by heart or mech-anically repeat mystic texts from the literature of the whole world' simply because they dare not face themselves.

Equally the hard road to self-knowledge could not be further from those two other major 'spiritual' growth in-dustries among the young in recent years – evangelical Christianity and left-wing or Trotskyite Socialism. Both of these 'quasi-religions' are deeply attractive to the confused, insecure young because they seem to offer such a simple path to instant salvation – by adapting to an external stereotype. Both, therefore, are inevitably collective move-ments (you cannot be a solitary Evangelical, any more than you can be a solitary Socialist).

Like all collective movements, both inevitably project a hostility on to the outside world ('We are the elect, who have the exclusive answer'). Above all neither of them allow any real growth of the individual personality.

But at Olympia I sensed that, in and among all the superficialities, there were a small number of groups which had at least caught some glimmer of the way to self-understanding. What they are offering is not something fashionable, or collective, but nothing less than the chance for ordinary people to transform themselves into extra-ordinary people, by discovering their true Selves – and thereby experiencing that most extraordinary liberation the world has to offer. The knowledge that all is one, that love is all, and that life here on earth is truly a sacred adventure. So sacred, indeed, that the very idea of 'life on earth' be-comes limited and meaningless, because we are already living life eternal.

50

Knowledge and Illusion

(9 April, 1977)

There is a strange mood abroad in Western civilization at the moment — a general sense that, after the frenzied forward rush of the Sixties, we have suddenly come — politically, artistically, morally, scientifically — up against something of a blank wall. All the great collective twentieth-century adventures — the myriad forms of political and social Utopianism, the modern movement in the arts, the great 'leap forward' of personal liberation and emancipation ('Self-Fulfilment the Freudian Way') — have lost their steam, and petered out in exhaustion. The ever-rising escalator of technological progress and eternal growth has faltered, if not stopped. Round the corner, we see the distant sky looking very black: overshadowed by over-population, nuclear holocaust, totalitarianism, all sorts of unimaginable horrors. But for the time being, the foreground is still reasonably sunlit. There is no extreme sense of urgency. We dimly sense that we have reached the end of all kinds of roads, but no one wants to admit it too loudly for fear that we might actually be forced to start thinking about it all.

One man who has given these deeply important questions some thought, however, is Stuart Hampshire, in his recent lecture called 'The Future of Knowledge'. Professor Hampshire's thoughts are a fine starting point for considering where we have to go to, and where we might be going, if only because, as one might expect from such a distinguished philosopher, he gives such eloquent voice to what might be called the conventional wisdom on these matters.

He begins by claiming inspiration from his seventeenth-century predecessor as Warden of Wadham, John Wilkins, founder and first secretary of the Royal Society in 1662. Hampshire sees Wilkins's enthusiasm for the 'new science' as a symbolic landmark: 'three hundred years of accelerating understanding of nature as a rational system had begun'.

But today we are at another such turning point. In the past decade there has been 'more authoritative questioning of technology and even of the future of natural science than ever before in the last three hundred years'. Here the Professor adduces two examples, in rather strange juxtaposition: the first is that 'after two centuries we still have not come anywhere near to an exact understanding of human behaviour and of social change'; the second is that, by 'scientific calculation', we still cannot 'design a new town, or even a housing development ... as a centre of pleasure in living, or as a fully human environment'. Some might say that a truly scientific attempt to understand human nature might well begin from an attempt to grasp precisely why it is that we cannot create 'fully human environments' by 'scientific calculation', but let that pass.

Professor Hampshire goes on to talk about the way in which, in the past 300 years, scientific knowledge has become so fragmented. All very natural, he admits, but we cannot afford to let this go on indefinitely: 'The time to provide for the survival of the nation and of the species is too short.' We must learn how to re-synthesize. Could we perhaps set up a 'Supreme Academy to oversee inquiry'? Oh beautiful Enlightenment thought – an Academy of Lagado, a Super-Pugwash, to ensure that all future research should be coordinated for the good of mankind! One of the first aims of such an Academy would be to study human nature. It would (of course) accept that 'mathematics is the language of the intellect', which, coupled with recent advances in linguistics (in search for some common basis for the study of man) should give up 'the beginnings of a new self-understanding which could have an extensive feedback effect'.

But even Professor Hampshire realizes that this is scarcely the Panacea he is searching for. What about the 'social sciences', which have let us down so badly? Alas, psychology is not much good. 'If you want to understand states of mind and their causes ... you cannot expect to make them the subject of an exact, experimental science unless you find their physical equivalents.' He flirts with the idea that all mental processes are 'ultimately to be explained in terms of physics and chemistry'. If only it were true. Just a few more experiments, a little more money on research, and bingo! We should understand Man, the Physical and Chemical Being! We might even be able at last to design the Ideal Housing Estate for him to live in!

So where is the Panacea? Of course 'the Academy will encourage economics'. Why? Because 'when it has confined itself to carefully abstracted aspects of human behaviour, economics has avoided the uncertainties and vagueness of psychological explanation'. Economics, the exact social science! No messy, unpredictable human psychology round there!

Then there is history. This is important because ... why is history important? Because, in our 'bored', trivial, 'modern advanced industrial civilization', cut off from the rhythms of the seasons (and from the 'beliefs, principally religious, associated with such rhythms'), we need an identity, which we derive from 'the consciousness of a long history'. 'Every time a street or building that incorporates a considerable history is destroyed ... some future happiness is destroyed along with it.' So we must all become conservationists, to preserve our sense of identity.

But we must also find a way forward, 'some pride in the monuments of the present age', not just in architecture, but in all the arts. And here at last, Professor Hampshire leads us, almost before we notice it, into his Panacea. What has gone wrong with our culture? It has become one-sided, too rational, too technocratic. We have missed out something vital. 'Adult reason, employed in administration and technology' must be counter-balanced. And with what? Creativity! The wonderful arts, summed up in the most revealing sentence of Hampshire's entire lecture, as 'opportunity for free imagination, for fiction, deceit, illusion, showmanship, irresponsibility'. Oh, Ed Berman, with your street theatres, you have not lived in vain!

To revive our culture we must revive our arts. That is the Professor's final prescription. And how? 'By a great central push.' 'A change of attitude is needed, both in the taxpayers and in the government, towards supporting the arts as a source of glory and as a necessity of continuing life.' The English language, finest jewel of our heritage, is sustained by those who extend its resources and refine it by their inventions, 'the poets, dramatists and novelists of our time'. Stand up Harold Pinter, Samuel Beckett, Brigid Brophy! You are the saviours of our culture, and Professor Hampshire thinks you should all get a huge increase in subsidies so that you can keep us all (and our little language) refined, extended and alive.

It would be hard to conceive of a more eloquent parody of the utter bankruptcy of our present conventional wisdom, than this mish-mash of rationalism, materialism, utilitarianism, and finally crazy Utopianism. Professor Hampshire's lecture is indeed the very last gasp of the Enlightenment, as it subsides into total exhaustion. Such men (for Hampshire is by no means alone, but has merely said out loud what most distinguished minds in our culture would say if they dared to think about it) know that 'the smile of reason' has led us to a sense of spiritual bankruptcy and intellectual disillusionment unique in the history of the human race – but they cannot see that it is precisely their faith in 'reason' (as they would define it) which has led us there. They see the 'creative' part of man (as opposed to the physics and chemistry which may still 'explain' human nature) as simply a desire for 'fiction, deceit, illusion' – and not as stemming from those very forces in his psyche which, cruelly repressed and distorted as they have been for so long, may yet lead him back to a sense of wholeness, integration, meaning and all the things which the rationalists know they have lost without knowing why. They cannot see that the ultimate 'illusion' is precisely the kind of rationalism to which they themselves so desperately cling, and yet which has led humanity up such a dreadful cul-de-sac that we even face extinction.

51

Beyond the Riddle

(16 April, 1977)

There is a view, so common that it must be regarded as the implicit orthodoxy of our time (admirably reflected in Stuart Hampshire's recent lecture on 'The Future of Knowledge') which sees the present plight of mankind as a great riddle.

On the one hand, says the conventional wisdom, we stand here in the late twentieth century as heirs to the greatest adventure of the 'human spirit' ever known: 500 years of ever-advancing scientific knowledge about ourselves, the world and the universe. By the consequent advance in our technological skills, we have won an incredible mastery over our environment, annihilating almost all our enemies, from disease to discomfort, and emancipating us, to a wonderful degree, from our previous nasty, poor and brutish 'dependence on nature'.

Similarly we stand as heirs to 500 years of social and political advance, liberating us from age-old subjection to ancient hierarchies and feudal monopolies of power. We stand as heirs to a great, remorseless artistic advance, so that from the time of, say, Giotto or Josquin des Prés, each generation in turn has built on and extended the achievements of his predecessors in an almost logical progression – each step in turn giving a new sense of liberation and understanding. We stand as heirs to 500 years of spiritual advance, so that we have been gradually liberated (via the Reformation, Deism, Secularism and Couldn't-Care-Lessism) from our ancient subjection to superstition and belief in a supernatural order.

All in all, these 500 years of the increasing 'light of reason' have given us (deny it if you will) the sense that we stand at the top of a long climb out of darkness, and that it is somehow open to us to 'fulfil ourselves as individuals', and to order things better to our advantage, than any generation which has ever gone before.

And yet somehow (*vide* Professor Hampshire's lecture) we are left deeply baffled by the upshot of this wonderful advance. Instead of feeling like gods, in total, self-assured control of our environment, we have to fight off, repress or otherwise ignore a growing sense of hopelessness, which in the past ten years has begun to attack us with unprecedented force.

Our great advance in perception of the physical universe has certainly brought within our collective grasp a fantastic accumulation of physically undeniable facts. But at the same time it has not brought us any glorious new synthetic illumination, but merely a helpless sense of fragmentation – so that we feel we know everything, and also nothing.

Our 'conquest of nature' by technology has assuredly brought us health, comfort and power of a kind which to our medieval forefathers would have seemed positively magical – but at the same time it has mysteriously made our world progressively uglier, noisier and more dangerous, brought us face to face with the immeasurable perils of the population explosion and the strong possibility of nuclear extinction, and at the very least, by the rate at which it exhausts natural resources, has ensured that our present state of industrial civilization cannot be more than a very short-lived phase in the history of mankind.

Our political and social advances in the name of equality and toleration have left us with the knowledge not that the countries of the world are now free and properly ordered for the first time in history, but at best that they are socially confused and potentially chaotic, and at worst that more of them now languish under totalitarian tyrannies than at any time before. Our great artistic 'advance', while bringing many miracles along the way, has left us with the uneasy sense not just that we are now facing such a final and total disintegration of forms that there is no freedom left to win, but that our poor artists have really nothing of profound interest left to say. While finally our spiritual 'liberation' from the forms and content of a fundamentally religious view of the world and ourselves has left us not exhilarated and triumphant, but only with a dull sense of shallowness, lack of meaning and our own insignificance.

Such is the nature of the twentieth-century riddle. We have dreamed a dream and created a nightmare, and we cannot see any connection between the two. Like poor Mr Stephen Gardiner, whose letter to last week's *Spectator* could see no connection between the visions of Le Corbusier in the 1920s and the hell that was made of our cities in the 1960s, or like those sentimentalists of revolution who can see no connection between the paradise promised by Lenin and Marx and the hell of post-revolutionary Russia, we have in our century shown no more consistent and profound intellectual characteristic than our quite literally schizophrenic desire to separate human actions and ideas from their inevitable consequences.

The 'solution' to the twentieth-century riddle is in fact very simple. It merely requires a complete shift of our centre of intellectual and spiritual gravity – to recognize that the great 'emancipation of man' over the past 500 years and its consequences, the dream and the nightmare, are in fact inextricably intertwined. We are in fact living under a set of rules, which Pythagoras and the philosophers of the ancient world perceived very clearly, but which the modern world has tried completely to ignore. If one looks at the modern world through the framework of those rules, instead of seeing just an insoluble riddle, everything that has happened to mankind in the past 500 years makes perfect sense.

The essence of that ancient view of man was that he is part of a beautifully harmonious whole, a sense of which is imprinted deep in his psyche. But in some unique way he is 'separated' from that whole – and he can either spend his life in search of re-establishing the sense of wholeness, or he can be determined to become just a part, separate from and somehow 'against' the rest. If he does this, as the ancient Greeks would have said, he is guilty of *hubris*, and sooner or later an inevitable nemesis will fall upon him, re-establishing the whole by the extinction of the 'rebellious' part.

In recent years there have been many signs that modern man is beginning to recapture a dim sense of that ancient perception (although to accept it entirely involves such a blow to the ego of poor little modern man, and involves such a large-scale junking of all the paraphernalia of the conventional wisdom that it is going to be a long haul). Nevertheless it is only by beginning from such an acceptance that one can hope to make any 'sense' of what is happening to us all today. It is only thus, for instance, that we can see how it is not just malign chance that our great technological conquest of nature (oh, hideous *hubris*) should have produced not only colour television and DDT and oil-fired central heating, but also pollution, ugliness and enough nuclear weapons to kill us all a thousand times over. And it is only thus that we can see how, in his one-sided pursuit of more physical knowledge and material comfort (which are ultimately what the great modern ad-

venture is all about), that man has himself become so disintegrated, and so out of touch with literally vital parts of
his psyche that we have reached that ultimate point of
bankruptcy where Professor Hampshire can talk of 'creativity' in man as being merely an adjunct to an otherwise
full materialistic life (what the Professor calls the need for
'fiction, deceit, illusion, showmanship, irresponsibility').

Would Rembrandt, or Dante, or Beethoven, or Shakespeare (or any of the men whose 'creativity' makes any
artist of today seem like a poor stunted victim of mental
disorder) have viewed 'creativity' as the need for 'fiction,
deceit and illusion'? Of course not. They would have seen
'creativity' as the fundamental drive in man to establish his
relationship with what, when he finds it, he knows and
feels beyond any argument to be 'reality'; the reality both
of his own nature and of the entire universe that is both
outside us and inside us. Of course distinguished philosophers have long since defined and logic-chopped any
such absurd notions out of existence. Of course they have!
For a crucial part of that 'sense of reality' is a perception
of the true relationship between *all* the parts of man's
psyche (reason, sensation, feeling, intuition – or, if you
prefer, mind, body, heart and soul) and that he who aspires
to perceive the universe through only one window (such
as 'reason') is doomed to a sense of ultimate meaninglessness and death.

If our upholders of the conventional unwisdom, be they
Professor Hampshire or whoever, persist in their desire to
differentiate, they will continue to see our plight as an insoluble riddle to the end of our civilization (which may
not be very far away). 'Who sees the variety and not the
unity must wander on from death to death', as the old
sages used to say. Fair enough. It's a free country, as we
say. But let us no longer make the mistake of considering

the one-sided, arrogant, limited little rationalistic view of man and the universe that has increasingly dominated our culture for the past 500 years as having anything to do with the *true* light of reason — which can only shine as part of a much wider apprehension altogether.

Part Seven

Epilogue

I had originally intended to write a special epilogue to this account of the Seventies – an attempt to weave together and to sum up the themes which have run through these past few hundred pages, to look to the future and to end, if it were possible after so much gloom, on a note of cautious hope. I had a number of tries at such an epilogue; but each in turn threatened to become almost a new book in itself. Then, when the Seventies were almost over, came a week the events of which somehow seemed to sum up better than anything else in the decade almost everything I have been trying to say. I decided there could be no more appropriate way for me to round off this book than simply to reprint the 'Saturday Column' I wrote for the *Daily Telegraph* on 6 October 1979 – after seven days when our television screens and newspapers had alternately been filled with reports on the Pope's tour of Ireland and the U.S.A., and the Labour Party's first conference following its defeat in the May 1979 General Election. I hope its implicit challenge may serve as an appropriate epigraph to the decade of the Eighties which lies ahead.

(6 October 1979)

For those of us in Britain, two images have dominated this past historic week.

The first has been the deeply depressing spectacle of the Labour Conference at Brighton – the sight of men and women driven by negativity and hostility, diminished as human beings, possessed by that manic infantility which is the most alarming thing about any Left-wing movement in full cry after power, the psychic state where collective ego-demands are taken for reality.

In psychological terms, the only thing missing from the brilliant *Guardian* cartoon showing Wedgwood Benn as Peter Pan, flying off with his childish followers into the Never-Never Land, was that it could not also somehow convey the shadowy underside of the psychic disease which always infects the Socialist Left – that constant unconscious need for antagonism and hatred which is what gives totalitarian Socialism its most terrifying, inhuman aspect.

The second dominant image of the week could not have provided greater contrast. I am referring, of course, to the spectacle of Pope John-Paul II on his triumphant progress through Ireland and the United States.

A year ago, in the week when Karol Woityla became Pope, I wrote that his election promised to thrust the Papacy back into the centre of 'the psychic drama of mankind'.

Seeing this week the remarkable effect of this burly, strong, smiling, gentle figure as he passed through the incredible crowds at Drogheda and Knock, Boston and New York, that prediction has come true to an extent which even a year ago would have seemed inconceivable.

It is important that we should recognize and reflect on just why it is that this truly extraordinary man is having such an impact on us all. One point which has not escaped commentators, particularly in America, is how the Pope seems to diminish all our present generation of political leaders – the Carters, Kennedys, Reagans *et al*. He seems to tower above them because he is so solid, so authoritative, so mature – a 'real man' in a world of posturing, weak, egotistical children.

The real significance of John-Paul II is that, in an age when we seem to have lost the art of growing up, he has called us back to recollection of what it means to be a proper human being.

The Pope is in fact the most 'complete' man who has occupied a position of world prominence for a very long time – certainly since the coming of the mass-media. The reason why he seems so complete, why he shines forth with such authority, is that he shows us what a man is capable of becoming when he develops all the main parts of a human personality.

In psychological terms, regardless of our sex, we all have four main psychic functions, two 'masculine' and two 'feminine'. On the 'male' side of the psyche, the first is that which relates us to our bodies, to the physical world – that which, when fully developed, gives physical power and authority.

The second masculine function is to do with the mind and rationality, that which gives intellectual authority.

The 'feminine functions' are, on the one hand, sympathetic and compassionate feeling – the heart; on the other, that vastly underrated and important function, our intuition, that which teaches us of the true, hidden connections between things.

Now, in any fully-developed human personality, *all* these functions have to be brought into balance, or the person remains in some way lop-sided, immature and egocentric. It is only when all the functions are developed that a man or a woman emerges as, in Jungian terms, the full Self, transcending the limitations of the ego.

The point about John-Paul is that he is so transparently a man in whom all four functions – body, mind, heart and soul, as one might put it – are equally in balance. He has a tremendously easy and powerful relationship with the physical (in his ski-ing and mountaineering, his healthy appetite, his sheer physical presence). He has a first class rational mind (trained in philosophy, a voracious reader, a true intellectual).

While on the 'feminine' side, he has equally well-developed those two gentler functions which are essential to make the male functions life-giving – his real (i.e. in no way sentimental) sense of compassion, and that intuitive 'inner eye' which ultimately gives an awareness of the spiritual, the transcendent dimension of all existence.

That is why the spectacle of the Pope has proved in the past few days so hugely impressive. Of course in reality no human being is perfect. No doubt in the months and years to come we shall hear much criticism of Pope John-Paul II (particularly when it becomes clear just how 'conservative' a Catholic he is on moral and doctrinal matters).

Nevertheless, it is not on this level that he has had such extraordinary impact in the past week. Just as when he returned earlier this year to his native Poland, the Pope has been transformed into a symbol – the most powerful symbol known to man. Like Christ his master, he has come amongst us as a symbol of the fully-developed human Self

– what we all may strive to become – which is why he constantly exhorts each of us to become 'kings', in our own inner kingdom.

Nor is it any accident that Karol Woityla (like that grimmer, but not totally dissimilar figure, Solzhenitsyn) has worked towards his present state of Self-realization through long ordeals under totalitarian regimes. For what we are seeing in the world at the moment is a polarization, not of political systems, but of the two extreme states to which human beings may aspire. On the one hand, there is that state of true human fullness and maturity, which can only come from the realization by each individual of his or her own human potential.

On the other hand are those ideologies which offer precisely the opposite – those collectivizations of the ego which keep men frozen in a state of incompleteness and infantility, make it impossible for them to grow to their full stature, and fill them with all that is negative – not with warmth and openness but with greed and envy, not with love but with hatred.

This is why the images this week of Brighton and of the Pope have presented such a contrast – because they have shown us in such striking terms the two roles in the psychic drama of mankind which each of us must choose to play. We can either become true 'kings', or we must remain miserable slaves, dreaming false dreams of a 'liberation' which can only be vainly pursued at the price of untold suffering. Ultimately, of course, this is not a matter of 'politics', whether of Left, Right or even Centre. It is how we each of us dispose ourselves towards that kingdom which is within us. From that alone, everything else follows.

More About Penguins and Pelicans

CHARMED LIVES
Michael Korda

The story of Alexander Korda and the fabulous Korda film dynasty starring Garbo, Dietrich, Churchill and a cast of thousands.

'Charmed lives, doubly charmed book ... Comments, jokes, experiences; and at the heart of it all there is Alexander Korda, powerful, brilliant, extravagant, witty, charming. And fortunate: fortunate in his biographer. Few men have the luck to be written about with so personal an appreciation, so amused, yet so deep an affection' – Dilys Powell in *The Times*

NANCY CUNARD
Anne Chisholm

The rebellious only child of an American society hostess and an English aristocrat, Nancy Cunard became the darling of high café society in the twenties and thirties. She knew Eliot, Joyce and Louis Aragon, she sat for Cecil Beaton and was an Aldous Huxley heroine in *Antic Hay*; a poet and a writer, she was the *avante-garde* publisher who 'discovered' Beckett, a passionate advocate of racial equality and a journalist in the Spanish Civil War. In her acclaimed biography, Anne Chisholm brings to life this extraordinary woman, Nancy Cunard, who, by the time of her tragic death in 1965, had become the dazzling symbol of her age.

THE AMERICANS
Letters from America 1969–1979
Alistair Cooke

With his engaging blend of urbanity and charm, Alistair Cooke talks about Watergate and Christmas in Vermont, gives opinions on jogging and newspaper jargon, creates memorable cameos of Americans from Duke Ellington to Groucho Marx and discusses a host of other topics – all in that relaxed, anecdotal style which has placed him among our best-loved radio broadcasters.

'One of the most gifted and urbane essayists of the century, a supreme master' – Benny Green in the *Spectator*

CLEMENTINE CHURCHILL
Mary Soames

Lady Soames describes her book as 'a labour of love – but I trust not of blind love', others have acclaimed it as one of the outstanding biographies of the decade:

'Perceptive and affectionate, shrewd and tender . . . a joy to read' – Elizabeth Longford

'Lady Soames has carried out the extremely delicate and difficult task of writing the real story of her mother. I found it particularly moving because I had a very deep affection for her father and mother' – Harold Macmillan

'A triumph . . . her subject, unknown yet well-known, is enthralling' – Eric James in *The Times*

A PORTRAIT OF JANE AUSTEN
David Cecil

David Cecil's magnificent and highly enjoyable portrait of a writer who represents for us, as no other, the elegance, grace and wit of Georgian England.

'A masterpiece which ought to be in every educated home. Nobody could have done it better, nobody will be able to do it so well again. The book is a monument to subject and author' – Auberon Waugh in *Books and Bookmen*

THE BRITISH IN LOVE
An Amorously Autobiographical Anthology
Jilly Cooper

From the magnificent poetry of Donne and Shakespeare, to the rolling iambics of Shelley and the nostalgia of Yeats and Hardy, from the needle-sharp wit of Nancy Mitford, to the subtle prose of Anthony Powell and the hilarity of George and Weedon Grossmith, it is all here brought to life by the irresistible and irrepressible Jilly . . .

'Brilliant as well as adorable' – John Betjeman

'Sad, funny and sensual' – *The Times*